Additional Praise for *The Risk-Wise Investor*

"Risk—you must live with it, you can't invest without it. Mike's book does an excellent job explaining risk, and why we as investors (and real, live people!) need to understand this most basic element of our financial lives."

—E. Blake Moore Jr.
CEO, Allianz Global Investors Fund Management

"When investors are terrified, fight or flight—or freeze—are typical reactions, all of which destroy wealth! Mike Carpenter's *The Risk-Wise Investor* offers a new and refreshing alternative, one investors (and their advisors!) can learn and profit from."

—Charlotte B. Beyer
Founder & CEO, Institute for Private Investors

"A valuable guide for navigating uncertain times that every investor should read and add to their investment library."

—Peter Jones
Franklin Templeton Investments

"When Michael Carpenter, a savvy, seasoned, and successful investment professional talks about risk, attention must be paid! This book is not a "how to" guide to becoming wealthy, but a rich compendium of tested strategies for protecting and growing your nest egg. Investors saving for retirement, for their children's education, or for any long term goal will profit from it"

—Burton Greenwald
BJ Greenwald Associates

"Financial risk has been a subject that is intimidating and not well understood, yet today has become *the* financial topic! Individual investors want financial risk to be defined, assessed, and managed. This book allows the investor to accomplish each of these and build a financial roadmap to calibrate their personal risk exposure."

—Phillip D. Meserve
Financial Strategist

The Risk-Wise Investor

How to Better Understand and Manage Risk

MICHAEL T. CARPENTER

WILEY

John Wiley & Sons, Inc.

Published by John Wiley & Sons, Inc., Hoboken, New Jersey.
Published simultaneously in Canada.

For general information on our other products and services or for technical support, please contact our Customer Care Department within the United States at (800) 762-2974, outside the United States at (317) 572-3993 or fax (317) 572-4002.

Wiley also publishes its books in a variety of electronic formats. Some content that appears in print may not be available in electronic books. For more information about Wiley products, visit our web site at www.wiley.com.

Library of Congress Cataloging-in-Publication Data:

Carpenter, Michael, 1947–
    The risk-wise investor: how to better understand and manage risk/Michael Carpenter.
      p. cm.
    Includes bibliographical references and index.
    ISBN 978-0-470-47883-7 (cloth)
1. Investments.   2. Risk management.   3. Investment analysis.   I. Title.
    HG4521.C2824 2009
    332.6–dc22   2009013315

Printed in the United States of America

10 9 8 7 6 5 4 3 2 1

To Cindy
Wonderful wife, mother, and best friend
The smartest, sweetest, most patient
and understanding person I know

Contents

Preface

When you change the way you look at things, the things you look at change.

Max Plank
Nobel Laureate in Physics

Welcome and congratulations on your decision to read this book. Many people don't realize that one of the most common characteristics of truly *successful*, long-term investors is their appreciation of the importance of investing their time, before they invest their money. Many of those investors learned the hard way the necessity of spending at least as much time understanding the risks of any potential investment, as well as the rewards, before investing their capital. They have found that the more they know about both the potential downside and the upside, the better decisions they make, and the more likely their investment decisions will pay substantial rewards.

User-Friendly Risk Management

Initially, risk management may appear to be a complex, highly technical, and daunting discipline. However, once you become familiar with the "Risk-Wise" approach you'll see how user-friendly, nontechnical, and effective it can be. The fact that you are now investing your time to gain insights and improve your knowledge level of the enormously important subjects of uncertainty, risk, and risk management is a very positive step. Quite simply, not being aware of or ignoring the critical role risk management plays in successful investing is itself a primary investment risk. So you should congratulate yourself for identifying that overriding risk, acknowledging its importance, and investing your time in gaining a better understanding of risk and risk management. Those few steps alone set you apart from most investors and serve as a key predictor of your future long-term investment success.

The principal objective of this book is to help you become a true "Risk-Wise" Investor. It is focused on helping you to better identify risks, to reduce the likelihood and impact of risks that do occur, and to turn risks into inconveniences and even potential opportunities.

What Is a "Risk-Wise" Investor?

The term "Risk-Wise" Investor refers to any investors with the power of judging their risk/reward decisions correctly, and following the soundest course of action based on broad *knowledge, understanding, experience*, and *preparation*. Those simple, nontechnical attributes are the foundation of the entire "Risk-Wise" approach. They are the key to better understanding risk, and the risk management methodologies discussed in this book. They are also the very same factors that helped you learn how to become a master of risk management in dealing with the risks you face in your everyday life. In fact, it's a fundamental truth of human existence that we are naturally fearful of what we aren't familiar with or don't understand. So the more you know and understand about anything, the less fear, better decisions, and fewer missteps you'll experience, and the more successful you'll be. That is especially true of risks. In the heat of our fast-paced modern lives, and our fascination and dependency on technology, we may have neglected to apply what has been known about effective risk management for centuries. Almost 150 years ago the great thinker and writer Ralph Waldo Emerson articulated a key foundation concept of effective risk management that is just as valuable today. He observed: "Knowledge is the antidote to fear." Since fear is integral to our natural risk management system, that insightful observation reinforces the fact that improving our knowledge of risk is key to reducing our fear of risk and to opening the door to better risk management and becoming less anxious, more comfortable and confident investors. When increased knowledge of risk is paired with deeper understanding and thorough preparation, risks are managed much more effectively and our fears and anxieties are dramatically reduced. Simply stated, and with very few exceptions, *what we know, understand, and are prepared for cannot harm us*.

This important precept is extremely valuable to "Risk-Wise" Investors today. It serves as a guidepost in the continuous search for better ways to identify, understand, manage, and control risks. This strategy is also just as effective in addressing the newly evolving, and sometimes frightening risks emerging from our rapidly changing, faster-paced, more interconnected, and less certain world.

In reading this book you'll become familiar with the basic practical knowledge, understanding, and preparation methods you'll need to become a more effective "Risk-Wise" Investor, including:

- Using a new empowering definition of *risk* to improve your investment success.
- Finding a time-tested way to reduce unpleasant, negative surprises.
- Reducing the severity of negative surprises, should they ever occur.
- Converting risks into "inconveniences," and even potential opportunities.
- Improving your investment success by understanding your risk biology.
- Seeing where and how to best focus your risk management resources.
- Learning how to know which risks should you avoid, accept, or manage.
- Creating a personalized, systematic process to better identify, manage, and neutralize the risks you face.
- Managing ongoing, ever-changing, and new risks.
- Better navigating extraordinary crisis events, bear markets, frightening volatility, and extremes of the business cycle.

Again, congratulations! Once you finish reading and absorbing the contents of this book, you'll know and understand more about uncertainty, risk, practical risk management, and how to implement it for your personal benefit than the vast majority of investors. You'll become a more "Risk-Wise" Investor. That knowledge and those insights will serve you well. They will help you better identify, understand, prepare for, and manage risk. You'll enjoy the greater peace of mind that comes from truly understanding what you are doing and why you are doing it, plus you'll avoid many of the potential pitfalls and investment nightmares that can occur along the way. Best of all you'll improve the likelihood of reaching your personal financial objectives, regardless of the investment environment.

Acknowledgments

The fact that this book was conceived in the first place, let alone completed is due the ongoing encouragement, support, and help of numerous friends, neighbors, and associates all over the country.

Enormous thanks are due to great friends John Riordan, John Nicholson, Rahoul Banerjea, and John Paolucci, whose continuous encouragement, questions, and comments helped me so much when I first became interested in researching and developing a user-friendly, nontechnical approach to understanding and managing risk. A tremendous debt of gratitude is owed to my friends and authors Jim Huguet for his sage counsel and educating me on the many issues facing a potential author, and Beth Birkman for graciously familiarizing me with the book publishing process, and for saving me an enormous amount of time and trouble in researching all that she was happy to share with me over a cup of coffee. Special thanks to wordsmith, author, and now retired risk management professional and consultant, Felix Kloman, for sharing his life-long passion for studying, observing, speaking, and writing about the multidisciplinary and ever-fascinating subjects of risk and risk management. His generosity in providing some key information on the history of risk management made my job much easier. Deep appreciation is also extended to friends and portfolio managers, Tom Goggins and Bill Hamilton, who shared their invaluable perspective as very experienced investment and risk managers. Thanks also to Jack Kenney, for his inspiration, counsel, and fine example of investment professionalism; Janice Reals-Ellig, for her encouragement; Dawn Kahler, for providing the efficient frontier studies; Todd Hiller, for his always thoughtful perspective and comments; and Ed Boudreau, for his suggestions and observations on risk management, from a private pilot's viewpoint. Special thanks to former submariner Dave Wilson, Fire Chief Ken Willett, and Deputy Police Chief Barry Neil, for their insights into the unique challenges and risk management methods used by professionals whose job is to deal with life-threatening risks on a daily basis.

The deepest gratitude to my parents, Tom and Betty Carpenter, for their encouragement to always follow my dreams, and my brothers, John and

Jim, and sisters, Cindy and Kim, for their love and unwavering support. Many thanks are also due to Nannette, Dean, and Ashley Carpenter, and Elizabeth Brodsky, for their technical help and support; senior management consultant, Paula Camara, for her always thought provoking questions and enthusiastic encouragement; and the extremely knowledgeable, helpful, and always friendly staff at the Boston Public Library and the library's Kirstein Business Branch.

My appreciation is immeasurable for Tom Thomas and Dick Forbes, the two investment industry veterans who many years ago gave me the opportunity to first enter their incredible business, actually train on Wall Street, and build a career as an investment professional. I must also thank all the investors, financial advisors, and former associates, team members, executives, portfolio managers and consulting clients I've been unbelievably privileged to work with and continued to learn from over the years. You have made me feel truly blessed.

Last but not least, special thanks to Senior Editor David Pugh, Development Editor Kelly O'Connor, Senior Production Editor Michael Lisk, and Editorial Assistant Adrianna Johnson of John Wiley & Sons for their responsiveness, ideas, editorial assistance, professionalism, and help in making this book a reality.

CHAPTER 1

The Increasing Importance of "Risk-Wise" Investing

May you live in interesting times.

Ancient Chinese Curse

Our world, investment markets, and investing itself have changed dramatically in just the last decade. Investing has been irreversibly altered by a number of powerful, interrelated factors including:

- Enormous growth in the volume, availability, and instant dissemination of investment information.
- Unprecedented expansion of the number and types of investment vehicles.
- A dramatic increase in the sheer number of investors, domestically and worldwide.
- An explosion in the total size of investment holdings.
- Huge increase in investors' interest in, and knowledge of, investments and investing.
- The ongoing and remarkable lengthening of human life spans, raising the stakes and critical importance of investing successfully.
- The increased global interconnectedness of all investors, economies, markets, countries, and continents, and their growing interdependence on one another.
- The accelerating pace of worldwide change and all the uncertainties it generates.
- Enormously increased market volumes and at times gut-wrenching volatility.

1

These historic changes have created wonderful new investment opportunities and new challenges. They've increased the likelihood and impact of old familiar risks and totally new types of risks when the stakes for what's at risk are now even bigger. With those dramatic and continuing changes, understanding and managing risk is more important than ever before.

The Holy Grail?

Based on what we see, hear, and read virtually every moment of every waking hour, each and every day, achieving outstanding investment performance is the Holy Grail of investing. It's held up as the foundation of investment success. Enormous time, energy, and resources are devoted to identifying and urging us to take advantage of the newest, hottest investment ideas, best performers, and the next big investment winners all over the world.

For instance, the media overloads and overwhelms us 24/7 with analysts, pundits, seers, and prognosticators (often contradicting one another). They urgently forecast economic and market moves for the next year, quarter, month, week, hour, day, and unbelievably, even minutes, so that we can rush to take advantage of their insights. Simultaneously, we're experiencing an enormous explosion in the number of new investment vehicles, trading tools, and information sources. We're also seeing a deluge of new active and indexed investments strategies, all designed to "help us" make more money on both the positive and negative price movements of almost everything. We now live in an investment world offering more distinct types of investments to choose from, and more and different ways to make or lose money investing, than ever before in history. As more sophisticated active and index investment alternatives attract more assets and compete more intensively with one another, the range between strong and weak investment performance is also shrinking.

The same phenomenon is occurring with private equity, alternative investments, and hedge funds as well as many other investment types. As more managers with more assets under management chase similar opportunities, the range of performance narrows and gradually reverts to a tighter range, more closely grouped around the mean.

The Game Has Shifted

There is another change that's occurred in the investment world over the last 20 years, which has been overlooked by many investors. The nature of this subtle, but very important change was first pointed out by renowned institutional investment consultant Charles Ellis in his thought-leading book, *Winning the Losers Game.*[1] In his book, Ellis reviews why and how investing has shifted from a "Winner's Game" to a "Loser's Game." He describes how the nature of the investment world has changed to now favor those investors who make the fewest mistakes rather than the investors focused on gaining the highest returns. He observes that the key driver of investing success has become similar to the success drivers in activities like golf and amateur tennis. In all these pursuits the winners win not by outplaying their opponents but by making the fewest mistakes. If you have ever played golf or tennis, you are undoubtedly familiar with this phenomenon, because the harder you try to win, the more mistakes you tend to make.

Investing changed to a loser's game when large numbers of very bright people, with lots of resources, access to timely information, and lots of money to invest began competing with one another to achieve the best performance. The advantage now goes to investors who understand the benefit (using a baseball analogy) of the more consistent winning strategy of hitting lots of singles and doubles, getting on base regularly, and avoiding errors and missteps rather than having everyone of the team swing for the fence, attempt to hit home runs, and then strike out.

Ellis strongly emphasizes that the primary objective of investment management is risk management. Managing risk has always been important, but now emphasizing risk management and "Risk-Wise" investing is *the most important* investment success factor in achieving your long-term investment goals. Of course, this concept isn't new or just limited to investing. It is also the fundamental core of the Hippocratic oath made by physicians for thousand of years: "First, do no harm." Even real estate mogul Donald Trump has stated, "Protect the downside and the upside takes care of itself."

That viewpoint is now also shared by the world's largest business enterprises. In fact, the advantages of proactive risk management have become so important that within the last 10 years more and more large companies have created and staffed a totally new C-Suite level function focused on risk management. Adding to the long established positions of CEO, COO, CFO, CIO, CMO is the totally new position, and firm-wide department of the Chief Risk Officer (CRO). The underlying question though, is why? Why have these very sophisticated global enterprises felt the need to create a new senior executive position to oversee risk and risk management?

These multinational firms are placing such a big emphasis on risk management because they see and understand its tremendous value and realize:

- In today's world almost anything is possible (both positive and negative).
- Today's stakes have never been higher, and risk management never more important.

- Offense wins games, and defense wins championships.
- If something can happen, it typically will happen (often at the worst possible time) unless action is taken on it in advance.
- It is critical to be ready and prepared for any contingency, no matter how extreme.

These huge enterprises understand how much more efficient and ultimately less costly it is to invest time and effort in being proactive, prepared, and ready for risks. It's much preferable to paying the enormous tangible and intangible costs of being caught off guard, being unprepared for negative surprises, and furiously scrambling around to recover from risks when some of them inevitably become reality.

If major worldwide corporations, with all their resources and capabilities, are now focusing on risk and risk management throughout their entire enterprises, isn't it even more important for individual investors to do the same? Individuals investing for their own and their family's future carry the full responsibility of their future quality of life and prosperity, and it is all riding on their understanding and effective management of the investment risks they face. So where do you go to gain that critical understanding of such a multifaceted, multidisciplinary, and important a subject as managing uncertainty and risk?

The New Way to Gain Mastery

The big challenge for most investors in improving their knowledge of risk and risk management is that the subjects can seem complex, confusing, and even intimidating. When the unpredictability of the future is also factored in, the entire process can seem overwhelming and almost fruitless. As a result, many investors either give up on the effort right away or lose interest over time when confronted with the challenge. They just don't have the extra time to dedicate to educating themselves on the complexities of the subject, with all the other demands on their attention. Even investors who are fully committed to improving their understanding of the subject are often disappointed, because most sources of information on risk management either oversimplify the subject or offer varying forms of technical overload. At one extreme are the sources that discuss the subject of risk and risk management simplistically and skim over it much too lightly. At the opposite extreme are sources that elaborate on highly technical, detailed, quantitative approaches (the details of Modern Portfolio Theory, the Efficient Frontier, quantitative analysis, variance, alpha, beta, and correlation coefficients, standard deviation) that don't resonate even with many sophisticated investors, unless they also happen to be engineers, mathematicians, or statisticians.

The single most important thing to remember is that for any risk management approach to work, you must not only understand how the method works, but also why it works, so that you can understand its strengths and weaknesses. It also helps if, through personal experience, you know that it works under a full range of environments and circumstances. Next you must have enough knowledge of and confidence in the method to believe it will work, and then fully commit to it.

The most critical point to keep in mind is this: *Any risk management system that any investor uses and does not understand, or does not have confidence in, will not work.* The reason it won't work is because investors who don't truly understand and have confidence in their risk management methodology will many times abandon it, at the worst possible time. As a result, there is an enormous need for a user-friendly, knowledge-based, easy-to-understand, and easy-to-implement risk management approach. A new middle way is needed between the extremes of oversimplification and technical overload. That new knowledge-based, user-friendly alternative is the "Risk-Wise" Investor method.

The "Risk-Wise" Investor approach is specifically designed to help you and investors everywhere build a strong, knowledge-based understanding of risk and risk management in a practical, user-friendly, nontechnical, and easy to understand way. It is designed to increase your knowledge and understanding of risk management, and your confidence in your risk management abilities. It will also help its users make better informed investment decisions, reduce the number and impact of negative surprises, and improve the likelihood of investors achieving their long-term investment objectives. What makes the "Risk-wise" Investor approach so easy to understand and use is that you have and are already using it, very effectively, in numerous aspects of your daily life.

Release Your Own Natural, Everyday Risk Management Power

You are a very successful Master of Risk Management. Although you may be surprised by that statement, and may not actually feel like an expert risk manager, you indeed are one. In fact, you are an accomplished and very successful Master of Life-Risk Management if you are a normal adult human being. You are a Risk Management Master because you successfully deal with all kinds of risks (big, small, and some life threatening) multiple times, every single day. Your risk management skills are so well developed that many times you use them unconsciously. Just think about the life-threatening risks you take just driving to and from work or going out for simple errands, every single day.

You started learning about risks and risk management when you were very young. You survived all the risks of early childhood. You learned some of your risk management skills from your parents and siblings. They taught you about a full range of risks you faced and how to manage them. Unfortunately, some risks you had to learn about the hard way, and even today you may still carry the physical and mental scars from those painful lessons. If you have been or are now a parent, you know how often and how quickly small children can unknowingly place themselves in highly risky situations.

You've survived and learned to successfully manage the many dangerous risks of adolescence and the challenging teen years, when your emotions and raging hormones overruled your logic and controlled your actions. You may even remember some former personal friends from those days who weren't as good at risk management or risk decision making as you and as a result didn't survive their teens. In fact, teenagers are such a documented high-risk age group that auto insurance rates for teenagers and young adults are significantly higher than any other age group, except for those people well into their later senior citizen years.

When you graduated into adulthood you faced many new risks and learned how to manage them as well. The key point is that as adult human beings, we are all Masters of Life-Risk Management and very skilled in dealing with life risks. Not perfect by any means, because risk management is never perfect and accidents and mis-steps do happen. Even then, because we are prepared, we have mechanisms in place to minimize the impact of those surprises and almost inevitable accidents.

In general, adult human beings have extremely well developed risk management skills that are very easy to take for granted. Have you ever driven home, pulled in your driveway or garage and realized you don't recall making any conscious decisions on your drive home? It's as if you were on automatic pilot the entire trip. What's really quite fascinating are the responses you get when you ask most people to describe what process they use so skillfully to manage the life risks they face every day. Most, even after thinking for a moment, can't describe their risk management process because they don't know it. They don't think about it. They just do it. Those individuals have internalized their risk management process so much and become so comfortable with it that they can't articulate what it is.

What would it be like if you could reconnect with the process you use so effectively to manage everyday risks and apply that same process and those same impressive risk management skills in the investment world? You would:

- Better understand and manage risk.
- Make better, more knowledge-based investment decisions.
- Have more confidence in your risk management skills.

- Make fewer investment mis-steps and experience fewer negative surprises.
- Reduce the impact of the unpleasant surprises that do occur.
- Improve the likelihood of achieving your long-term investment goals.
- Be a happier more successful, less anxious, ready for anything "Risk-Wise" Investor.

The core of the "Risk-Wise" Investor method, and what makes it so different, is how it refamiliarizes and reconnects you with the very same process you have used in learning and developing your own everyday, and natural, life-risk management skills. It then provides you with a nontechnical, and easy to implement, step-by-step process to use in creating your own personalized risk management plan, and ongoing risk managed decision-making process. Let's now review the steps in our everyday, natural life-risk management process and see how easily they transition into the "Risk-Wise" Investor method discussed in the next chapter.

CHAPTER 2

Introduction to the "Risk-Wise" Risk Management Process

If a man empties his purse into his head, no one can take it away from him. An investment in knowledge always pays the best interest.
Ben Franklin

What would it be like if you could be as accomplished and comfortable managing investment risks as you are managing the risks you face in your every day life? You'd make fewer investment missteps, and reduce the severity of the risks that did occur. You'd also increase the likelihood of achieving your financial objectives, and you'd be a happier, less anxious, more confident, more successful investor.

That's the objective of the "Risk-Wise" Investor risk management method. My purpose is to show you how to use this user-friendly, easy-to-implement way to release your innate, natural, and highly developed life-risk management skills in the world of investments.

As adult human beings, we are all very accomplished, and very successful managers of the many risks we encounter in our everyday lives. Yet as comfortable and accomplished as we are with managing these everyday risks, we often feel quite uncomfortable and ill-equipped to manage the challenging and sometimes very painful risks of investing. Many investors have become so frustrated by their inability to effectively manage investment risks that they've come to see the investment markets as giant casinos, and investing as a crap shoot or game of chance. Although that's not the case, those feelings of exasperation, frustration, and second-guessing our investment decisions are only natural. They result from the growing uncertainties generated by our increasingly faster-paced, rapidly changing modern world.

Frequently those feelings are further amplified by surprise crises, economic shocks, natural disasters, and geopolitical or economic turmoil. The added concerns generated by gut-wrenching market drops, and increased market volatility, which defy even the forecasting skills of the most experienced investment experts, can intensify those feelings to the extreme.

So what is the process we use to so effectively manage our everyday life-risks? Why and how can those same skills work just as well in the investment world?

That's exactly what we cover in the rest of this chapter. We start by refamiliarizing you with your own highly developed life-risk management process. Then we review how to use the elements of that ingrained system as the foundation of your own, user-friendly investment risk management method, and close by introducing you to the basic steps of the "Risk-Wise" Investor risk management process.

Releasing Your Natural, Everyday Risk Management Skills

The more you become familiar with and use the "Risk-Wise" Investor risk management approach, the better you'll understand and more effectively manage the risks you face now and in the future.

First, you need to refamiliarize yourself with the natural, step-by-step process you used in gaining your skill and comfort in managing everyday life-risk. However, that can be challenge for anyone; since by the time we reach adulthood the vast majority of us have internalized our risk management process so much that it has become automatic. We've become so comfortable managing life-risks; we do it on an instinctive level without even thinking about *how* we do it. In fact, when asked what process they use in managing their everyday life-risks, many people say that they don't have a specific process. They just do it.

As such, I encourage you to take a moment right now to think through the steps you personally use in successfully managing the life-risks you face everyday. Then write those steps down. (Give yourself a little time to think about it and let it resurface, then write each step down in the spaces provided.)

1. _____

2. _____

3. _____

4. _____

5. _____

6. _____

Now, did the steps in your own risk management process come to mind easily, or did they require serious effort to recall? How successful were you in listing all the steps? How long did it take? If you are like most people, you found it surprisingly difficult for a process that you use so many times each and every day.

Although our bodies are hard-wired with many built-in, involuntary life-risk management systems (like our natural reaction to blink when something moves rapidly in front of our eyes or our instantaneous reflex reaction when we touch something hot), most of our life-risk management skills are learned skills. We learn them from our parents, friends, by watching others, and by ourselves.

Below is a quick review of the step-by-step process we humans use in learning how to so effectively manage the life-risks we face.

The Everyday Life-Risk Risk Management Process Steps

1. **Identify Risks.** Determine, and remember for future use those things that may cause harm or interfere with your physical health, goals, or objectives.
2. **Understand Risks.** Learn as much as you can about each potential risk, including its likelihood of occurring and its impact should it occur.
3. **Review Risk Reduction/Risk Management Strategies Available.** Become familiar with any and all strategies that can be used to avoid each risk, reduce the likelihood of a risk occurring, and minimize a risk's impact should it still occur.
4. **Evaluate the Risk/Reward Tradeoff (with and without risk management).** Review the rewards of an action, or inaction, and the risk reduction options available to use versus the risks (likelihood and impact) of the potential action or inaction.
5. **Make Your Decision to Act or Not Act.** Once you identify and understand the rewards and the risks (likelihood and impact), have evaluated the effectiveness of the risk management strategies available to use, and have a full understanding of your risk/reward trade-offs, you then make your decision to either act or not act. You can then decide to avoid the risk entirely, act and accept the risk with risk reduction initiative(s) in place (reducing the risk likelihood and/or impact) or act and accept the risk with no risk reduction.
6. **Implement** your decision.
7. **Learn and Adapt.** Continuously learn from actual experience, then use what you learn to make better risk/reward decisions in the future.

Although these steps may at first seem simplistic, their ultimate risk management success is the result of each step building sequentially on the foundation of the one before to create a very powerful and effective risk management system.

Releasing Your Everyday Life-Risk Management Skills in the Investment World

As a result of its effectiveness and flexibility, you can apply that same basic, step-by-step, life-risk management process to managing investment risks, while paying special attention to some of the differences in managing investment risks versus real world, life-risks (Which we'll cover in-depth soon.)

In addition, it's very important to be patient with yourself. You gained your facility with managing life-risks over at least several decades. So remember, just like learning to do anything new, managing investment risks may initially feel a little awkward, cumbersome, and slow. However, the more you use it and repeat it, the faster, easier and more comfortable you'll become. Then, over time, it becomes so automatic, internalized, and second nature, that you won't even have to even think about it any more. You'll just do it.

The Fundament Principals of "Risk-Wise"Investing

Before reviewing the "Risk-Wise" Investor risk management process it is very important to consider some basic facts about risk and its management. First, life, risk, and reward are inseparable, interconnected elements. In fact, just to live at all exposes each of us to numerous risks, not the least of which is day-to-day survival.

In discussing risk management, Walter Wriston, Former Chairman of Citicorp, Chairman of the Economic Policy Advisory Board for President Reagan from 1982 to 1989 and recipient of the Presidential Medal of Freedom said at www.online.citibank.co.in/portal/co/var.ppt: "All of life is the management of risk, not its elimination."

This means that since it's impossible to eliminate risk in life, we are all exposed to numerous kinds of risk whether we like it or not. As a result, since we can't eliminate risk, we each must decide to either manage risks or be subject to their raw and potentially painful impact. Below are a few basic principals of risk management that are very important to keep in mind as you go about managing risk.

- Risk and reward are a normal part of life, of everything we do, including investing.
- Risk/reward trade-offs are integral to every decision, action, or inaction.

- Effective risk management is critical to long-term investment and life success.
- Risks can be managed, but never eliminated.
- You cannot effectively manage risk or uncertainty without understanding it.
- The more you know about risk and risk management the more effective you'll be.
- Risk management will not work effectively if you do not understand how and why it works or have confidence in it.
- The most effective method of managing risks is to:
  - Directly face risks.
  - Become familiar with risks.
  - Understand risks.
  - Prepare for risks *in advance*.

When investing, the practical implementation of these risk management principles can best be achieved by using the same logical sequence of steps all of us use in our everyday life-risk management processes. The "Risk-Wise" Investor risk management method follows those steps, and in addition integrates into each step the special, unique considerations necessary for successful "Risk-Wise" Investing.

Building a Solid Foundation

Although the following process may at first glimpse appear simple and straightforward, don't allow its simplicity to deceive you into underestimating its value and power.

Just because something is complex or quantitatively based, doesn't mean it is necessarily better or more effective. Keep in mind what Benoit Mandelbrot, distinguished Sterling Professor of Mathematical Science at Yale University, one of the fathers of chaos theory, the inventor of the new field of fractal geometry (the geometry of nature), and extensive researcher of market price changes said in his excellent 2004 book *The (Mis)Behavior of Markets*. In discussing the efficient market hypothesis, which has been embraced by Wall Street, and become so popular with many academics, consultants, market analysts, and portfolio managers over the past 30 years, Professor Mandelbrot says, "Alas, the theory is elegant but flawed, as anyone who has lived through the booms and busts of the last decade can see."[1]

As with any successful multistep process, each step of the "Risk-Wise" process is built on the previous one. The quality and effectiveness of your end results, and the risk management benefits you enjoy will depend entirely on how well and how thoroughly you complete each preceding step. With each step in this risk management process being the foundation of the next step, the book devotes considerable additional time to familiarizing you with key information, valuable insights, and important facts you'll find essential in effectively building a solid foundation at each step of the "Risk-Wise" risk management process.

The "Risk-Wise" Investor—Risk Management Process Steps

Now that you've refamiliarized yourself with the steps in your own, everyday, life-risk management system, and reviewed the fundamental principles of effective risk management, it is time to introduce you to how to apply those insights in managing the risks in the investment world. Once you become familiar with the "Risk-Wise" Investor approach and begin using it more and more, you'll gradually find yourself becoming as accomplished at managing investment risks as you are managing the everyday life-risks you face.

The "Risk-Wise" Investor Process

1. Personal Risk Assessment
   - Define risk (your definition of risk is the foundation of the entire process).
   - Identify risks (you can't manage a risk you haven't identified as a risk).
   - Understand risks (their likelihood and their personal impact should they occur).
   - Determine which risks to avoid, accept, and/or manage.
2. Review risk reduction/management strategies available (their strengths and weaknesses).
3. Evaluate your risk/reward trade-offs (while avoiding common evaluation pitfalls).
4. Make your decision to act or not act — then implement it (while avoiding the common decision-making traps of many investors).
5. Effective ongoing risk monitoring and decision making (continuously being on guard for the emergence of new risks or threats and the evolving nature of known risks).

Building on this basic outline of the "Risk-Wise" Investor risk management process, the rest of this book will focus on how you can put each step of that process into action with extensive practical insights and valuable additional information that will help you build you own personal, customized risk management plan. We'll review how to apply a new empowering definition of "risk" used by some of the top corporate chief risk officers (CROs) to your lifetime risk management and investment success. We'll also discuss insights and lessons from the new field of behavioral finance and how to use them in avoiding very common risk/reward decision-making traps. In addition, we'll cover a simple way to determine which risks you personally should avoid entirely, which risks to take and manage, and which ones to just accept.

On completing this book you'll have also learned how to manage the full range of risks occurring in roaring bull markets; frightening bear markets; uncertain markets; and sometime the most challenging risks of all, the risks, traps, and pitfalls of our own, frequently flawed, decision-making biases. You'll have everything you need to create and implement your very own customized, comprehensive, ready-for-anything investment risk management plan, and will be well on your way to becoming as accomplished and comfortable in managing investment risks as you are in managing your everyday life-risks.

CHAPTER 3

The Evolving History of Risk and Risk Management

Better to be wise by the misfortune of others than by your own.

Aesop

O f course risk and risk management are nothing new to human experience. They are as much a part of being human as living and breathing. Yet most of us know very little about how risk management has developed and evolved over time. So the very first step in improving our own knowledge and understanding of risk and risk management must be to become familiar with the history of this very important subject. Only then can we benefit from that knowledge in managing the risks we ourselves face today.

Rather than review the history of risk and risk management in detail, we'll be taking a multidisciplinary, highlights approach. However, it can still benefit you greatly to study this very important subject in further detail. Therefore, I strongly recommend you read works such as Charles Kindleberger's classic book on the history of financial crises, *Manias, Panics, and Crashes*, Peter Bernstein's excellent history of risk, *Against the Gods*, and the classic, *Extraordinary Popular Delusions and the Madness of Crowds*, by Charles Mackay, and any of the many other fine books on the history of money, investing, and risk. You'll be very glad you did.

Historical Highlights

In reviewing this chronology, you'll also see just how our world is becoming both safer and riskier at the same time. This seeming paradox occurs because as we live with established and familiar risks we gain control and mastery over them, and gradually we become less concerned about them. However, the accelerating pace of change and the ever-more-interconnected nature of our modern world means that new, unfamiliar, and often frightening risks we've never experienced before can pop onto the scene to challenge our risk management abilities. Simultaneously, we can also very easily fall victim to overconfidence in our risk management abilities, let down our guard, and end up paying a very high price for erroneously assuming that some of our old, familiar risks were fully under our control.

This overview of the history of risk and risk management addresses the gradual evolution of our risk management knowledge and skills over time. It highlights examples of our triumphs over some risks, as well as instances where risks have surprised us, harmed us, and taught us how to better deal with them in the future. This review is divided into three general sections, each coinciding with the three main eras in the evolution of our growth in understanding risk, risk management, and uncertainty:

Part 1: A brief review of the ancient world through the Middle Ages.
Part 2: The pivotal role of the Renaissance
Part 3: The post-Renaissance period to the present.

This review is not meant to be a comprehensive study of the history of risk management but rather a quick, high-level overview of the growth of our knowledge of risk and risk management over time, better understanding, and a deeper knowledge of how we humans are gaining a better understanding of risk and how to manage it more effectively.[1]

Part 1: The Ancient Past (Pre-600 B.C.)

The fragile, and challenging nature of the hunter/gatherer lifestyle of very ancient times placed enormous demands on the ability of people to survive from day to day. Often referred to as the Ancient Past, this period lasted until about 600 B.C. in most parts of the world. Listed below are a few insights into what life was like for humans during that ancient period of time.

- People lived at the mercy of their environment and were consumed with the basic, continuous struggles of finding enough food, providing shelter for themselves and raising their offspring.
- The seasons, weather, and the availability of food dictated peoples' lives.
- Human life spans were considerably shorter than they are today.
- One day was very similar to the next, with little change over time.
- Decisions were driven by instinct or the necessity to follow food sources.
- Men and women were truly passive before nature.

- Oracles, witchdoctors, astrologers, and soothsayers read the stars, entrails, smoke, dreams, and animal bones in an effort to help people gain insights into their uncertain future, and/or what the gods had in store for them.
- During this period people viewed their future as a matter of random chance, luck, and/or the vagaries of the forces of nature or the gods. Humans took what was dished out to them and did the best they could to deal with the conditions that were presented.
- People invented unseen forces and ascribed divine intelligence to natural phenomenon, which they then could blame for misfortunes, praise and thank for good luck, or sacrifice to in order to gain indulgences, favors and special requests.
- Gradually, people began to see natural patterns and began to use that knowledge to their benefit. They developed mechanisms and systems to deal with what they could expect as well as the occasional surprises that could occur, even if they couldn't predict the exact timing or form of those surprises.
- People were unable to conceive of having any real influence or control over the circumstances of their lives.

Over thousands of years, farming, and then the domestication of livestock gradually developed. Those innovations led to the establishment of permanent villages, then towns, cities, states, and eventually empires. Even when towns and cities developed, people still had little or no control over their lives. Their futures were set out for them from birth. They were born into the vocation of their families, and even those individuals of noble birth had no real alternative but to live the life they were born into, in their particular locale. In fact, traveling outside their immediate home base was rarely done because of travel's many dangers, perils, and uncertainties. People literally had little or nothing to say about their futures. Life was simple, hard, generally very short by today's standards, and offered people few options and few opportunities to influence their fate.

Early History (600 B.C.–A.D. 500)

By 600 B.C. cities, kingdoms, and civilizations had developed. Many of the modern characteristics of civilized societies we know today were already in place and reasonably well developed. Yet humans still possessed very limited ability to control their lives or determine their own futures because so much of what happened to them was beyond their personal control.

In fact, generation after generation of Chinese, rather than use their own judgment, depended on the teaching and guidance offered in the *I Ching*. During their classic era even the Greeks, as culturally sophisticated as they were, still consulted the Oracle at Delphi for insights into the future on their most important issues. Here are some other insights into life during this period of early human history.

Sixth Century B.C.: The Chinese sages Confucius and Lao-tzu developed and taught their principles. Confucius emphasized self-cultivation and a preference for sound judgment, equilibrium and harmony, while Lao-tzu, the father of Taoism, was greatly influenced by nature and taught the benefit of letting events follow their natural course. This period also saw the beginnings of Greek philosophy.

Fourth Century B.C: Plato asserted that all things partake of two worlds: the visible world that is always changing and the intelligible world that remains unchanged

333 B.C: Alexander the Great expands the limits of what was ever thought possible, from the scope of his conquests, to demonstrating how effective out-of-the-box thinking can be in solving problems, when cleaving the Gordian knot with his sword.

49 B.C: Establishing a historic example of unalterable decision making, Julius Caesar crosses from Gaul into Italy over a stream called the Rubicon, breaking a Roman law forbidding any general to lead his troops onto Italian soil.

The Middle Ages (A.D. 500–A.D. 1500)

The Middle Ages lasted about a thousand years from the fall of the Western Roman Empire in the fifth century to the beginning of the Early Modern Period. The Reformation of Western Christianity, the growing view of the "dignity of man" in the Italian renaissance, and the beginning of European overseas expansion signaled its end.

This was truly a multiphased transition period lasting almost one thousand years. The following timeline briefly highlights some of the important characteristics of life during each of the major phases of the middle ages.

The Dark Ages (500–800) directly following the fall of the Romans was characterized by:
- Elevated political uncertainties (in the vacuum left by Rome's fall).
- A reduction in economic activity.
- Successful incursions into Europe by non-Christian peoples.
- The general loss of learning and literacy.
- The church and clergy were *the* unifying cultural influence, which also maintained the arts and knowledge of writing and reading.

The High and Later Middle Ages (800–1400): were characterized by:
- A revival of urban and commercial life.
- The development of the institutions of lordship and vassalage.
- Castle and cathedral building.
- Mounted warfare and the Crusades.
- Growth of royal power.
- The rise of commercial interests.
- The great plague of the fourteenth century.

800–900: The Arabic number system (originally developed by the Hindus), which includes the new invention zero, becomes accepted throughout the Arab empire, and energizes the use of mathematics due to its ease of use compared to previous systems.

1066: The Norman conquest of England and the age of feudalism.

Eleventh Century 1100-1200: The foundations on which algebra is developed are articulated by the Persian poet, polymath, philosopher, teacher, and mathematician Omar Khayyam
- The precursors of Universities like Oxford and Cambridge were first established as scholastic enclaves by religious monks
- Literacy started becoming more available to a wider class of people.

1215: The Magna Carta becomes the basis of constitutional government.

1291: Two hundred years of Crusading ends with the fall of Acre. While tens of thousands died in them, the Crusades led to Europeans being introduced to many new technologies, developed trade routes, and improvements in navigation. Silk, which was known to the Romans much earlier and new items such as gunpowder and navigational aids were discovered by the West, which made the great Age of Exploration possible.

Twelfth and Thirteenth Centuries: A dramatic increase in the rate of new inventions and innovations began taking place. These included invention of the cannon, spectacles, and cross-cultural introduction of the compass and astrolabe.
- Improvements were made to the design and construction of ships, improving seafaring.
- Great numbers of translations of Greek and Arabic medical and scientific works were distributed throughout Europe.
- Aristotle and his rational, logical approach became very important.

Part 2: The Renaissance

The major transition period between modern times and the past was the Renaissance. It began in the 1300s in Italy, spread to the rest of Europe in the 1400s and 1500s, and generated revolutions in art, science, culture, religion, and thinking. Listed below are a few high points of the period.

- Beliefs of more than 3000 years were openly challenged and left behind.
- Humans began to believe they could actually understand and gain control over their world and manage the risks they faced.
- Artistic expression blossomed.
- Scientific inquiry, knowledge, and interest exploded.
- Printing press is invented.
- New world is discovered.
- The incredible Age of Exploration begins.
- Commerce and trade blossomed.
- People could now earn wealth and were not limited to inheriting it.
- Superstition and tradition lost their strangleholds over people's thinking.
- Serious study of risk and risk management began.
- A fourteenth-century English friar proposed Occam's Razor, a rule of thumb for scientists and other trying to analyze data: *The best theory is the simplest one that accounts for all the evidence.*

Part 3: Entry into the Modern Age and Up to the Present

The late renaissance in the 1600s marks the beginning of the western world's transition into the modern age. From this period onward, the pace of humankind's growth in knowledge, progress and change has continued to accelerate up through the present day. The growth in our knowledge, understanding and management of risk is no exception. The following timeline reviews developments and events of note in that continuously evolving process. As you review this segment of the timeline, don't focus so much on the details of each event; concentrate on the flow of events, the increasing pace of change, and the escalating importance of proactive risk management.

1620: Francis Bacon, English philosopher, lawyer and politician promoted the advantages of scientific study over inductive reasoning.

1630s: The Dutch issued and traded options securities virtually identical to those we use today.

1641: René Descartes, French philosopher, mathematician, and scientist proposed reason as a better way of gaining knowledge and established the foundation of the scientific method we still use today. He popularized the fundamental precept of sound reasoning, that anything must be doubted until it can be demonstrated or proved.

1650s:
- Printing and books had ceased to be a novelty.
- The Amsterdam stock exchange was flourishing.

- Blaise Pascal and Pierre de Fermat developed the basic concept of calculating probabilities for chance events from gambling.

1660: Pascal's wager on the existence of God showed that the consequences of being wrong can be the most important factor to consider for a decision maker, rather than the likelihood.

1687: Edward Lloyd founds Lloyd's of London in his coffee house. He creates a risk marketplace where first ship owners, and then others seeking insurance against financial risk, could acquire that protection from a risk taker (underwriter) for a mutually agreed premium payment by the insured.

1693: Edmund Halley, The astronomer famous for Halley's comet, developed the first mortality (life expectancy) tables.

1703: Gottfried von Leibniz's comment, "Nature has established patterns originating in the return of events, but only for the most part," to math genius Jacob Bernoulli prompts Bernoulli to invent the Law of Large Numbers and statistical sampling. Bernoulli's work then leads to the modern activities of statistical polling, wine tasting, stock picking, and the testing of new drugs.

1720: The "Bubble Year." The South Seas Bubble in England, the Mississippi Bubble in France, and a remarkable range of other new investment ventures, many financed with borrowed money, all creating enormous speculative frenzy throughout England and Europe, finally collapsed. They financially devastated large numbers of individuals and institutions alike.

1730: Abraham de Moivre first demonstrated the structure of normal distribution of random events, introducing what we know today as the bell curve.

1738: Daniel Bernoulli created the basics of risk analysis by observing random events from the personal standpoint of how much an individual desires or fears each possible outcome, and he introduced the term *utility* to risk management. He stated that the desire of any individual for more over less is inversely proportional to the quantity of goods the individual already possesses.

1763: Housing, turnpike, and canal speculation throughout Europe.

1774: Dutch merchant Adriann van Ketwich creates the first investment fund, which he named *Eendragt Maakt Magt* or "unity creates strength," on the principle that diversification and its resulting reduction of risk would appeal to smaller investors.

1793: English canal mania hits (bubble).

1797: Collapse of the French Assignat currency from hyperinflation.

1822: King Wilhelm I of the Netherlands launches the first closed-end mutual fund.

1825: Latin American bonds, mines, and cotton mania.

1847: Railway and wheat speculative excesses in England.

1848: Carl Frederick Gauss studied the blell curve, earlier described by de Moivre, and developed a structure for understanding random events that are large in number and independent of one another.

  ▪ Continued railway and public land speculation.

  ▪ California Gold Rush began with discovery of gold at Sutter's Mill.

1873: Railroad, homesteading, and Chicago building booms in the United States.

1875: Francis Galton (the first cousin of Charles Darwin) discovered the concept of regression to the mean. That concept is based on his observation that although values in a random process can differ from the average value, in time they will move back to it. This concept will influence a number of areas, including investing, and can be recognized in everyday observations such as:

  ▪ Why Pride goes before a fall and clouds tend to have silver linings.

  ▪ Why we make decisions based on extremes returning to normal.

1890: Silver and gold speculation leading to inflation (Sherman Silver Act in the U.S.).

1893: The Panic of 1893 and repeal of the U.S. Sherman Silver Act, which reversed previous excesses.

1900: Sigmund Freud's analysis of the unconscious mind found that people's decisions and actions can frequently be effected by factors concealed in the mind rather than by pure logic.

  ▪ The great Galveston, Texas, hurricane and tidal surge killed more than 5,000 people and destroyed the city in less than 12 hours, leading to dramatic changes in the scope and nature of weather prediction in North America and the world.

1906: 5:12 A.M., April 18, the Great San Francisco Earthquake began its 45–60 seconds of shaking, massive destruction, and raging fires. It led to over 2000 deaths, the demolition of the largest city in the western United States, and key lessons on the importance of managing the secondary and tertiary earthquake risks of weak building design and construction methods and poor fire preparedness.

1907: Coffee and rubber booms in Brazil and the United States. The Union Pacific Railroad boom.

  ▪ **The Panic of 1907** A number of Wall Street brokerage firms went bankrupt, The Knickerbocker Trust and Westinghouse Electric failed, the Dow-Jones Industrial Average dropped 45 percent from its previous high, and J.P. Morgan brought together leading financiers to save the banking system and the economy.

  ▪ **Irving Fisher,** an American economist developed the concept of net present value as a tool to help make better decisions. He proposed discounting expected future cash flow at a rate that considers an investment's risk.

1913: The U. S. Federal Reserve Bank was created to actively manage the very common boom and bust swings of the U.S economy and to act as lender of last resort to the banking system, should the need arise again.

1921: Frank Knight published *Risk, Uncertainty, and Profit*. The book became a keystone in the library of risk management. He distinguished uncertainty, which is not measurable, from risk, which is. He celebrated the prevalence of "surprise" and cautioned against over-reliance on extrapolating past frequencies/probabilities into the future.

- *A Treatise on Probability* by John Maynard Keynes appeared. He derided dependence on the Law of Large Numbers, emphasizing the importance of relative perception and judgment.

1923: The Germany Weimer Republic experienced hyperinflation, with prices for everything doubling every two days at its peak. Banknotes had lost so much value they were used as wallpaper.

1924: The first modern mutual fund (open-end investment company) was started in Boston by MFS Investment Management. Later the same year, State Street Investors Trust launched the second mutual fund.

1926: John von Neumann presented his first paper on a theory of games and strategy at the University of Gottingen, suggesting he goal of not losing is superior to that of winning.

1928: The first antibiotic drug, Penicillin, was accidentally discovered by Dr. Alexander Fleming, beginning the antibiotic revolution in medicine, reducing the risk of lethal infections and saving tens of millions of lives worldwide ever since. Example of logical risk management; First method to effectively reduce the common risk of death from infection.

- The first no–sales charge mutual fund was launched by the investment firm of Scudder Stevens and Clark of Boston.
- The first mutual fund to include both stocks and bonds, *The Wellington Fund*, was launched.

1929: There were 19 open-end mutual funds competing with 700 closed-end funds.

- In late October the stock market bubble, which had been building for over 10 years burst, dropping from a DJIA high of 381.17 on September 3 to a low of 41.22 on July 8, 1932. That drop created a total loss of 89.19 percent over that three-year period. It took until 1954, almost 22 years, to once again reach its previous 1929 high.

■ With the stock market crash, the highly leveraged closed-end of the time were wiped out although smaller open-end funds managed to survive.

1933–1934: The Great Depression in the United States reached its deepest point.

■ The U.S. Securities and Exchange Commission was created to regulate the securities markets (and improve risk management).

■ The Securities Acts of 1933 and 1934 were enacted to safeguard and protect the interests of investors, and mutual funds were required to register with the SEC and provide disclosure in the form of a prospectus.

1944: John Von Neumann (also see 1926) and Oskar Morgenstern published their paper, "The Theory of Games and Economic Behavior," which describes a mathematical basis for making economic decisions. They embraced the view that decision makers are *always* rational and consistent, in general agreement with most economic thinkers before them.

1945: The Atomic Age began; and the enormous rewards, risks, responsibilities, and related risk management issues raised deep concerns for all humankind.

■ The Nuclear Arms Race initiated between the United States and the U.S.S.R.

1946: The Magic 8 Ball decision-making aid was invented by The Alabe Crafts Company of Cincinnati, Ohio. It was designed to help people make decisions under uncertain conditions.

1947: Rejecting the classical notion that decision makers behave with perfect rationality, Herbert Simon argued that because of the costs of acquiring information, executives make decisions with only "bounded rationality," and make do with *good enough* decisions.

1952: Dr. Jonas Salk began human testing of his new (killed virus) polio vaccine, designed to neutralize the risk of polio, which at the time was everyone's second-greatest fear after the fear of nuclear attack. Dr. Salk's vaccine was finally declared safe and effective in April 1955. His vaccine, over time, virtually eliminated the risk of Polio, saved million of lives and untold suffering around the world.

■ The *Journal of Finance* published "Portfolio Selection," by graduate student Harry Markowitz, who later won the Noble Prize in 1990. It explained aspects of return and variance in an investment portfolio and why diversification works, leading to many of the sophisticated quantitative measures of financial risk in use today.

1956: The *Harvard Business Review* published *Risk Management: A New Phase of Cost Control,* by Russell Gallagher, then insurance manager of Philco Corporation. It highlighted the cost savings of risk management.

1960s: Edmund Learned, C. Rowland Christiansen, Kenneth Andrews, and others created the SWOT (strength, weaknesses, opportunities, and threats) model of analysis, and it became widely adopted as a practical decision-making aid.

1961: The term "Catch-22," from Joseph Heller's best-selling book, became popular for describing bureaucratic, frustrating, and illogical procedures that impede good decision making and risk management.

1962: Dr. Albert Sabin saw his oral polio vaccine (live-attenuated virus) approved by the FDA. Along with the Salk vaccine, it further contributed to the virtual elimination of the risk of polio throughout the world, within 40 years.

- *Silent Spring* by Rachel Carlson was published, challenging the public to seriously consider the risks of the degradation of our air, water, and ground from both inadvertent and deliberate pollution. This led to the creation of the U.S. Environmental Protection Agency in 1970 and the global Green movement so active today.

1964: Bill Sharpe articulated his Capital Asset Pricing Model in the *Journal of Finance*. He also developed what becomes known as the Sharpe Ratio, and eventually is extensively used to characterize how well the return of an asset compensates the investor for the risk taken. (Sharpe subsequently received the 1990 Nobel Prize in Economics along with Harry Markowitz.)

1965: The rear engine, compact car, the Corvair, manufactured by Chevrolet was exposed. Ralph Nader's book *Unsafe at Any Speed* appeared and gave birth to the consumer movement in the United States, then throughout the world.

1966: "Nuclear option" became a widely used new term (based on the massive impact of atomic weapons) used to indicate the most extreme option when making a decision.

- The insurance Institute of America developed a set of three examinations that led to the designation Associate of Risk Management, the first such certification.

1968: *Decision Analysis,* a book by Howard Raiffa, reviewed many decision-making techniques, including the use of decision trees and sampling to aid in decision making.

1969: In a triumph of stunningly successful risk management, focused effort, and technical achievement, in just about eight years President Kennedy's 1961 challenge to "land a man on the moon and return him safely to the earth by the end of the decade" was spectacularly achieved.

1972: Dr. Kenneth Arrow and Sir John Hicks won the Nobel Prize in Economics. Arrow imagined a perfect world where every uncertainty was identified, the Law of Large Numbers worked without fail, then pointed out that our knowledge will always be incomplete and "comes trailing clouds of vagueness."

1973: Fischer Black and Myron Scholes in a breakthrough academic paper, showed for the first time how stock options can be accurately valued. Their work began a transformation in the field of investment risk management. It took until the 1987 stock market crash and then again in the 1998 financial crisis (which was punctuated by the collapse of the hedge fund Long-Term Capital Management, where Black and Scholes were partners) for the flaws in their theoretical model to be exposed by actual financial panics.

- The OPEC oil embargo skyrocketed oil and gas prices, fuel rationing, high inflation, and extremely high interest rates.

1974–1975: Crash in the price of stocks, REITs, office buildings, and 747 jetliners. (The Dow Jones Industrial Average dropped to 577.)

1976: *Fortune Magazine*, with the support of the Risk and Insurance Management Society published a special article entitled "The Risk Management Revolution" articulating many ideas, which took over 20 years to be adopted.

- Hayne Leland and Mark Rubinstein, fellow finance professors at U.C. Berkeley developed the revolutionary idea for a new investment concept called *Portfolio Insurance,* which was designed to provide the upside potential in stocks with the downside limited only to an insurance premium (*see the notes under 1987 to learn how well this innovation worked*).

1979: Amos Tversky and Daniel Kahneman published their Prospect Theory, which established Behavioral Finance as a new academic discipline. They showed how the traditional rational model of economics incorrectly describes how people arrive at decisions when facing real-world uncertainties.

- The cover story "The Death of Equities" in *Business Week* magazine's August 13 issue became a famous example of a contrary indicator, since within a few years the stock market began a 20-year bull run, increasing over 1000 percent by the end of 1999.

1980: The Society of Risk Analysis formed in Washington, D.C., to represent public policy, academic, and environmental risk management advocates.

- Through the SRA's efforts the terms *risk assessment* and *risk management* became more familiar in North America and Europe.

- Monte Carlo simulations became popular in the theories of random walk, asset pricing, and finance, as a way of exploring a range of possibilities.

1983: William Ruckelshaus, the former director of the Environmental Protection Agency, delivered his speech on "Science, Risk, and Public Policy" to the National Academy of Sciences, launching the risk management idea in public policy.

- Risk management reached the national political agenda.

1984: The horror in Bhopal— 40 tons of poisonous methyl isocyanate gas were accidentally released from a Union Carbide chemical plant in Bhopal, India, killing 3,800 people and injuring 11,000 people. The accident served as a bellwether to the entire chemical industry and a catalyst for increased focus on risk management and safety reforms.

1986: Meltdown at Chernobyl: The Soviet nuclear power plant experienced a core reactor explosion as the result of a planned experiment that went bad. It sent a huge radioactive cloud into the atmosphere, immediately killing 31 people from radiation poisoning, forcing the evacuation of 130,000 people, and spreading radiation over most of Europe.

- Space Shuttle *Challenger* exploded just after liftoff on January 28, killing all crewmembers on board, setting the shuttle program back over two years, and becoming a horrific example of how even small errors in managing risk in complex systems can have catastrophic consequences.
- The Institute of Risk Management began in London establishing the first continuing education program in all facets of risk management.

1987: "Black Monday," October 19, 1987, hit the U.S. stock market. Its global shock waves reminded all investors of the risk and volatility in the markets.

- The Dow Jones Industrial Average (DJIA) dropped 508 points, to 1739 on record volume. The 22.5 percent one-day DJIA drop was the largest one-day percentage decline in stock market history and also set off record declines in stock markets around the world.
- The flaws of portfolio insurance, invented in 1976 (based on the quantitative Black/Scholes options pricing model) and then broadly used by institutional investors to reduce risk were widely exposed by the market crash. The inability to implement its strategies in a market route and the cost of portfolio insurance turned out to be much higher than the paper calculations had predicted, which invalidated the model. With the concept

failing to prevent large losses, it totally fell out of favor and has not been used the same way since. As Michael Lewis said in the introduction of his book, *Panic, The Story of Modern Financial Insanity*, copyright 2009, and published by W.W. Norton & Company, "The very theory underlying all insurance against financial panic fell apart in the face of an actual panic."

- Important assumptions concerning human rationality, the efficient market hypothesis, and economic equilibrium were brought into question by the event.
- Debate as to the cause of the crash of 1987 still continues many years after the event, with no firm conclusions reached.

1989: The *Exxon Valdez* super tanker ran aground on a reef in Alaska's Prince William Sound and punctured eight of its cargo holds, spilling over 11 million barrels of crude oil into one of the world's most pristine natural areas. The severity of the spill and the ineffective response to it created an economic and environmental disaster, leading to subsequent improvements in the design and construction of oil tankers and oil spill response preparation around the world.

- United Airlines Flight 232, while flying en route to Denver from Chicago, experienced an engine explosion, which expelled debris that severed all three hydraulic systems on the aircraft, leaving the pilot without any control of his DC-10. Through very unconventional methods, courageous effort, skill of the cockpit crew, and a highly coordinated emergency response, the plane was able to make a crash landing at the Sioux City, Iowa, airport. Due to outstanding risk management practices, both in the air and on the ground, of the 296 passengers and crew onboard, 184 people survived the crash. This event reaffirmed the importance of risk management planning and preparation.

1991: The spectacular bull market in Japanese stocks, The Nikkei Bubble ended, beginning a 14-year bear market.

1993: The title of Chief Risk Officer is first used by James Lam, of GE Capital, to describe the function of managing "all aspects of risk." Today there are hundreds of CROs, globally responsible for the multiple risk management functions of their organizations.

1995: Rogue trader Nick Leeson, in Singapore, found he was disastrously overextended and managed to topple Barings Bank (known as the Queen's Bank) within a couple of days, becoming a glaring example of insufficient financial risk management. Founded in 1762, the bank had financed the Napoleonic Wars, the Louisiana Purchase by the U.S. government, and the Erie Canal. At its demise, Barings was the oldest merchant bank in London.

1996: Risk and risk management made the best-seller book lists in North America and Europe with the publication of Peter Bernstein's *Against the Gods: The Remarkable Story of Risk*. Now in paperback and translated into multiple languages, this single book, more than any preceding papers, speeches, books, or ideas popularized the understanding of risk and the attempts over the centuries to manage it.

- The Global Association of Risk Professionals (GARP) representing credit, currency, interest rate, and investment risk managers, began in New York and London. By 2002, with over 5,000 members and 17,000 associate members it had become the world's largest risk management association.
- In the March–April issue of the *Harvard Business Review*, Peter Bernstein warned in his piece "The New Religion of Risk Management," about the replacement of "old world superstitions" with a "dangerous reliance on numbers."
- At the December meeting of the American Enterprise Institute, in discussing the strong stock market, Federal Reserve Bank Chairman Alan Greenspan said, "But how do we know when *irrational exuberance* has unduly escalated asset values, which then become subject to unexpected and prolonged contractions as they have in Japan over the past decade?"

1997: The Asian Financial Crisis (Asian Contagion) gripped much of Asia beginning in July, and raised fear of a worldwide economic meltdown (financial contagion). The IMF stepped in with a $40 billion program to stabilize the region. It resulted in President Suharto of Indonesia stepping down after 30 years in power, widespread rioting, dramatic price increases, and weakened economic conditions that lasted well into 1999.

1998: Long-Term Capital Management/Russian Crisis.

- The investment dream team of John Meriwether, former head of bond trading at Solomon Bros., Myron Scholes, and Robert C. Merton, who shared the 1997 Nobel Prize in Economics and David W. Mullins Jr., former Federal Reserve Vice-Chairman, saw the highly leveraged hedge fund they formed in 1994, Long-Term Capital Management, lose $4.6 billion in a few months.
- Despite being based on sophisticated quantitative financial models and overseen by Nobel laureates, with annualized returns of over 40 percent, before fees, in its first years, it still failed.
- In order to avoid heavy losses to its lenders and a wider collapse in the financial markets, the Federal Reserve Bank of New York organized a bailout of $3.625 billion by the fund's major creditors.

- After the creditors recovered their bailout investments, the fund was liquidated.
- In a far-sighted observation, some industry officials said that the Federal Reserve Bank of New York's involvement in the rescue, however benign, would encourage large financial institutions to assume more risk, in the belief that the Federal Reserve would intervene on their behalf too, in the event of trouble.

1999: The dot.com and Internet boom reached a true feeding frenzy, even though some observers were calling it a classic bubble. To their future great regret, many investors disdained any need for risk management because "this time it's different," "the sky is the limit," and "we are in a brand new era of mankind."

2000: In a great success for risk management, the widely anticipated Y2K bug failed to materialize, mainly due to the billions spent to update software systems worldwide.

- The dot.com bubble and its "irrational exuberance" finally burst, with devastating effect on business, high-tech industries, investors, and the national economy at large.

2001: The terrorism of September 11 and the collapse of Enron reminded the world that nothing is too big to collapse. Risk management became a more important concern for everyone.

- September 11, terrorists attacked the World Trade Center Towers in New York City, and the Pentagon in Washington, DC, killing more than 3,000 people. A similar aerial attack targeting the U.S. Capitol building was prevented by passengers on the highjacked plane. Those events led to a complete shutdown of domestic air travel for several days, closure of the U.S. securities markets, and economic dislocation, and increased security.
- Closure of the New York Stock Exchange, American Stock Exchange, and NASDQ markets from September 11 until Monday, September 17, which was the longest closure of the stock markets since the Great Depression in 1933.
- When the markets reopened, the Dow Jones Industrial Average stock market index fell 684 points, or 7.1 percent, to 8920, its biggest-ever one-day point decline.
- By the end of the week, the DJIA had fallen 1369.7 points (14.3 percent), its largest one-week point drop in history. U.S. stocks lost $1.2 trillion in value for the week.
- At the end of 2001, just over three months following 9/11 the DJAI was back over 10,000.
- *Fooled by Randomness: The Hidden Role of Chance in Life and in The Markets* by Nicholas Taleb was published by Random House. Taleb presented the thesis that humans are often unaware of the very existence of randomness. We frequently explain random

outcomes as nonrandom and view the world as more explainable than it really is. The book's ideas have profound implications for better risk management. Later, *Fortune* magazine selected it as one of "The Smartest Books of All Time."

2002: A major earthquake struck Alaska along the Denali fault, which passes directly under the Trans-Alaska Oil Pipeline, which carries up to a million barrels of oil per day. Yet, because of successful risk management in the design of the pipeline system and the quality of the maintenance, surveillance, and emergency preparedness, not a drop of oil was released, and a potential catastrophe was averted. This event served as a powerful example of the many benefits and cost effectiveness of properly executed risk management.

- Daniel Kahneman was awarded the Nobel Prize in Economics for his work in Prospect Theory and the study of judgment and decision making under uncertainty, heuristics, and biases. He and his collaborator Amos Tversky were recognized as the founders of Behavioral Economics.

2003: Space Shuttle *Columbia* disintegrated on re-entry after a 16-day scientific mission, killing all seven crewmembers. Although the danger of insulating foam falling off fuel tanks at launch was known to be a common problem, even before *Challenger's* launch, the accident served as a vivid reminder of how even small risks, if not addressed, can have catastrophic consequences.

- Northeast U.S. Blackout, August 14, 4:15 P.M. EDT: An enormous, widespread power outage affecting 10 million people in Canada and over 40 million people in eight northeastern and mid-western states became the most widespread electrical blackout in history. The ultimate cause was determined to be a cascade of events starting with high electrical demand, tree pruning issues around power lines in Ohio, the subsequent shutdown of an Ohio power plant, a software bug that prevented alarms from alerting controllers of an energy management network, which led to the failure of primary and backup computer control systems. Fortunately power was restored the next day.

2005: Hurricane Katrina slammed into the gulf coast of Florida, Mississippi, and Louisiana. The combination of storm surge, wave action, and high winds created broad destruction, which was unusually severe in New Orleans. The storm caused nearly 2,000 fatalities, an economic loss of $125 billion, and displaced hundreds of thousands of people from their homes and workplaces.

- Because of easier financing standards, prices of U.S and European residential real estate, European, and emerging market stocks all begin to increase dramatically, attracting even more investors and speculators, driving prices higher.

2007: Nassim Taleb's second book, *The Black Swan: The Impact of the Highly Improbable*, was published by Random House, became a best seller, and helped us look in a different way at how our world works. It was a warning that "our world is dominated by the extreme, unknown, and the very improbable, while we spend our time engaged in small talk, focusing on the known and repeated."

2008: The first truly global housing, credit, and commodity bubbles all burst simultaneously. The greatest financial crisis since the Great Depression (79 years earlier) gripped the United States, then the world. It began with the bursting of the residential real estate bubble, declining home prices, tightening credit, and record numbers of adjustable rate mortgages resetting at higher rates. Those events then led to record foreclosures nationwide and their negative effect on all the highly leveraged mortgages on large numbers of homes where the mortgages exceeded the homes' market values. Uncertainty generated by these issues then caused a collapse in the credit and lending markets nationwide.

- A nationwide $150 billion U.S. economic stimulus package was approved early in the year to help consumers jump-start the economy, but had little to no long-term positive effect.
- The U.S. Federal Reserve Bank bailed out Bear Stearns—appearing to many as an admission of failure of conventional risk management in financial institutions.
- Fannie Mae and Freddie Mac were bailed out by the U.S. Government; Lehman Brothers was allowed to default; and AIG was bailed out.
- The general confidence level of lenders dropped precipitously, leading to severely reduced lending activity and a slowing economy.
- Residential real estate prices in the United States and Western Europe extended their price declines.
- Dramatic commodity price increases (especially oil prices) began collapsing in the fall as the global economic slowdown spread and accelerated.
- The $700 billion, Troubled Asset Relief Program (TARP) was enacted.
- By October the Dow Jones Industrial Average was down over 30 percent from its high a year earlier, almost all asset classes saw large loses, and individual retirement plan and 401(k) assets levels were down dramatically.
- The U.S, economy slowed and appeared to be entering a prolonged recession.

- The Big Three U.S. automakers appeared before Congress seeking a bailout.
- December 1, the Dow Jones Industrial Average dropped 680 points, –7.7 percent in a single day, and the National Bureau of Economic Research declared the economy was in a recession and had started its economic decline in January 2008.
- Some forecasters even began talking about another depression being possible.
- Unemployment reached levels not seen in decades.
- Risk and risk management became a critically urgent issue to everyone from federal, state, and local governments, to businesses large and small, and individuals and families everywhere.

2009: The miracle on the Hudson River—On the afternoon of Thursday, January 15, Captain "Sully" Sullenberger, pilot of U.S. Air Flight 1549, and First Officer Jeffrey Skiles, with 155 people on board, accomplished a perfect emergency "splash" landing of their Airbus A320 aircraft on the Hudson River, adjacent to midtown Manhattan's 48th Street. Along with the incredible preparedness and actions of the New York City and New Jersey emergency services response teams, everyone on the aircraft survived, and the incident was universally declared an miracle.

- More than a miracle, the entire incident was a remarkable testament to the importance and the benefits of implementing the proven risk management principals of identifying, assessing, planning for, and thoroughly preparing for risks in advance. Just a few examples:
- Captain Sullenberger's skills and judgment gained in 19,000 hours of flight experience and service as an aviation safety expert combined with First Officer Skiles and their flight crew's emergency situation training, turned a potential disaster into a frightening inconvenience. (Crew preparation included flight attendants trained to only open an aircraft's front doors in a water landing, because opening the back doors, which one passenger attempted, can make the aircraft fill with water and sink much faster.)
- A320s are equipped with a ditch button in the cockpit, so just prior to a water landing the cockpit crew can hit that button and seal up the plane's fuselage, allowing the plane to stay afloat longer; the planes are also equipped with passenger escape chutes at all aircraft doors, which also function as life rafts in case of water landings.
- In another example of thoughtful emergency contingency planning, the A320's builders also installed an emergency power generator, called a ram-air turbine, which is designed to supply

emergency power to a plane's flight control systems in the rare event that both engines stop working, as did Flight 1549's engines. Had that in-flight, emergency power generator not been on board or not been deployed, the pilot would have been unable to control the plane and the outcome would have been a disaster.

- The continuous emergency response training and immediate actions of the Hudson River Ferry crews, the New York City and New Jersey Police, Fire, EMTs, Coast Guard, plus all the other emergency responders was critical, given the freezing weather and icecold water conditions. As one first responder, ferry captain said, "We train, train, train, and this is where it pays off."

Observations from the History of Risk and Risk Management

What can this historical overview teach us about risk and risk management? It's easy, just review the ten key historical lessons about risk and risk management outlined below:

1. Instability, not stability, is the norm throughout history. Instability and progress are very closely linked. Progress leads to "creative destruction" and instability, which are byproducts of the growth and improvement in our quality of life. In essence, instability is a price of growth.
2. Surprises and rare occurrences (both positive and negative) happen all the time, should be expected, planned for, and prepared for. We know they will occur. We just don't know when they will happen.
3. Crisis events, bubbles, busts, panics, crashes, wars, natural disasters, and all manner of surprise events are the norm throughout investment history.
4. Stability is the exception, as much as we may prefer it to be otherwise. Stability is actually very unnatural.
5. Risk cannot be eliminated. It can only be prepared for and managed. (There are risks in both acting and not acting.)
6. The pace of change in the world is accelerating, leading to increasing uncertainty, and more surprises worldwide.
7. With the complexity and interconnectedness of our world accelerating, breakdowns and accidents in our increasingly complex and worldwide systems are becoming more frequent, far-reaching, and potentially catastrophic.
8. When risks are ignored, trivialized, or danced around, they never become well managed.

9. Where risks are identified, directly faced, studied, and understood, risk management knowledge improves, leading to more effective and reliable risk management.
10. In our more complex and interconnected world, the stakes at risk have never been higher, and managing risk has never been more important.

So let's now continue with how to actually put this knowledge to work for our own, personal risk management benefit.

CHAPTER 4

"Risk"—What Is It, and How Does It Work?

Greater knowledge of a danger creates greater safety.
Dr. Benoit Mandelbrot
The (Mis)Behavior of Markets,
Basic Books, 2004

R isk is a very broad, deep, and multidimensional subject area. It has so many aspects that it can be extremely hard to pin down. Yet having as concise as possible an understanding of what risk is, how it works, and a sense of its behavioral characteristics is one of the most important steps in effectively managing risk.

Your Definition of Risk Is Crucial

How can you effectively manage risk without first defining it and then understanding it? The more we know about risk and risk management the more effective risk managers we become. Since history has taught us over and over again that the better we understand anything the better we can control it, we must first dedicate some time to better understand the true nature of uncertainty and risk. (Although a distinction is often made between those two terms, in that risk can be measured, while uncertainty cannot, for our current purposes I treat the terms interchangeably.) Once we have a deeper understanding of our subject we can then review risk management alternatives from a much more knowledgeable perspective.

When it comes to risk, the basic definition of risk you use is *the critical foundation* on which your entire risk management approach will be built. With a strong and solid foundation, what you build will make your risk management job easier and more effective, serve you better, and stand the test of time. With a weak or inferior foundation, even the grandest, most sophisticated risk management methodologies will not work, and will lead to frustration, disappointment, and unnecessary loss. Now you may believe that I'm making a big deal out something quite minor. Just think a moment however, about how the old, inferior, pre-Galileo celestial mechanics definition of the universe revolving around the earth, would have greatly frustrated mankind's space exploration efforts; about how the assumption of a flat earth stifled global exploration for centuries or even the common belief for thousands of years that man was not meant to fly, and never would. Your basic definition determines how you look at a question, and is the first step to ultimate success. It is the frame through which you view your challenge and can either complicate your efforts and restrict your success or empower and facilitate your efforts. Using the right definition is in fact, very, very important.

The Many Meanings of Risk

In their April 2002 paper "Perception of Risk Posed by Extreme Events," prepared for the Risk Management Strategies in an Uncertain World conference in Palisades, NY, Paul Slovic and Elke U. Weber discuss the multiple concepts of risk. In other words, the term *risk* itself can carry different meaning depending how it is used. They cite the most common uses as:

- Risk as a hazard
  - Example: "Which risks should we rank?"
- Risk as a probability
  - Example: "What is the risk of getting AIDS from a contaminated needle?"
- Risk as consequences
  - Example: "What is the risk of letting your parking meter expire?" (Answer: "Getting a ticket.")
- Risk as a potential adversity or threat
  - Example: "How great is the risk of riding a motorcycle?"

With that background perspective, let's review some of the general, high-level definitions of risk now in use:

- The possibility of harm
- Something bad might happen
- Possibility of a loss
- Negative surprise(s)
- The likelihood, impact, and timing of a negative event
- An indicator of a threat

- A possible threat
- Plus, from a different source: the probability that exposure to a hazard will lead to a negative consequence[1]

With so many different potential meanings for risk in general, it is not at all surprising that people find it challenging to understand and manage risk; however, the term has even more implications when we discuss it in relationship to investments. Used in this way, risk is alternatively described as:

- Unexpected market volatility
- Variations in investment returns
- Standard deviation
- Loss of capital
- Below benchmark performance

In reviewing these concepts and definitions, do you see any common characteristics among them? How do these definitions make you feel about your ability to deal with risk? Do they empower you and give you and your risk management abilities a sense of control, or do they make you feel as though you have little or no ability to manage such a multifaceted, intangible, and sometimes amorphous phenomenon as risk? Do they provide a better understanding, or do they actually complicate understanding?

Treat the Cause Not the Symptom

The reason these definitions may not empower us is first and foremost is that they really don't define risk as much as they describe the results of risk(s). Volatility, loss, variations of returns, negative surprises, harm, and negative consequences are the secondary or in some cases, even tertiary results of the actual risks manifesting themselves. Medical students learn very early the critical importance of treating the underlying disease rather than the symptoms, because otherwise they will never cure their patients. We need to do exactly the same thing and learn to focus on the risk itself, not the result(s) of the risk.

Using a recent, real-world example, tens of thousands of people lost their homes, and around 2,000 lost their lives, when Hurricane Katrina hit the gulf coast of the United States in 2005. New Orleans, Louisiana, experienced torrential rains, hurricane-force winds, extraordinarily high tidal surges, levy breaks, widespread flooding, and a disorganized emergency response effort. It all resulted in a catastrophe of massive proportions, with enormous human, cultural, economic, and environmental cost. Of all the various factors mentioned above, which were the actual risks and which resulted from the risk(s) occurring?

The three true risks were as follows:

1. New Orleans is almost totally surrounded by water, which averages a height of 14 feet above sea level, while much of the city is located below sea level. (The city is constantly fighting a centuries-long battle to stay dry.)
2. Hurricane Katrina itself (the 38th time a hurricane has flooded New Orleans since 1759).
3. The failure of the city's flood protection system.[2]

The results of the risk were the massive flooding; tens of thousands of people losing their homes; thousands losing their lives; and the enormous human, economic, and environmental costs.

Though this is an extreme example it graphically illustrates why it is so important in risk management to focus first on risks themselves rather than be distracted by results of risk. That focus is so important because you must first identify the risk(s), then successfully avoid, prepare for, neutralize, or manage the risk, so the results of that risk occurring are either entirely prevented from occurring or dramatically reduced.

An Empowering Definition of Risk

Given those facts, where can we find a definition of risk that meets our needs? Where can we find a definition of risk that's practical, empowering, focuses on the risks, and provides us with a high level of control? An outstanding answer came from right among the top ranks of corporate America, from the executive suite of one the best-known brands and most innovative and successful companies in the world, Apple.

Knowing that a unique definition of risk originated from a senior officer of Apple, you know it has to be something out of the ordinary, and it is. That's likely due to the fact that Apple and this executive have been successfully dealing with enormous business opportunities and practical everyday business risks for a very long time, and along the way they have done a lot of thinking, and a lot of work, on better understanding risk and risk management. The Apple senior executive I'm talking about has been with the firm since 1996 and is currently their chief financial officer, Peter Oppenheimer. He defines risk as:

"The degree to which an outcome varies from expectation."

Although initially that simple definition may not seem particularly profound, it is outstanding when you consider its far-reaching implications.

- It's a tremendously empowering definition of risk. It's empowering because although we have little to no control over the future, we alone determine our own expectations of potential outcomes based on our knowledge, understanding and preparation.

- Our expectation of the possibilities is under our control, which is not the case when we abdicate the control to totally random occurrences.
- The greatest impact typically comes from those risks that we don't expect or aren't prepared for.
- This definition helps us think through the full range of possibilities, both the expected and unexpected while recognizing how surprises happen all the time.
- We have total control over our expectations and full responsibility for them.
- More realistic expectations lead directly to better and more effective risk decision making and risk management.
- We have the power to ignore, accept, or prepare for what we expect.
- This definition has the flexibility to deal with both negative and positive variations from expectation.
- When we know, understand, and are prepared for risks, the very nature of that understanding and preparation converts them, should they occur, into inconveniences, and even potential opportunities.

Now that we've found a definition of risk that meets our objective, let's focus in on the nature of risk and its behavioral characteristics to see what we can learn that can help us better understand risk.

Understanding the True Nature of Risk

Although we typically think of risk or uncertainty as a singular phenomenon, according to Professor Benoit Mandelbrot, in *The (Mis)Behavior of Markets* (2004), uncertainty is actually more complex than that.

Understanding his breakthrough perspective, however, can make an enormous difference in understanding and managing risk. The real beauty and power of his observation is that it makes what we see happening more understandable, and ultimately helps make managing risk, easier and more logical. Please allow me to explain. . . .

After many decades of studying uncertainty in many markets, Dr. Mandelbrot (who is also renowned for inventing the newest form of geometry, fractal geometry) observed that uncertainty (risk) comes in more than one form. In fact, he came to the conclusion that instead of having only one form, uncertainty actually has three forms or "states." Initially that concept may seem a little hard to grasp. However, multiple states or forms are a quite common natural phenomenon. A tangible example of this characteristic is the very physical matter that composes our world and the entire universe. At a fundamental level, all matter has three basic states: gas, liquid, and solid. Just as water has three distinct states, ice, liquid, and gas (steam), with each phase exhibiting very different physical properties and behavioral characteristics from one another. Dr. Mandelbrot has identified three different states of uncertainty. Each of the states exhibits properties and characteristics as different from one another as ice, liquid water, and steam are from each other, even though they are all H_2O. The three states of risk identified by Professor Mandelbrot are *mild*, *slow*, and *wild* uncertainty.

The States of Risk

Doctor Mandelbrot's breakthrough description of risk in his book The (Mis) Behavior of Markets, 2004 is a classic example of thinking outside the box and the power of unbiased, scientific observation. Pointing out the similarities between the multiphase states of matter and the multiple phases of uncertainty and risk, he clarifies risk in a fundamental and important way. Once you become familiar with the three phases of risk he describes in The (Mis) Behavior of Markets, 2004, which are reviewed below, you'll never be able to look at risk the old way again.

> *Mild* uncertainty is like the risk in calling a series of coin tosses. This form of risk/uncertainty adheres to the normal bell distribution. It has well defined parameters, low variability, no big surprises, and is predictable. Dr. Mandelbrot says that it "is like the solid state of matter because it has low energy and stays where you put it." It is the kind of risk, price variability, and volatility that are periodically found during normal, random walk stock market periods. In his thought-leading 2007 book *The Black Swan*, Nassim Taleb characterizes this type of uncertainty as Type 1 randomness. Among the examples of this type of uncertainty he cites in that book are the height, weight, and calorie consumption of people, car accident rates, mortality rates, and IQ. This type of risk is characterized by the routine, the obvious, and the predicted.
>
> *Wild* uncertainty is the opposite of the mild form. It is unpredictable, irregular, outside what is normally expected, high energy, not structured, and has fast seemingly limitless and frightening fluctuations from one value to the next. In his book, Professor Mandelbrot states that "its like the gaseous phase of matter, no structure, no volume, no telling what it will do." This form of risk is typical of extreme, highly unstable, hypervolatile stock markets like the one in the fall of 2008. Nassim Taleb, in *The Black Swan*, also provides examples of this type of randomness. Examples of what he calls Type 2 randomness are the enormous range of wealth, personal income,

book sales, name recognition as a celebrity, damage caused by earthquakes, deaths in war, death in terrorist incidents, financial markets, commodity markets, and inflation rates. This risk type is subject to the accidental, the unseen, the unpredicted, surprises, and the extreme.

Slow uncertainty is the form of risk between *mild* and *wild*. Dr. Mandelbrot describes it as like the liquid state of matter.

Looking at risk and uncertainty in this multistate way, with each state of risk having different behavioral characteristics can be an enormous advantage in helping us understand not just the way risk works, but also the world we live in, the wide variances we can experience, and the range of market behaviors we can expect over time. It can also greatly help us in determining and implementing effective risk management methodologies.

Now that we have a practical, empowering definition of risk, and an understanding of the various types of risk and their behavioral characteristics, let's now direct our focus toward risk management.

CHAPTER 5

Which "School" of Risk Management Is Best?

The feeling of having done a job well is rewarding; the feeling of having done it perfectly is fatal.

Donley Feddersen

Rarely do we humans agree on there being only one right way to do things, and managing risk is no exception. Over time, numerous approaches to risk management have been attempted, with some more effective in certain situations than others. As time has progressed, these many different approaches have evolved into a couple of basic philosophies or schools of thought as to the best and most effective way to manage risk. This chapter objectively examines each of those "schools" of risk management to determine which is most effective for our use as individual investors. Before beginning that study however, we need to make certain we are very clear on exactly what we mean when we use the term *risk management*.

What Is Risk Management?

What characteristics do we want to see in a good definition of the management of risk? Besides being as brief as possible, it must be compatible with the following six statements:

1. Risk is not about the past or the present, but about the future.
2. The future offers no certainty, and as much as we hope or plan on it developing in a certain way, we really don't know what it will bring.

3. Risk is a measure of possibility and potential impact.
4. Risk can lead to a range of both good and bad possible outcomes.
5. Those outcomes can be mild or wild, and can include possibilities of extreme events that we can't even imagine (e.g., Black Swans).
6. Risk is a relative phenomenon, meaning that even when two people are both facing the same situation at the same time, the risk to one person is often entirely different from the risk to another. (This difference is caused by a number of factors including each individual's age, experience, level of exposure, understanding, knowledge, and confidence level when facing a threat, as well as their level of preparation.)

Considering all these factors let's consider a few different definitions of risk management, starting at the highest and most all encompassing level. The high-level definition of risk management developed by Felix Kloman, lifelong student of risk management, former risk management consultant and corporate chief risk officer (CRO), and worldwide authority on risk management, is outstanding. In his book, *The Fantods of Risk*, Seawrack Press, 2008, he shares this definition:

Risk Management is a discipline for dealing with uncertainty.

Another, somewhat more detailed definition incorporates the importance of risk exposure analysis and using a process-based approach. It comes from the InvestorWords.com online investment dictionary. There, risk management is defined as:

The process of analyzing exposure to risk and determining how to best handle such exposure.

Also, with risk management professionals in Australia and New Zealand being among the true thought leaders on risk management issues, the Australian Standards/New Zealand Standards 4360:2004 articulates a definition that recognizes the universal interlocking relationship of risk and reward, and the importance of using a risk management process and embracing a risk conscious culture. That definition reads:

Risk Management is the culture, processes and structures that are directed toward realizing potential opportunities while managing adverse effects.

For our purposes, the last definition may be the best because it highlights the five key elements of any successful risk management effort:

1. A focus on the future
2. A culture where risk is always kept in mind
3. The development of a risk management process to build consistency and effectiveness
4. Decisions that are based on a balanced understanding of both potential rewards and the potential risks
5. Advance preparation for potential adverse effects and potential opportunities

Risk management at its most fundamental starts with a continuous awareness of possible risk because surprises happen all the time. Then, after building on that foundation, comes the next step of determining what, if anything, needs to be done to avoid, prevent, or manage the risks identified, as well as initiatives to minimize their impact should any of them occur.

The Big Question

Over many years, two very different approaches, philosophies, or "schools" of risk management have developed. One has evolved and been used successfully over the last thousand or so years; the other has gained prominence, popularity, and widespread use in just the last half century. Proponents of each of these different risk management approaches tend to be dedicated believers in their particular method. They are strong proponents of what they perceive to be their chosen philosophy's numerous advantages and superiority over what they see as the inferior qualities of the other. The acolytes of these two, polar-opposite risk management "schools" are very adamant in their views and have rather heated debate with one another as a result. We, however, will explore and get to know both of them.

Given that no one approach is perfect and there are advantages and strengths, as well as disadvantages or weaknesses to any "school," rather than just select one or the other, we'll explore how we may be able to exploit the advantages and minimize the weaknesses of each approach. You should become more familiar with both methods and better able to manage the risks you face more effectively than investors who doggedly adhere to just one philosophy or the other.

Let's first look at the foundational underpinning of each of the risk management "schools" independently. We'll follow that examination with a dive into the nature of risk itself. Then we'll circle back to review how both these two opposing approaches to risk management can benefit your risk management effectiveness. Capitalizing on each one's strengths while minimizing their weaknesses will give you a big advantage as you pursue becoming an even more knowledgeable and effective "Risk-Wise" Investor.

Quantitative versus Subjective

The two schools of risk management are the *quantitative school* and the *subjective* or *qualitative school* of risk management. The quant school is embraced by those who see quantification of past occurrences, relationships, trends, correlations, mathematical relationships, and numbers as the best way to make risk/reward decisions about the future. By contrast, the Qualitative School encompasses those who believe that in a rapidly changing world it is more effective to base risk/reward decisions on subjective degrees of belief about a subjective future rather than relying exclusively on quantifications of the past. With just that short description, it should be easy to appreciate how controversy and tension have developed between these two very different approaches to risk management.

As our first step, let's review the most dominant investment risk management approach used today, the quantitative risk management method. We'll explore what it is, how it works, and some of its history. When we've completed that exercise with the quantitative approach we'll shift our attention to the qualitative or subjective risk management method, and go through the same process. Once you have a good understanding of both approaches, and with an understanding of the fundamental nature of risk (see Chapter 4), we'll review how both risk management methods may be use in concert to enhance your investment risk management effectiveness.

Trust the Numbers?

The quantitative approach to risk management initially evolved out of efforts in the late Renaissance to gain an advantage in gambling by better understanding the internal workings of games of chance. Quantitative techniques accelerated their early development in the mid-1600s with the expanding use of the more sophisticated mathematics made possible by the "new" Arabic numbering system. During that period, Blaise Pascal and Pierre de Fermat developed their concepts of calculating probabilities of chance events, based on gambling. They were followed in the early 1700s by Jacob Bernoulli's development of statistical sampling techniques, and the Law of Large Numbers. Bernoulli was then followed by Abraham de Moivre and his bell curve and then by Daniel Bernoulli (Jacob's younger brother) and his application of the concept of "utility" to risk decision making. In the 1800s Frederick Gauss worked out his more detailed analytics of the bell curve, and Francis Galton discovered, then articulated the natural process of regression to the mean and its application to business analysis and risk/reward decision making.

The quantitative method of risk management and its potential applications in the investment world gained a big surge in momentum in 1952 with the work of Harry Markowitz on return and variance in investment portfolios, on the efficient frontier, and on why diversification works. Then in 1964, Bill Sharpe introduced his capital asset pricing model and the Sharpe ratio that is still widely used today to characterize how well the return of an investment compensates the investor for the risk taken. With its comprehensive set of theories and mathematical elegance, the quantitative approach was subsequently embraced by the academic community and within a decade by the investment management world. The quantitative approach received still further reinforcement when in 1973, Fischer Black and Myron Scholes jointly showed how to accurately value stock options, just before the opening of the first true stock options exchange, the Chicago Board Options Exchange (CBOE) in 1974.

The quantitative approach to risk management including the "capital asset pricing model," "modern portfolio theory," "the efficient frontier," and defining risk using the statistical term standard deviation, all became mainstream. Its approach to constructing, monitoring, and adjusting investment portfolios based on mathematical formulae, numerical technical measures such as alpha, beta, Sharpe Ratios, and correlation coefficients made investment management and risk management seem much more like a science than an art. The quant method when embraced, promulgated, and perpetuated by academicians, became virtually the only method of investment risk management that has been taught in our universities and business schools over the last 30 years.

The quantitative approach has also become the *default* risk management approach of the majority of the global investment community. This quantification seems so logical, neat, tight, tidy, and well . . . appealing. It's so gratifying and reassuring to see the highly complex, ever changing, and complex, multidisciplinary subjects of risk and uncertainty reduced to rock-solid numbers and mathematical equations that allow us to manage risk more effectively than ever. Maybe Benjamin Disraeli was wrong when he remarked, "There are three kinds of lies—lies, damned lies, and statistics."

There, is however, one important question we have to ask ourselves: Has what works in theory and elegant equations actually worked in the real world? Fortunately, we now have over three decades of real-world experience to show us how well it works. Unfortunately, the real-world experience in using the quantitative risk management method has been mixed. Quite simply, what works beautifully in theory, in reality works sometimes and sometimes doesn't work well at all. In fact, the quantitative method works well in routine and reasonably stable markets (periods of mild uncertainty).

When this approach tends not to work well or becomes less effective is when markets begin behaving badly, when volatility increases, previously established relationships begin rapidly changing, and instability raises its ugly head (periods of wild risk). Of course, that is exactly when investors need effective risk management the most.

Now let's examine some of the assumptions that form the foundation of the quantitative theories and hypotheses.

Basic Assumptions Behind the Quantitative Risk Management Approach

While examining some of the basic assumptions behind the quantitative risk management approach, be sure to keep in mind that since there are literally thousands of real-world variables that impact investment and portfolio performance, assumptions must be made by the quantitative theoreticians to simplify the math enough to make the theoretical numbers work. However, if these assumptions are in fact inaccurate, then the entire structure built on them must be called into doubt.

Here are six assumptions on which the quantitative method depends:

1. The past is the best model for the future. So looking backwards is the best way to determine the future.
2. The efficient frontier is a valuable tool for determining the optimum asset allocation to maximize return and minimize risk in the future.
3. All price variations follow the standard bell curve distribution pattern.
4. Each value (trade/price) is independent of the previous or subsequent value (trade).
5. Markets are always efficient at determining the true value of a security.
6. Investors are always rational.

Strengths of the Quantitative Approach

The quantitative school of risk management has some very compelling advantages, including the following five:

1. An enormous amount of current and historic data available for analysis
2. Theoretical logic
3. Mathematical elegance
4. Excellent applications for use with computers
5. Practical applications in portfolio construction

Investment Reality

In reality, the quantitative method of risk management works reasonably well in normal markets, but has broken down, and has over and over again disappointed investors, when markets begin to change rapidly and extreme volatility raises its ugly head.

Another reality is that although future financial markets will have some things in common with past financial markets, the future will be different from the past (and at times behave very differently). So, relying too heavily on past relationships and trends in managing risks in the future, during the most rapidly changing period in human history, is a recipe for disaster.

Additionally the quantitatively based efficient frontier model of asset allocation (which defines a portfolio being efficient when it produces the most profit with the least risk) looks solid and stable over the 48-year time horizon presented in Figure 5.1. But when you examine the numbers decade by decade as in Figure 5.2, it's an entirely different story.

Figure 5.1 depicts the efficient frontier of equity and bond portfolios illustrated in 10 percent increments. Equity returns are based on the returns of the S&P 500 Index, which includes the reinvestment of dividends. Bond returns include the reinvestment of interest and are based on the Barclays Capital Aggregate Bond Index.

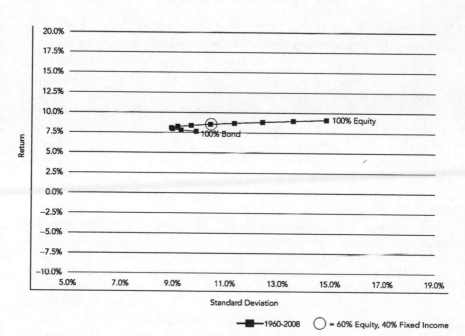

FIGURE 5.1 The Efficient Frontier 1960–2008 (48 years)

Source: Reprinted by permission from Rydex Investments 2008.

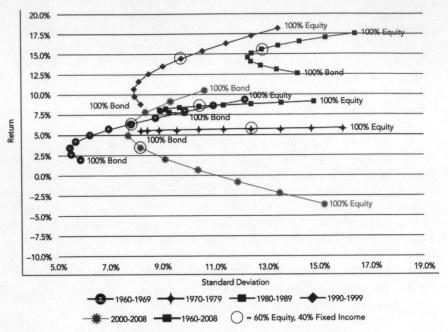

FIGURE 5.2 The Efficient Frontier Decade by Decade (1960–2008)

Source: Reprinted by permission from Rydex Investments 2008.

The standard deviation axis of the chart in Figure 5.1 represents annual portfolio volatility (sometimes volatility of returns is also called "risk") and the annual return axis represent annual percent returns. Each of the symbols represents a 10 percent change in the equity (stock)/bond mix between a 100 percent equity portfolio at one extreme, a 50 percent equity/50 percent bond portfolio in the middle and a 100 percent bond portfolio at the other extreme. In this example, a mix of 30–40 percent bonds and 60–70 percent stocks provided the best return for the least risk over the 47-year time frame.

However, when you look at shorter, decade-long time horizons, you see a highly variable and ever-changing environment. As you can see in Figure 5.2, the efficient frontier has moved around dramatically from decade to decade over the last 47 years. In fact, in the nine years from 2000 through 2008 the efficient frontier actually inverted (which is very unusual), so that a portfolio of 100 percent bonds actually generated a higher return with less risk than a portfolio composed of 40 percent fixed income and 60 percent equities. That constantly changing range of risk (standard deviation) and return in the relative performance of stocks and bonds over decade-long time frames can be very unsettling and quite a challenge for individual investors with shorter investment time horizons (20 years and under) and possible interim liquidity needs.

Figure 5.2 depicts the efficient frontier of equity and bond portfolios illustrated in 10 percent increments. Equity returns are based on the returns of the S&P 500 Index, which includes the reinvestment of dividends. Bond returns include the reinvestment of interest and are based on the Barclays Capital Aggregate Bond Index.

The standard deviation axis of the chart represents annual portfolio volatility (sometimes volatility of returns is also called "risk"), and the annual return axis represents annual percent returns. Each of the symbols represents a 10 percent change in the equity (stock)/bond mix between a 100 percent equity portfolio at one extreme, a 50 percent equity/50 percent bond portfolio in the middle, and a 100 percent bond portfolio at the other extreme. In this example, a mix of 70 percent bonds and 30 percent stocks provided the best return for the least risk over the last 9-year time frame.

On a decade-by-decade basis there are dramatic changes to the shape, risk, and return of the efficient frontier that are masked by looking at only the longer 47-year institutional time frame.

All price variations *do not* follow the standard bell curve (mild risk/Type 1 uncertainty) distributions depicted in Figure 5.3

In reality, *wild* risk, outliers, black swans, and tail risk are real and happen with unpleasant regularity, even though modern finance theory assumes that only mild randomness exists.

Figure 5.3 shows a classic representation of the normal bell curve distribution. The vertical axis represents the number of occurrences of each particular random sample value, and the horizontal axis represents

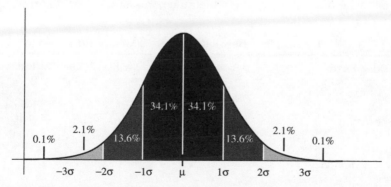

FIGURE 5.3 The Normal Distribution Bell Curve, with Standard Deviations Indicated

both the positive and negative distribution of samples around the mean, with 1 standard deviation either (+) or (−) encompassing 68.2 percent (34.1 + 34.1) of all values. 27.2 percent (+13.6 percent + (−)13.6 percent) representing 2 standard deviations, and so on.

In his 2004 book, *The (Mis) Behavior of Markets*, Dr. Benoit Mandelbrot pointed out some specific examples of how the normal distribution depicted in Figure 5.3 *is not* an accurate explanation of reality of uncertainty in the securities market.

Reviewing Table 5.1, it's clear that bell curve theory does not reflect reality in the investment world. As an example, bell curve theory predicts a greater than 4.5 percent daily market move occurring only 6 days in 87 years (which is approximately 21,750 days) or .027 percent of the time. When in fact from 1916 through 2003 the Dow Jones Industrial Average experienced a daily move greater than 4.5 percent 366 times (on average, about 4.2 days every year for 87 years, or about 1.7 percent of the time). That's about 60 times more frequently than theory predicts. So clearly theory does not reflect reality. Dr. Mandelbrot's examples demonstrate that real-world events inconveniently expose the bell curve as being not up to the job of properly representing the brand of wild uncertainty found in the investment markets.

Additionally, reality demonstrates the some of the assumptions necessary to make the quantitative model function are flawed. As examples consider:

- Although quantitative theory assumes that each value or price change of a security is independent from the previous value, reality inconveniently demonstrates that *security trades are not independent of one another* and can and do impact the next value. In fact, very often a previous security price movement or string of price movements will impact the next and following price movements (which theory assumes does not occur).

TABLE 5.1 Real-World Examples—Dow Jones Industrial Average 1916–2003 (87 years)

Daily Price Moves	Bell Curve Theory Predicts	Reality
>3.4 percent	58 days in 87 yrs	1,001 days
>4.5 percent	6 days in 87 yrs	366 days
>7.0 percent	Once very 300,000 years	48 days
(−)21 percent—October 19, 1987—the largest one day drop in history	Once in 10^{50} days (It should never happen)	1 day

Source: The (Mis)Behavior of Markets by Benoit Mandelbrot, p. 13, copyright © 2004. Reprinted by permission, Basic Books, a member of the Perseus Group.

- Quantitative theory assumes that market are always efficient, while reality demonstrates that markets are efficient sometimes and *very inefficient* other times. (Generally speaking free markets are efficient pricing mechanisms. However, many times individual securities as well as markets can become extremely oversold or overbought, and very inefficient pricing mechanisms develop in those situations where emotion rule over logic.)
- Investors are not always rational. They are both rational and emotional beings. At times they are quite rational and at other times their emotions override their logic, and they become irrationally exuberant or irrationally pessimistic.

Therefore as elegant as the quantitative method is theoretically, it just doesn't hold up and in fact becomes inelegant under the intense light of investment reality.

Sample of Weaknesses in the Quantitative Risk Management Approach

The fundamental weakness of quantitative method is that its calculations are based on the flawed model of reality represented by the bell curve. In fact its flaws are most obvious when extreme market moves occur, and risk management is needed the most. Following are some examples.

For individual investors, the major decade-by-decade shifting of the efficient frontier's shape, risk/reward levels, and optimum asset mix visibly demonstrates this weakness because the future is frequently very different from the past. This finding is evidenced by the time periods listed here:

- See the 2000–2008 period in Fig.5.2 where the efficient frontier "fishhook" actually inverts and a portfolio of 100 percent bonds provides an almost four times higher return with less volatility than a portfolio of 100 percent equities over a nine year period of time.
- Also In Fig.5.2 see 1970–1979 when there was effectively no difference in return between a portfolio of 100 percent equities and a portfolio of 100 percent bonds although the bond portfolio enjoyed over 50 percent less price volatility than the equity portfolio.
- October 1987: Quantitatively based portfolio insurance was completely discredited because it dramatically failed to deliver the downside protection it was calculated to deliver.
- Fall 1998: The hedge fund Long-tem Capital Management collapsed, even though it counted among its partners and founders two winners of the Nobel Prize for their quantitative expertise.
- December 2006: Bill Sharpe, original developer of CAPM, published a new book *Investors and Markets* articulating—his flexibility is

admirable—that he now prefers a "state/preference" approach to his original capital asset pricing model (CAPM) because his newly favored scenario-based approach allows for unforeseen crisis events and wild risk, which CAPM does not.

- October–November 2008: The historic, gut-wrenching, hypervolatile market meltdown, across almost all asset classes (foreign and domestic) and the bursting of the housing bubble, credit bubble, and commodities bubble, demonstrate the flaws in using the backward-looking, quantitative risk management approach as an effective risk management method during periods of wild/Type 2 risk.

Quantitative Risk Management Approach Summary

In summary, the quant school approach can be helpful in constructing portfolios and managing risk in generally normal (mild risk) market conditions. However, its effectiveness breaks down and becomes ineffective at managing risks during extreme (wild risk) market conditions or when previous market patterns and relationships are changing rapidly. The numbers, mathematical formulae, and apparent rigor of the quantitative method can easily entice investors into trusting it implicitly. If you're not familiar with its track record and flaws, it is very easy to believe that its theories, models, and analytics have neutralized uncertainty and tamed investment risk in all market environments, which is demonstrably not the case.

Trust Your Gut?

The subjective or qualitative approach to risk management is a very natural and intuitive method of risk management. It's not a numbers based method. In fact, it has a great deal in common with the way we adult humans manage our everyday life risks. The qualitative school is based on the belief that since the world is always changing and every situation is different, it is more effective to base risk/reward decisions on subjective degrees of belief about a subjective future rather than on observations of the past. Although the past can be helpful in making decisions about the future, that knowledge and experience when combined with a forward-looking view and sound judgment will improve the quality of our risk/reward decision making and overall risk management success.

The heart of the subjective method is probably best described by combining the essence of the precept I introduced in the Preface of this book: "What we know, understand, and are prepared for cannot harm us," and utilizing the full potential of the empowering definition of risk provided by Peter Oppenheimer we reviewed in chapter 4, where your "risk is the degree to which and outcome varies from (your) expectation." By combining and implementing these two foundational observations, we become focused on building our knowledge and understanding of risk, developing more realistic expectations, and better preparing for the risks we expect and even the ones we don't. This improvement in knowledge, understanding, and preparation, provides us more comfort, control, flexibility and fewer surprises in dealing the risks we'll face.

Basic Assumptions Behind the Qualitative Risk Management Approach

In reviewing the eight qualitative model's assumptions in the following list you'll see they are generally broader, more flexible, personal, and practical than the quantitative model's assumptions.

1. Looks forward while referencing (but not exclusively) past experience and practical knowledge.
2. Naturally skeptical, avoids reliance on any one method or possible outcome.
3. Assimilates the reality that both negative and positive surprises can be expected.
4. Incorporates current information and forward-looking judgment.
5. By directly facing possible risks, studying them, and working to understand their nature and character, risks can be more successfully managed.
6. The more you know about a risk, the better decisions they'll make.
7. Make realistic, knowledge-based assumptions in evaluating the range of possibilities, risk mitigation alternatives, and risk/reward tradeoffs.
8. Recognize that risk and risk reward decision making is a very personal and subjective process.

Strengths of the Qualitative/Subjective Approach

As you would suspect, the 10 strengths of the qualitative system outlined here confirm its practicality, flexibility, and ability to factor in personal judgment:

1. Forward looking
2. Flexible and easy to adapt and/or incorporate new information or situations
3. Experience, knowledge and judgment can be incorporated in decision making
4. Not as constrained by an over-reliance on only numbers, formulae and the risk of using flawed assumptions necessary to make the model work

5. Leverages our own well developed, life-risk management experience and skills
6. Easy to understand and implement
7. A straightforward, user-friendly, and intuitive method
8. Complements our control over what we expect, including expecting the unexpected
9. Works in both *mild* and *wild* risk conditions
10. Recognizes that we each can understand and manage our own unique and ever-changing, personal risk management priorities better than anyone else

Investment Reality

Although certainly not perfect, over the thousands of years humans have used and improved it, the qualitative method has demonstrated its applicability in all market conditions. Its functionality and success are directly related to the familiarity and understanding of its users with the nature of the risks expected, and the time and resources those individuals have to prepare for those risks. Its flexibility and ease of use make it an attractive risk management alternative.

Sample Weaknesses of the Qualitative/Subjective Approach

The qualitative approach's four prinipal weaknesses are:

1. Requires an initial basic knowledge of how to use it
2. Requires an effort to stay current on the business, economic, and geopolitical environment
3. Cannot manage risks that are not expected (just like quantitative method)
4. Cannot predict timing of a risk, but can predict its existence and potential personal impact

Qualitative Risk Management Approach Summary

The qualitative approach incorporates the often misunderstood problem that the risk/reward tradeoff can often be very different from one person to the next. The level of risk can vary dramatically based on an individual's own knowledge, skill, experience, and exposure in dealing with a risk. The actual risk each individual takes, even when facing an identical threat, can range widely from little to enormous risk. The subjective risk/reward analysis can also be influenced by the relative value of what one can potentially lose versus what might gain in taking a given risk. (Remember Daniel Bernoulli's utility theory: One with more to lose sees a risk/reward decision as less attractive than one with very little to lose, even though they are both looking at the same potential gain.) The qualitative method also benefits from both an individual's logical and intuitive decision-making processes. Often, with enough information knowledge, and experience, and after weighing all the factors, trusting your gut can be a very effective risk management decision-making strategy.

It is important to keep in mind that the subjective risk management method should not be confused with the practice of guessing. It's not guessing when you're using familiarity, knowledge, and/or personal experience as the basis for your risk management decision-making process or when using the advice of an expert who's knowledgeable in the discipline appropriate to the decision. Of course, it is definitely guessing, and should always be avoided, when you're tempted to make a risk management decision with little knowledge, practical experience, or expert advice. In cases where you are making a risk management decision and lack the appropriate knowledge or have insufficient information, the decision should either be deferred until your knowledge/information gap is rectified or a knowledgeable subject-matter expert can be consulted.

Two Is Often Better than One

Given that each of these approaches to risk management has both advantages and disadvantages, which school of risk management is best? Like so many other things in life, that depends on you. Remember what I mentioned earlier in this book about how critical it is, for the success of any risk management method, that each one of us know, thoroughly understand are comfortable with, and have confidence in the method we use (understanding both its strengths and weaknesses). If you are an engineer, statistician, mathematician, or are quantitatively oriented and more comfortable with the quantitative method, then by all means use it. If, on the other hand, you are more intuitive, have business and investment experience, confidence in your business judgment and experience, stay current on the business and investment worlds, and prefer more personal control and flexibility, then the subjective method will be the best for you.

The very best way to proceed may be using both methods at the same time because they complement one another so well. The quantitative method is helpful in portfolio construction and works well in mild risk environments, whereas the qualitative method is more intuitive and more effective during the inevitable periods of *wild* risk. In addition, the subjective approach gives more control in terms of what risks are expected (even in planning for rare or unexpected risk too) and how to specifically avoid, manage, or accept those risks. Another way to benefit from both schools of risk management is to use quantitative techniques for periodic portfolio rebalancing, while using the qualitative approach to manage big picture risks and for making the occasional tactical decisions to defensively raise cash, hedge, or become more aggressive when appropriate. Just as diversification is a proven risk reduction technique in portfolio construction, and one can reduce overall portfolio risk further by owning stocks-bonds-cash, value and growth, large capitalization stocks and small caps, domestic and international, it makes the same sense to diversify your risk management methods as well.

CHAPTER 6

How Your Body Can Work Against You

Our civilization is still in the middle stage, scarcely beast, in that it is no longer guided by instinct, scarcely human in that it is not yet wholly guided by reason.

Theodore Dreiser in *Sister Carrie*, 1900

W hy do investors invest with confidence, enthusiasm, and even eupho- ria when markets are advancing, yet avoid investing when those same assets drop in price? Why are investment returns typically higher than investor returns? Why do we love to buy cars, TVs, clothing, and all manner of consumer merchandise on sale yet are appalled at the thought of buying investments when they are down in price and on sale? We'll explore answers to these age-old questions as well as many others in the next few chapters.

Both Beast and Human

Even though humans are the most knowledgeable and advanced creatures to have ever existed, at the most fundamental level we're still animals. We are composed of two different natures. As Theodore Dreiser points out, we're "scarcely beast and scarcely human." Our higher thinking powers are continuously in battle with our basic animalistic tendencies and ingrained instincts, working to rein them in. Most of the time these conflicting forces balance against one another. In extreme situations however, our animal nature often overtakes our higher logical nature, which many times leads to trouble. Investing is one of our human activities that can bring out the full range of our animalistic and emotional extremes. Although experienced investment practitioners strongly advise against letting emotions and feelings impact investment decision making, it is extremely difficult for even savvy investors to do so because emotions and feeling are such an integral part of our everyday human decision making. In fact, almost anyone who is even briefly exposed to the investment world is struck with how emotionally charged investing can be. Our own basic instincts and emotions, as well as those same instincts in the universe of all other investors, play a critical role in whether we succumb to investment pitfalls or maximize our investment opportunities and enjoy long-term financial success. Greed, hope, fear, denial, remorse, pride, joy, anger, despondency, avarice, and all our basic survival instincts are commonplace in our modern investing landscape. Sometimes you can even see all of these various phenomena in the investment markets within as short a time frame as 24 hours. Although we continually strive to use our higher powers of logic to rise above our base animal instincts and raw emotions, those base instincts can many times overwhelm us to the point where we can become our own worst enemies. In answering the big questions of why and how this happens and how can it be avoided, we must first invest our time in better understanding the functioning of our own bodies, brains, and minds—and how they interact. Once we become familiar with and understand those details, we'll be better prepared to deal effectively with those situations where our bodies and/or our brains are working against our own best long-term investment interests.

Our bodies are amazing in their capabilities, complexity, adaptability, and incredible self-healing power. Think about all our highly integrated organ systems. They range from food processing, nutrient distribution and waste removal, information collection and analysis to temperature stabilization, advanced and integrated communications capabilities, to reproduction, threat analysis and risk response systems, all operating so well that we don't even have to think about them. Even though modern medicine has learned a tremendous amount about how our bodies work, there is still so much more to learn that tens of thousands of scientists all over the world are dedicating their lives to advancing our knowledge, and they know their work will go on indefinitely.

Model T Biology in the Internet Age

Our bodies have developed enormously sophisticated hard-wired automatic, reflex systems to control our blood sugar and oxygen levels, heart rate, hormone levels, and literally thousands of other substances in order to give us the maximum opportunity to survive, reproduce, and prosper in the natural world. These natural, built-in capabilities have given us an incredible advantage in dealing with the challenges of the world our species has faced as humans have navigated through their daily lives throughout history. As wonderful, amazing, and powerful as these automatic systems and built-in hardwiring are, it is very, very important to understand how they can easily cause us to act against our best interests in the non-natural world of investments.

Those same very strong, automatic systems that developed to help us survive and prosper in the natural world can often work against us because our biology has been left in the dust by the enormous advances we've made in the development of our modern lives in just the last few hundred years. Our bodies have been preprogrammed for a hunter-gatherer life style and the risks and threats of the natural world our distant ancestors faced and dealt with for more than 50,000 years. Now, however, we live in an incredibly different, extremely fast-paced world with a completely new array of challenges and issues where our Model T biology is working overtime to help us survive and prosper in our super mobile, multitasking Internet/high-tech/space age. That divergence creates a number of challenges that are critical to understand if we want to manage those internally generated risks. It is somewhat like the issues you might run into were you to use computer punch cards to load software on a state-of-the-art super computer or to connect your old trusty analog TV to a high definition video feed. The old technology will have trouble adapting to the new reality. Fortunately, we are a very smart, fast-learning species and have been able to adapt in many ways. However, the investment world in particular offers special challenges and common pitfalls directly resulting from the gap between our hard-wired biology and the realities of the modern investment world, which "Risk-Wise" Investors need to address. These include pitfalls that are directly related to the automatic reflexes built into the internal hardwiring of our brain and our body/brain interface.

Understand the Enemy Within

The best way to face these challenges is to continue to apply the fundamental philosophy of "Risk-Wise" investing to the special class of investment risks that originate inside our own bodies. Our true enemies within. (Remember that the best way to understand and manage risks is to face them directly, get to know them, and understand as much about them as you can. Because the more you know and understand about risks, the better decisions you'll make in identifying, avoiding, neutralizing and/or managing them.)

We'll start by identifying these ingrained, preprogrammed, internal risks. Then we'll review each one in more detail. The ultimate objective is to help you to better identify, understand, prepare for, and effectively manage any of these risks when they manifest themselves. However, there's both good news and bad news on this subject. The good news is that because most of these risks involve your own internal decision-making ability, they are totally under your own control. The bad news is that because they are instinctive, hard-wired, and automatic ways of thinking/reacting, it's very easy to be influenced by them, and it can be extremely challenging to overcome them. Fortunately, just the knowledge of their existence and an understanding of when and how they activate can help you manage or avoid these internal decision-making traps more easily.

The ingrained, internal risk factors we'll highlight and review in more detail in this chapter are:

- Misunderstanding the non-natural characteristics of the investment world
- How your brain works for you and can work against you

The internal risk factors we'll review in subsequent chapters include the perception versus reality gap, the herd instinct, ingrained decision-making biases, pattern finding in randomness, and the extrapolation trap.

The Non-Natural World of Investing

It is critical to emphasize the importance of taking into full account and understanding the basic fact that human beings have been hard-wired by evolution over tens of thousands of years to deal with the risks, rewards, and realities of life in the harsh, natural world we humans have lived in for over 98 percent of human existence. Our innate physiology and behavior were formed in the unforgiving natural world where the focus of life was on surviving from day to day, and on only the here and the now. It was an environment full of countless challenges and dangers, including bloodthirsty beasts that viewed human beings more as prey than predators. It demanded focusing on the present, because the past and the future had absolutely no relevance. It was typically a life of feast or famine with relatively calm periods periodically peppered with short, surprising, highly stressful, life-threatening situations that ingrained the instinctive freeze, flight, or fight responses that we still posses today. The only priority was to focus on the daily struggle to pull through and live for one more day. Early humans' bodies and brains evolved to survive in that demanding, now-focused, survival-of-the-fittest kind of world. Even though our world has improved dramatically in the last few hundred years, that ancient hard-wiring still serves us reasonably well in dealing with the challenges we face in our day-to-day, natural existence. Of course, we also now live with new, persistent, and potentially more harmful global risks that our progenitors could never have imagined. However, dealing with those newer risks is a subject we'll return to later.

Investing does not operate in a natural-world setting. Instead, investing exists in a non-natural world, and the big difference is related to time. Unlike the real, natural world where we spend a lot of time and effort to hold onto and preserve the past, while living and taking action in the present, the investment world is not at all about the past or even the present. Investing is all about and only about the future. Investing is not about what happened yesterday or even what is happening now. The non-natural investment world is all about the future and what is likely to happen in that future. The past, and even the present, may offer a convenient reference on the future, but the future will always be different from that past. To successful investors, spending too much effort on the past and even the present is pure folly, an enormous distraction, and an extremely seductive trap. Most investors, analysts, and the press spend a great deal of time, energy, and effort focusing on and analyzing the past and the present, and not nearly enough time on the future and what is most realistically likely to happen over most investors' longer-term investment timeframes. When it comes right down to it, true investors are not investing today for today or even today for tomorrow. (Traders and speculators may take very short-term positions with the intention of benefiting from a few percentage points' move, but that's not investing. Those short-term speculators and trader are, pure and simple, just gambling. You'll also find that their ultimate long-term success is also about the same, and about as disappointing, as any gambler's.) When you are truly investing today, you are investing in anticipation of a world 3, 4, 5, 10, 15, or 20-plus years from today. In that future world, today's news, market fluctuations, movers and shakers, and screaming headlines will be totally forgotten, and have become inconsequential and unimportant random historic noise.

Now that's exactly the opposite of what the business and investment news programs and much of the financial pundits want you to believe. Their objective is to generate as many advertising dollars for their programs as possible by keeping as many eyeballs glued to their programs as possible. They are breathless, urgent, emotional, and unsettling because they want you to appeal to your animal brain and keep you focused on what the markets will be doing in the next minute, hour, day, or week. How successful would their programs be if at the end of the business day, they announced that the stock market was down 200 points today, but in the great scheme of things, it really doesn't matter for long-term investors?

As a result of our brain being preprogrammed for risk management in the right-now natural world and successful investing requiring a modified future-forward approach to risk management, our ancient and trusted, internal, natural-world, hard-wired risk management circuits and automatic responses run into real difficulty in the non-natural world of investing. I use the term *non-natural* because the investment world is a very different world in a number of important ways, and it requires a different set of success skills from the natural world where we spend the majority of our time. It is a critically important point to understand, because our natural-world hard-wiring just can't be as effective operating in a non-natural world that's so different from the one it was originally developed to address. That mismatch between the ingrained methods we use so successfully in the natural world, which work against our best interests in the investment world, is the primary reason so many investors can become frustrated, confused, and disillusioned with investing. Unless we become familiar with, and learn how to control our ingrained natural responses, and substitute them with the right non-natural approaches, we'll have problems. When using methods appropriate for success in a natural world, it is only natural to expect that we'd be incredibly frustrated, disillusioned and unsuccessful in the non-natural investment world.

How Your Brain Manages Risk

Let's take some time becoming more familiar with the ingrained, natural-world risk and threat management hardwiring of our own remarkable brains and bodies. Once that is accomplished, we'll review how to recognize those deep-rooted reactions that can work against us in the world of investments, how to manage them, and even how use them to our benefit.

Since we will be reviewing this subject at a relatively high level and rather quickly as well, I encourage you to seek out one of the best comprehensive sources on the subject of brain science as it relates to emotions, memory, fear, anxiety, and risk response. The books of Dr. Joseph LeDoux are outstanding. They include *Synaptic Self* and *The Emotional Brain*. As a university professor, and member of the Center for Neural Science and Department of Psychology at NYU, his books provide valuable additional insights in helping you better appreciate, understand, and manage your own magnificent brain.

Our brain's risk management and response system, sometimes called the fear system, is prepared for dealing with threats in two ways. Of course, we are hard-wired and preprogrammed in the womb with instinctive responses to some threats. In addition and throughout our lives we're also able to learn about new or different threats and then adapt to them by incorporating that new learned threat information into our fear and risk response system as illustrated in Figure 6.1.

Of course, risk management is a very broad and necessary ability in the natural world. That world strongly favors those species that can successfully manage the risks they face, because those species that are less successful risk managers just don't survive. Therefore the brain is preprogrammed to respond to dangers that can routinely occur in the life of a species, and

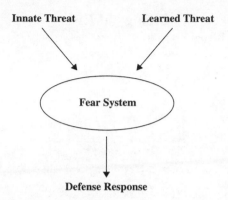

FIGURE 6.1 The Fear System Overview

Source: From Joseph LeDoux, *The Synaptic Self* (New York: Viking, 2002). Used by permission of Viking Penguin, a division of Penguin Group (USA) Inc.

fear/anxiety is the natural involuntary reaction to those real or potential dangers. Some of the potential threats that can activate our instinctive threat responses are falling; spiders; snakes; surprising loud noises; and facing people, places or things we've never seen before. In addition, our brains are so flexible, that we can even learn to fear potential threats like poisons, high voltage power lines, terrorists, and other potential hazards that are not part of our instinctive hard wiring. Our brains are so programmed to help us prepare for risks that after exposure to a danger our brains can also learn to fear elements of the environment (the context) in which the danger occurred. This phenomenon is called *fear conditioning*, and it is so powerful that once an animal is conditioned, the context itself can generate the same kind of fear reactions as the actual danger.

Over many decades of study, behavioral science has identified many other species that share very similar risk/threat management reactions with humans. These animals include fruit flies, marine snails, lizards, pigeons, rats, cats, dogs, monkeys, and baboons. All these creatures share the same high-level, risk/threat response behavior diagramed in Figure 6.2.

You may even recall experiencing "freeze, flight, fight" yourself or seeing it in others. It sometimes also occurs among investors experiencing volatile market drops or surprise negative news about their investments. In general, when animals or people sense a potential threat but do not have enough information to effectively assess whether it's an actual threat or not, they will freeze and remain totally motionless, minimizing the chance of being noticed. This strategy of freezing also gives the animal time to assess the risk, while not drawing attention to itself. Depending on the nature of

Biology of Risk

Humans Share Many Behaviors/Reactions with Animals

Hard-Wired Animal Reactions

Threats/Risk

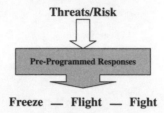

Freeze — Flight — Fight

FIGURE 6.2 Preprogrammed Threat/Risk Responses

the possible threat, the animal may decide to ignore, confront, or flee, once an accurate assessment has been made. Since predatory animals are hard-wired to detect motion, many times freezing by a prey animal will make it more difficult for a predator to detect it and thereby allow the risk to pass.

Although frozen and apparently idle from an external view, the innate risk management system of an animal in this state of aroused attention is far from idle. The threat response center of the brain is absorbed with enhancing and focusing the animal's senses on the potential threat, increasing its heart rate, blood pressure, and respirations rate, and beginning to release stress response hormones, which will improve its physical abilities. The flight option of running away as fast as possible is used by potential prey in those situations where they know they have been detected, the potential threat is real, and attack is imminent. In these situations energizing hormones are dumped into their blood stream, all body systems are ramped up to maximum, and the animal is running for its life. The same response will sometimes activate in people of even average size at accident scenes. In those situations, some people have been known to somehow gain the strength to lift cars off of loved ones who were pinned underneath the wreckage. Fighting is the final alternative and last resort, when no other options are left. In the wild, fighting is the last resort strategy because it carries with it the very real risk of serious injury that may not immediately be fatal, but can lead to eventual death from infection, disability, loss of defensive abilities, and/or starvation, even for the winner of a fight.

The key to understanding what is happening inside the brain when the threat/risk response is activated is to understand the workings of one of he oldest parts of our brain, the limbic system. It is such an ancient part of the brain that it is sometimes referred to as the *reptile brain*. The limbic system structures are located in the center of the brain and are responsible for our body's emotion and threat response systems. The seven principal parts of the limbic system are:

1. Amygdala
2. Cingulate gyrus
3. Fornix
4. Hippocampus
5. Sensory cortex
6. Mamillary bodies
7. Thalamus

This risk/threat management center of our brain is the master controller of our threat survival. It manages our body's threat response including our split-second decisions to freeze, fight, or run away and escape dangerous situations. It also helps us remember the details of situations that generate strong emotions. Figure 6.3 illustrates the location of the hippocampus and the amygdala (Greek for almond). The amygdalae are the *two* almond-shaped organs situated next to the ends of the hippocampus. The other risk center structures, not shown in this illustration, are packed directly around the structures shown.

The amygdala controls our emotions, including love, affection, friendship, the expression of mood, mainly fear, rage, and aggression. Each amygdala contains over 20 functional areas and is also linked to brain parts that govern senses, muscles, and hormone secretion. We know the amygdalae have a controlling role and a great deal of influence on other

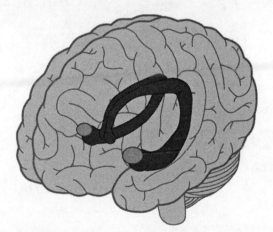

FIGURE 6.3 The Amygdala and Hippocampus Location

Source: Used with permission by Posit Science © Posit Science.

brain structures because there are many more neurons running *to* those other structures from the amygdala than those same structures have running to the amygdala. The *hippocampus* is directly involved with memory and specifically with the formation of long-term memory. Scientific studies have demonstrated that the hippocampus allows animals to compare the conditions of a present potential threat with similar past experiences. This context memory enables an animal to benefit from its previous similar experience(s) and choose the best option to maximize its survival in a similar future situation.

We are fortunate to live in an age when our knowledge of the brain is increasing enormously thanks to the technological advances in brain imaging technology, and the hard work of dedicated scientists. As a result we understand more than ever before about brain function as well as how and where risk management takes place in the brain. In addition to its many other benefits, that knowledge will help you better understand and manage the risks you'll face when investing.

Figure 6.4 reviews the steps of one of the hard-wired pathways our brains have developed to respond to risks, threats, and dangers that we *see*. Similar but slightly different pathways are followed with dangers/risks we identify through our other senses. The phenomenon of strong emotions taking over our physical actions is sometimes called hijacking the amygdala,

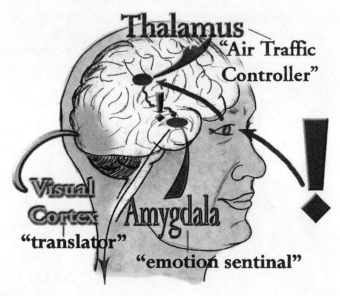

FIGURE 6.4 Hijacking the Amygdala

Source: Courtesy of Patricia Freedman and Joshua Freeman, Six Seconds (www .6seconds.org). Used with permission.

Figure 6.4 helps explain how visual signals lead to risk responses in the body.

Step 1. The eyes see the exclamation point (representing a possible threat the eyes detect) and convert it into a signal which is routed to ...

Step 2. The thalamus, which analyses the signal to determine if it is a potential danger or not (and acting like an air traffic controller) then routes the signal to the right place in the brain for processing, in this case ...

Step 3. The visual cortex then "thinks" about the impulse and determines if it is something the body should get excited about or not. In this case it thinks, "This exclamation point looks *dangerous* ... my body should get excited." The visual cortex then sends that danger signal to ...

Step 4. The amygdale, which on receiving the threatening stimulus activates its lateral nucleus, which begins a cascade of emotional and defensive reactions and actions throughout the entire body.

In summary, the thalamus is the "air traffic controller' for the signals coming into the brain from all the various senses. The sensory cortex (vision, smell, sound, touch, taste) initially interprets incoming signals as to whether they are either benign or threatening, and then if determined to be threats (or even potential threats) it alerts the amygdala. Once a threat alert is received by the amygdala (the emotional sentinel of the brain), it immediately stimulates numerous internal systems to insure that the body is emotionally and physically ready to do what is necessary to defend itself.

The Long and Short of It

Brain and behavioral scientists have now learned that information from external stimuli travel to the amygdala along two different pathways inside the brain, not just one. The short pathway is a very fast and nonspecific connection directly from the sensory thalamus to the amygdala. The long pathway runs from the sensory thalamus to the sensory cortex, looping in the hippocampus, before finally reaching the amygdala. Although this longer route is significantly slower, it is also more precise. In essence the shorter, more direct route provides an almost instantaneous response to a possible threat, allowing us to start preparing for it even before we know what it is. If, when the slower more detailed signal arrives at the amygdala with the sensory cortex's analysis and the hippocampus's context, and it confirms a danger, a significant time advantage has been gained. However, should the slower more information-filled rich signal arrive at the amygdala later and

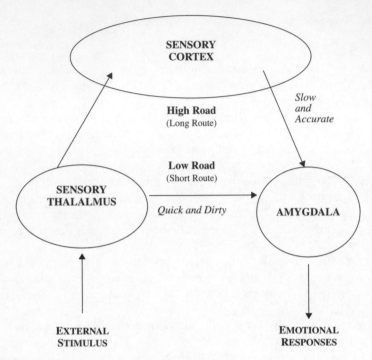

FIGURE 6.5 The Brain's Long and Short Fear Pathways

Source: Adapted from Joseph LeDoux, *The Synaptic Self* (New York: Viking, 2002). Used by permission of Viking Penguin, a division of Penguin Group (USA) Inc.

identify the perceived threat as a false alarm, that's even better. Particularly in high-risk or life and death situations, that speedier reaction time of the short route, even with the risk of reacting to a false alarm, is a big advantage over taking more time and being more certain before reacting to a potential threat. Figure 6.5 provides a simplified illustration of difference between the long and short fear pathways in the brain.

Get to Know Your Second Brain

Have you ever experienced a tense, upset, cramping stomach; stomach butterflies; a tight throat; or a strong intestinal urge before or during a stressful situation like an important job interview, presentation, a speech to a large group, an important test, or when investment prices move the wrong way? If so, you're certainly not alone. In fact, all those experiences and more are very common results of the extremely long and close relationship between our body's two essential brains. Those uncomfortable feelings are the result of your normally quiet and remarkably efficient second brain letting you know it's on the job. Of course, you are no doubt very familiar with the brain in your head. However, you may not be as familiar with your other brain, the very important but hidden brain in your gut, known as the enteric nervous system or ENS.

Now you may be asking yourself, what does this second brain in my belly have to do with investing and risk management? The principal reason we're reviewing it is the same reason why we've already discussed the human risk management process, the history of risk management, the two basic schools of risk management, and how our first brain deals with risk and threats. Quite simply, the more we know and understand about risk, our reactions to risks/threats, risk management, and the better prepared we are, the better risk managers and the more successful investors we'll become. Since the enteric nervous system can also generate physical manifestations in our bodies when we're facing threats, risk, or stressful situations, it is imperative that we also understand as much as we can about it as well.

Professor Michael Gershon, M.D., Chairman of the Department of Anatomy and Cell Biology at Columbia University Medical Center, a true expert on the ENS, coined the term *second brain* to describe this nervous system. Although the ENS sheaths the tissues lining the full length of the entire gut from the esophagus, stomach, and small intestine to the colon, it is considered one entity. The enteric brain neuron network sends messages back and forth along its length, allowing it to perform all its numerous, necessary, and complex functions and to learn, remember, generate gut feelings, and operate independently. This powerful second brain has over 100 million neurons (more than the spinal cord), and its only direct connection with the central nervous system and the brain is through the vagus nerve.

The nerves of the second brain were the very first nerves to develop in the bodies of primitive tubular animals hundreds of millions of years ago. Those early enteric nerves gave those first primitive animals a survival advantage in more efficient management of their food digestion. As animals evolved further the central nervous system developed in response to the need for additional brainpower for finding food and mates and for surviving. Over time the central nervous system and enteric nervous system developed connections, but the enteric system maintained its independence. Scientists believe that the earlier development of the gut brain, combined with the enormous complexity of efficiently digesting and excreting food material, plus the benefits of locating the control of digestive processes as close to the actual process as possible, are the reasons that the second brain has maintained its relative autonomy. Even so, both brains have a great deal in

common, including the fact that very early in our embryonic development
the brain in our head and the one in our gut both originate in the same
embryonic neural crest tissue, then separate and migrate to their designated
locations as embryogenesis progresses. The role the enteric nervous system
plays in risk management is very interesting and one of its primary purposes.

To view a color illustration of "The Brain in Our Gut" visit:http://www
.nytimes.com/imagepages/2005/08/22/science/20050823_GUT_GRAPHIC
.html

Applying This Knowledge

All these findings about our natural and ingrained threat response systems help to explain the uncomfortable physical phenomenon many
investors experience during major market drops. When humans' internal
risk management systems sense a threat or danger, a full complement of
emotional reactions (including fear, dread, and anxiety) and physical reactions (increased acuity of the senses, laser focus on the threat, increased
heart and breathing rate, elevated blood pressure, sleeplessness, queasy
stomachs, tense muscles, tension headaches, distrust, isolation, and threat
hormone release) are rapidly generated to deal with the threat. As a result,
these strong, automatic reflexive risk responses can activate investors' freeze,
flight, and fight response and easily override or hijack their logical thinking
as well. Of course, two, three, or more of these conditions occurring simultaneously can be very unsettling, because all the body's highly developed
survival instincts are kicking in and fully energizing it to freeze, flee or fight
a possible natural-world threat. You feel compelled to act, to comply with
what you body is telling you to do, because not only does it feel like the
right thing to do, but also taking action is the only thing you can do to
neutralize the risk management urgings generated by your body.

This happens in all potential threat situations because our brain isn't
hardwired to discriminate between a real-world natural risk and a non-
natural-world risk. It reacts the same to both. That's why it's so important
to get to know, understand, and be able to identify our body's ingrained
and natural risk management responses when they occur. You can then
apply that knowledge by letting those natural responses run their course in
dangerous natural-world situations, while controlling them by putting them
in context when the occasional non-natural risk (like a big, and always
temporary, market drop) occurs.

In a potentially dangerous situation, if you don't understand that what
is happening to you is a normal and natural reaction to a potential natural-
world threat, or if you don't know the importance of discriminating between
a natural threat and a non-natural threat, then you can easily fall victim

to a very common and costly investment pitfall, when your animal brain overcomes your logical brain. A natural risk like a fire in your house, and a non-natural threat, like a stock market drop when you are in your thirties are very different risks requiring very different responses.

Once you gain knowledge, comfort, experience, and then confidence in your practical application of this knowledge, you can even use those tangible threat response manifestations to your advantage as confirmation of potentially very attractive, non-natural investment world opportunities.

CHAPTER 7

Understanding the Risk Perception/Reality Gap

Three-fourths of the mistakes a man makes are made because he does not really know the things he thinks he knows.

James Bryce

R isk assessment is one of the foundations of effective risk management, and a cornerstone of risk assessment is an accurate and realistic understanding of the nature of the risks to be managed. It is so important because inaccuracies in understanding the nature and characteristics of any risk at the very beginning of our risk management process will lead directly to problems in effectively managing those risks. It's very much like the old "GIGO" axiom about computers, "garbage in equals garbage out." The better the quality of your basic input data, observations, or assumptions, the better the quality of your end results. If the basic information you start with is flawed or inaccurate in some way, how can you expect an accurate end result? Why even waste time going through the full exercise without first finding out whether the basic information you're starting with is accurate?

Our big challenge is that humans share a common and curious tendency to perceive risks very differently from reality, because our emotions and various experiences can impact the process so heavily. There are certainly risks that we perceive accurately. However, there are many risks that we perceive to be greater than they actually are (sometimes much greater), as well as an abundance of risks we perceive to be less then they actually are (sometimes much less). Quite simply, not understanding this very common risk/reality gap and not compensating for it can create some problems in effectively managing risk. The more accurate your understanding of the true nature and characteristics of a risk, and the smaller your risk perception/reality gaps, the better decisions you'll make in managing risk. The corollary is also true, in that the wider the gap between your perceived assessment of a risk and the true nature of that risk, the greater potential damage you're likely to suffer should that risk occur. That's why it's so extremely important to understand this common risk perception danger, so that you can minimize your perception/reality gaps when it comes to risk management.

Unfortunately for human beings, understanding and controlling the possibility of risk perception and risk reality gaps is much easier said than done. That's the case because risk perception is very much a case-by-case individual matter that can differ widely from person to person, based on a range of variables. There are no general answers. Each one of us has to honestly evaluate and the address our own strengths, weaknesses, and potential risks in this area. Since understanding and accepting that a potential problem exists is the first step in addressing it, the purpose of this chapter is to help you become more aware of and better understand risk perception/reality gaps, and then review how to minimize them in your investment risk management efforts.

How We Perceive Risks

Behaviorial scientists have documented that humans very frequently overestimate or underestimate the risks we face. We do so both individually and as groups, and it can have serious negative side effects, which could have been avoided. Although risk perception is an individual, person-by-person matter, behavioral scientists have discovered a few common denominators. Those commonalities can provide clues to the way humans determine, on a subliminal level, what we should fear and how fearful to be when we confront those risks. Outlined below are some behaviorial science findings about common risk perceptions as presented by authors David Ropeik and George Grey in their 2002 book: *Risk!—A Practical Guide to What's Really Safe and What's Really Dangerous in the World Around You*. In addition, I have included my own observations of common risk perceptions in the investment world. Although it's helpful to keep in mind that these are generalizations about most people, it is very interesting that these common risk perceptions/misperceptions are so widespread. They occur all over the world, throughout all cultures and age levels, and among both men and women. It is surely an indication of how these common perceptions must have provided our ancient progenitors with some significant survival advantages and have therefore been hard-wired by natural selection into the common risk management behaviors we all share today.

Common Widespread Risk Perceptions and Misperceptions

Generally, people have numerous ingrained risk perceptions and misperceptions. They include the following:

- Being more afraid of risks that are new than risks that have been lived with for a while. (Concerns about a potential nuclear war in the 1950s created a nationwide mania in building personal backyard bomb shelters. While today the world's combined nuclear bomb destructive power dwarfs what it was in the 1950s, we are much less anxious about the threat, even though its potential impact is much bigger, because we have lived with it so long.)
- Being less afraid of risks that are natural than those that are human made (People tend to be much more fearful of exposure to radiation from their microwave oven or high voltage electrical wires, yet they take a much greater and documented risk by laying out in the sun's radiation at the beach for pleasure.)
- Being less afraid of risk they choose to take than those that are imposed on them (like skydiving or scuba diving versus having to have major surgery).
- Being less afraid of risks that also confer some benefits they want. (Millions of people live in the southeastern and gulf seacoasts of the United States in the direct paths of devastating hurricanes, which occur every summer and fall, because they like the warm winter and spring weather.)
- Being more afraid of risks that can kill them in particularly awful ways (like being accidentally pulled into a wood chipper, crushed to death or decapitated, instead of being afraid of succumbing to the leading cause of death in the United States, heart disease).
- Being less afraid of risks they feel they have some control over (like driving a car versus being a passenger in a commercial airliner, when large commercial aircraft have proven to be one of the very safest form of transportation).
- Being less afraid of risk that come from sources they trust (places, people, organizations) such as hospitals, doctors, members of clergy, pharmacists versus chemical companies, weapons manufacturers, or nuclear power plants.
- Being more afraid of risks they are aware of (like terrorism *after* 9/11).
- Being less afraid of risks they are less aware of (like terrorism *before* 9/11).
- Being much more afraid of risks when uncertainty is high (such as just after a series of major stock market drops).
- Being less afraid when they know more (like following a series of consistent stock market advances).

- Parents are more afraid of risks to their children than to themselves.
- Parents are more afraid of potential toxins in their children's schools than in their own homes.
- Being generally more afraid of risks that can directly affect you than of a risk that threatens others.
- Disasters that affect people in a different part of the country are considered interesting news, while disasters that effect us personally are tragedies.
- Being less afraid of risks in investments and markets that have been rising in price. (Investors world-wide threw caution to the wind and saw little or no risk in the Internet bubble of the late 1990s and the real estate bubble that topped in 2006.)
- Being more afraid of risks in investments and markets that have been falling in price. (Many investors actually cashed out and/or then totally avoided investing in the stock market crashes of 1962, 1970, 1974, 1982, 1987, 1990, 1998, 2003, and 2008, all of which through 2003 eventually recovered to set new highs.)

In summary, because of our ingrained predilections, we often underestimate the actual risk in situations where we have personal control, that are known and familiar to us, are totally voluntary, are associated with a reliable and trustworthy source, and are natural. The opposite occurs, and we regularly overestimate the risks in circumstances that are unknown or we've never faced before, involuntary, not in our control, associated with an unreliable or untrustworthy source, or are man-made.

Of course, there are exceptions to these very common risk perception generalizations. These exceptions occur because we all have different experiences, upbringing, personalities, and confidence levels in the different threat situations we face. Our individual differences can either reduce or increase our particular fear level in various circumstances. These variations in individual fear levels are neither a negative nor a positive, they are just simply differences in our individual perspectives and feelings. The real problems come from the fact that we rely very heavily on our feelings in our daily decision making, leading us to sometimes trust those feelings too much when evaluating threats and risk. Our perceptions of and responses to threats, risks, and rewards are very powerful drivers of our behavior, thoughts, and emotions. Should those critical initial risk perceptions be wrong, they will compromise our risk taking judgment and lead to potentially very far-reaching and serious implications. The good news is that through greater awareness, knowledge, understanding, and preparation we can manage those risks and the factors that influence them. We can minimize future risk misperceptions, improve our risk management effectiveness, and become more successful "Risk-Wise" investors.

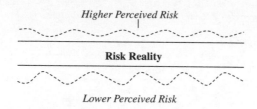

FIGURE 7.1 Innate Common Risk Perceptions vs. Risk Reality

Fluctuating Perceptions

One of the other facts behavioral scientists have discovered, other than the widespread and common risk perceptions we just reviewed, is that our risk perceptions are always fluctuating. Those fluctuating perceptions make our individual and group anxiety and fear levels cycle both up and down over time. The stock market is a perfect example of the kinds of swings we can observe from the peaks of joyful euphoria to the depths of utter despair. The graphic examples in Figures 7.1 to 7.4 illustrate the relationship between risk perception and risk reality. As you review the illustrations, please keep in mind that they are simplified for the purpose of easier visualization of the concepts and relationships presented. Even the real risk visuals depicted in the following figures are not as fixed and unchanging as they may appear in the illustrations. Actual risks can vary over time and from person to person, based on each person's particular knowledge of, comfort with, and preparation for dealing with a risk.

Figure 7.1 illustrates how risk reality for a range of risks remains unchanged while the perception of innate higher perceived risks fluctuates slightly higher than reality over time, and the perception of lower perceived risks fluctuates slightly lower than actual risk over time. (*Note that both the innate lower and higher perceived risks never fluctuate to match reality.*)

Figure 7.2 shows how experience-based, everyday risk perception (which can be altered by knowledge, experience, and risk exposure) fluctuates over time. (Notice that even though these everyday risk perceptions fluctuate over time, they rarely move to extremes.) They can move from being lower, equal to, and even higher than the actual risk, right back

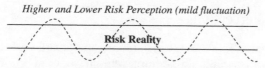

FIGURE 7.2 Mild, Experience-Based Risk Perceptions

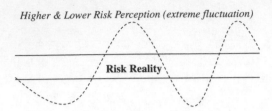

FIGURE 7.3 Extreme Risk Perception Fluctuations

to lower than real risk again, based on the changing nature of risk and a range of personal factors that can influence risk perception, including new exposure to the risk.

Figure 7.3 depicts a form of risk perception characterized by very big swings and extreme variations in risk perceptions, situations where one moment the perceived risk is low to moderate and the next moment the perceived risk becomes enormous. These wide swings in risk perception are typically generated in activities, settings, or environments that are exposed to one or more of the four emotionally charged situations where perceived risk can become enormous. These situations include the following four:

1. Where there are large-scale consequences to a risk
2. Where the risk is new, unfamiliar, or not understood
3. Where the risk is beyond our perceived control
4. Where the risk occurs suddenly and is unexpected

Can you think of any real-life situations that fit one or more of the risk perception–multiplying factors we have just reviewed? How about tornadoes, tsunamis, flash floods, landslides, earthquakes, natural gas explosions, terrorist attacks, accidents, and one example very close to the core subject of this book and familiar to experienced investors everywhere, the securities markets when major market collapses occur.

Granted, the time frames can be long between extremes, but one of the hallmarks of liquid securities markets for centuries is the fact that they are well known for moving from oversold and undervalued extremes at one end of their cycles to overbought and overvalued extremes at the other end of the cycle.

Upside-Down Perceptions

Normally, our natural, innate life-risk management skills can be relied upon across a range of potential threatening real-life, natural-world risk management situations. However, for reasons not yet fully understood, investing and investment markets are a different situation and a special case where the natural-world rules appear to be turned upside-down. In the world of investments our tried and true, natural life-risk management skills, methods, and perceptions can actually work against us, particularly in the extreme and emotional situations markets can generate. The causes of this unusual phenomenon may well include the strong emotional and well-being factors that many people associate with money, factors that can distort their values and thinking. It could be the fact that the investment markets themselves are driven by upside-down valuation factors (where what's good and bad in real-life situations are reversed in the investment world) or the extraordinary abilities of markets to anticipate and factor in fundamental economic and corporate development six to nine months in advance of the developments occurring. It may also be the result of what I mentioned previously about our real-life world being focused on actions and reactions that are more immediate or hear and now, whereas successful investing is not so much focused in the present but is about the future. At any rate there are profound differences in relative risk perceptions in the (non-natural) investment world from those in the real-life natural world. Those differences have frustrated generations of investors because despite their best efforts they have the tendency to do the wrong things at precisely the wrong times. Figure 7.4 shows graphically how this inverse or upside-down relationship between risk perceptions and relative market levels works in the investment markets.

The solid line in Figure 7.4 represents market action over time, and the dashed line represents how perceived risks have always fluctuated under changing market conditions for at least the last few hundreds of years.

Once you examine the figure, you'll observe how at stock market lows, when business news is weak and price performance has been weak for some time, risk perception is high, perceived risks are high, and actual risks are relatively low. (Presumably because most of the risks have been squeezed out of the market or are already factored into stock prices.) These periods of lower risk typically see investor disappointment commonplace, pessimism rampant, and investors questioning whether they should be investing at all.

Conversely, at stock market highs the business news is strong, stock price performance has been strong, risk perception is low, and actual risk is quite high. These periods of higher actual risk are typically characterized by investors aggressively buying-away with little or no concern for risk. Sometimes even euphoria is present as they buy into new market highs with abandon.

Why does this risk perception inversion take place? What makes it happen? Finally, what can we do about it to keep it from happening again? First, as to why this happens, there are a number of theories, and although no one

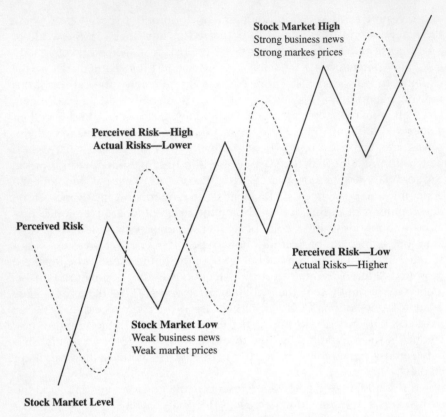

FIGURE 7.4 The Relationship of Perceived Risk and Stock Market Price Levels

knows for sure the best explanation so far is that our emotions get caught up in the negative or positive news of the day, and they and our innate fear circuitry create an internal feedback loop that reinforces itself and then finally overwhelms and overrides our logic and common sense. After all, in a previous chapter of this book on the physiology of risk we learned that our bodies have been hard-wired since ancient time to fear first and ask questions latter. Our strong and ancient survival instincts would rather we avoid potential hazards, risk missing some opportunities, and live to fight another day than expose us to something potentially harmful to us. What's fascinating is that there are some very successful investors who have been able to overcome their own innate hardwiring by using their knowledge and experience to effectively rewire their mental circuits so that their logic can override their natural fear mechanisms. Warren Buffett was widely crit-icized during the heyday of the Internet bubble for being too behind the times (and maybe too old) for not investing in the Internet frenzy. He was also publicly criticized in October 2008 for investing heavily in some large financial services firms in the middle of the market collapse when no one knows for sure what will eventually happen. However, Mr. Buffett cannot be criticized for not following his own advice, since he has been quoted many times as saying, "We simply attempt to be fearful when others are greedy and to be greedy only when others are fearful." What's fascinating is that the legendary investor and philanthropist Sir John Templeton said and did things very similar to Mr. Buffett. In commenting on his own investment beliefs Sir John said, "The time of maximum pessimism is the time to buy. The time of maximum optimism is the time to sell." Stepping back in time a bit further, there was another enormously successful financier, investor, and statesman of the 1920s, 1930s, and 1940s who shared the same philosophy as Buffett and Templeton. Bernard Baruch when asked his secret to successful investing simply stated the old Wall Street adage, "It's just like buying straw hats in winter." Clearly an investment approach based on doing the opposite of common perceptions, shared over multiple generations by world-class investment legends which has both its proven its success and longevity, deserves to be considered even when it flies in the face of typically incorrect common perceptions.

Outrage and Risk

Dr. Peter Sandman, the scholar and international expert on risk perception and risk communications, feels so strongly about the important role of risk perception that he has incorporated his thoughts into a formula for risk. The formula he personally developed is: "Risk = Hazard + Outrage." Rather than a mathematical relationship, his formula represents the qualitative relationship between the objective, factual characteristics of a risk (its probability and potential impact) or, as he calls it, hazard and the feelings (emotions) or outrage associated with it. Dr. Sandman maintains that the intensity of the emotion or outrage associated with a risk, and not its objective likelihood and impact, is the principal driver of our perception of risk and its ultimate acceptability level to each of us. The key point he makes with his formula is that whether the objective hazard is low or very high is not as important as the level of emotional outrage in determining how risky we see a potential danger.

As an example he sites the fact that we will accept the risks of driving, which is a statistically high, objective risk, because our outrage is low (since we are in control and 85 percent of us believe we are above-average drivers) where we do not accept a statistically very low objective risk like terrorism very well because our emotional outrage is so high.

Understanding and applying this aspect of risk perception, highlighted by Dr. Sandman is very important. It has profound implications, particularly regarding the level of emotional outrage associated with events that affect the markets, for our own personal investment buy/sell decisions and our overall effective risk management. (You can access a great deal more information about Dr. Peter Sandman and his work in risk perception and risk communications by doing a quick Internet search using his name.)

Final Thoughts

Being aware of the existence of gaps between our individual perceptions of risk and realty, as well as understanding how and why they exist are very significant first steps in our efforts to make better, knowledge-based decisions about risk. Now it's up to each of us to apply this knowledge to our own risk/reward decision making.

CHAPTER 8

Avoiding Common Pitfalls of Decision Making Under Uncertainty

Half our mistakes in life arise from feeling where we ought to think, and thinking where we ought to feel.

John Churton Collins

One of the fascinating things about investing is how much it can teach us each about ourselves, if we are willing to learn. As a result of its excellent liquidity and highly visible price changes the lessons of the public securities markets can both reaffirm our strengths, and expose our errors and weaknesses very rapidly. They teach us very effectively what works and what doesn't with a form of tough love, since when you learn those hard investment lessons well, that knowledge and the investment lessons you learn can reward you handsomely. Investing also tests a multitude of our skills ranging from our quantitative/analytical capabilities, and market knowledge to softer skills like business savvy, flexibility, realism, judgment, and conviction. It also tests our critical skill at recognizing the difference between what we know and or don't know, which is so fundamental to investment success. However, there is one high-level skill above all others, which pulls all the subordinate skills together to that pivotal moment when you take action or not. The ultimate skill I'm referring to is, of course, the all-important skill of decision making, and it's extremely critical to our investment success. It is the paramount skill because mistakes in decision making can negate the benefits of wonderful subordinate skills, and first-class decision making can make even make weak subordinate skills or information almost irrelevant. Granted, as we reviewed in Chapter 7, in decision making there is no substitute for good-quality information input. Many times, though, we find ourselves challenged by uncertain, threatening, or fast-moving situations where decisions have to be made even when we have incomplete information. Even in these uncertain conditions, good decision-making skills, coupled with an understanding of potential decision-making traps can make an enormous positive difference.

Decision-Making Patterns and Biases

As a result of its high importance, behavioral scientists and researchers have spent increasing time and effort over the last 40 plus years, working hard to better understand how our decision-making processes work in both stable and uncertain conditions. In studying how to improve decision making in general, these scientists have discovered a number of unexpected findings and common decision-making pitfalls. They have also learned that even if you do nothing else, avoiding those common decision-making pitfalls alone could have a very positive impact on your investment success. So, in the spirit of the "Risk-Wise" Investors credo we adapted from Ralph Waldo Emerson—"What you know, understand and are prepared for cannot hurt you"—we'll now embark on getting to know some of those decision-making risks better. In the process we'll better understand and become better prepared for the most common of those decision-making pitfalls and be better able to avoid their negative impact on our ultimate investment success.

The foundations of these decision-making traps are found in the hard-wired circuitry of our brains. They occur at the neurological level where our neurons interconnect with each other to form interlocking systems, which then develop and grow into various thought pattern pathways. Each of our brains literally wires their own thought pathways based on the patterns of our individual thoughts, feelings, experiences, and actions. In the interest of time, and so we don't have to think too much, our brain is always learning and working to make things as easy and simple as possible for us. The brain, via learning, even goes to the point of having pre-wired, ready-made response patterns all set up and standing at the ready for the situations and decisions we regularly encounter. These interlocking patterns of neural circuitry become the frame of reference we use to deal with the world. They become our gut feelings. Generally these neural systems work very well. However, where they can cause us some real difficulties is when our brain spontaneously gives us an answer to a decision or problem that is close to, but still different from, the true problem we're facing. So in effect, our brains give us a fast and confident answer to a similar but different question from what we're actually in the process of addressing. This type of pitfall can be especially tricky since the fast and confident answers our brains give us often feel intuitively right. Unfortunately these quick and top of the mind responses can be wrong because a key point or piece of information was missed.

A Lesson about Ourselves

One very interesting manifestation of this effect was demonstrated by Professor Shane Frederick, Associate Professor of Management Science, at the MIT Sloane School of Management, in the Fall 2005 issue of the *Journal of Economic Perspectives*. He created and conducted a test that he administered to 3428 respondents, in 35 separate studies, over a 26-month period, starting in January 2003.

Before we discuss an element of Professor Frederick's multielement test and its results, just for the fun it, why don't you take the same test yourself, which is presented in Figure 8.1. In taking this three-question quiz, you'll learn something about yourself and have some fun in the process. Please resist any urges you may have to skip ahead and preview the answers before taking the test. Doing so will neutralize the benefit you can gain. If you'd like additional people to take this test after you, without seeing your answers, you may want to locate a separate piece of paper where you can record your answers before you begin.

Once you've completed the test, please continue reading, and we'll review the answers, the result, and some important information that can benefit you. Please begin the quiz now.

> *Below are several problems that vary in difficulty.*
> *Try to answer as many as you can.*
>
> A bat and ball cost $1.10 in total.
> The bat costs $1.00 more than the ball.
> How much does the ball cost?
> _____ cents

> If it takes 5 machines 5 minutes to make 5 widgets,
> How long would it take 100 machines to make 100
> widgets? _____ minutes

> In a lake there is a patch of lily pads. Every day the patch
> doubles in size. If it takes 48 days for the lily pad patch to
> grow and cover the entire lake, how long would it take for
> the patch to cover half of the lake?
> _____ days

FIGURE 8.1 The Three-Question Quiz

Source: Courtesy of Professor Shane Frederick and the *Journal of Economic Perspectives* © 2005.

Finished? Thank you for taking the quiz. Well, what did you think? Were the questions easy or challenging to answer? Did the answers come to you quickly or did they take a little while to work out? Let's now compare your answers with the correct answers.

Question 1 Answer: The most common answer, the intuitive answer, and the wrong answer is 10 cents. It's incorrect because if the ball cost 10 cents and the bat cost $1.00, the bat would only cost 90 cents more than the ball. The correct answer is 5 cents. With a 5-cent ball and a $1.05 bat the bat would in fact cost $1.00 more than the ball, and fulfill one of the key conditions of the right answer.

Question 2 Answer: While the intuitive answer and most common answer, which is also an incorrect answer, is 100 minutes. The correct answer is 5 minutes.

Question 3 Answer: The most common and intuitive answer is 24 days, which you likely now know is the wrong answer, because of those very facts. The correct answer is 47 days, because the compounding effect of the lily pads doubling in size every day would mean from the 47th day to the 48th day the lily pads would grow from covering 50 percent of the pond to 100 percent of the pond.

Let's review the test background information and test results that Professor Frederick reported in his article in the Fall 2005 issue of the *Journal of Economic Perspectives*.

First, these three questions were posed to university students at some of the most selective universities in the United States, including Harvard, Princeton, Carnegie-Mellon, the University of Michigan, and others. Of the 3,428 individuals taking the test only 17 percent answered all three of the questions correctly, 23 percent answered two of the questions correctly, 28 percent answered 1 of the questions correctly, and 33 percent answered none of the questions correctly. So over 80 percent of the participants in the test (students at very selective universities) were unable to answer all three questions correctly. Since the students tested were attending elite schools, their general intelligence levels must have been relatively high. Why then would only 17 percent answer all three questions correctly and 33 percent answer none of them correctly. Clearly the quiz was providing a measure of something other than intelligence.

So what was Professor Frederick testing for? He was testing for our propensity to either accept our own very fast, first, and instinctive answer in making decisions or to reflect on the validity of those initial thoughts before reaching a decision. It's what researchers term *cognitive reflection* or *cognitive self-monitoring*. It's a built-in process, which only some people instinctively use to double-check their initial decisions in both everyday

life situations as well as in investing. The test also demonstrates and val-
idates the importance of developing that same habit of double-checking
your investment decisions, even if they feel intuitively right. As the simple
three-question quiz demonstrates, without cognitive self-monitoring the first
answer that comes to mind or the easy answer can frequently be wrong.
This pitfall also reinforces one of the most important reasons "Risk-Wise"
investors should work with a trusted financial advisor. Your personal advisor
can not only serve as a sounding board, information resource, and provider
of investment knowledge and wisdom, but can also help you double-check
your investment decision making. That advice alone can prove extremely
valuable in helping protect against falling into our own cognitive reflection
traps. The good professor found that people who have strong showings
on his cognitive refection quiz also have a tendency to be more patient in
making decisions between smaller, sooner rewards and larger rewards later.
(Sounds very similar to successful investing, doesn't it?) In fact, those same
people were also found to be more willing to take risk in financial settings.

In that same article and analysis, Professor Frederick pointed out that a
number of researchers in cognitive functioning have identified two types of
cognitive processes. System 1 processes are those in which decisions occur
almost instantly, with little conscious deliberation, effort, or even conscious
attention. System 2 processes are slower and more reflective, and require
serious effort and concentration because spontaneous answers just don't
or can't jump to mind immediately. Those distinctions may actually help
make it easier for us to identify and avoid cognitive reflection pitfalls when
investing. All we have to do is to stop and be just a little suspicious of, and
double- or triple-check any of our investment decisions that feel intuitively
right and occur easily and rapidly. Those, however, are the exact decision-
making situations when System 1 thinking is working and when we are at
the greatest risk of falling victim to cognitive reflection traps.

Pattern Finding in Randomness

Humans share the very common trait of not just noticing patterns but seeking
out patterns in randomness and many times imagining patterns or connections when none exists. Just as movement will instinctively draw the
attention of predatory animals, humankind has a very strong, hardwired
instinct that draws us to see patterns in our environments. We are continuously and subconsciously searching for patterns and meaning in all manner
of random occurrences. We're so attracted to patterns in events and even
natural phenomena that we will find meaning in them, even when there is
none. Its quite common for us to see things like canals on the planet Mars,
men in the moon, figures in clouds, faces on rock outcroppings, patterns in

star clusters. There's disagreement among experts in human psychology as to when and where this phenomenon originated although there is general agreement that the survival of early humans must have benefited from it. Being able to see short-, medium-, and long-term patterns in weather, seasons, river and ocean waters, the stars, and the behavior of wild animals all likely provided an edge in the battle for survival. Of course, if a survival advantage in finding patterns in randomness existed, the people who possessed it would naturally begin to outnumber the people who lacked that advantage. So, the thinking goes, it would become self-perpetuating.

Recognizing Real Randomness

We see this very old and established, natural pattern finding bias carried forward to this very day. Take for example a simple series of 10 coin tosses illustrated below. Review each one in Figure 8.2, then chose which sequence is most likely to occur. ("H" is for heads and "T" is for tails.)

Actually both series are equally likely to occur. Those apparent patterns are well within the statistical norms of randomness. It's just that our brain is hard-wired to find patterns and apply more significance to potential patterns.

Which Sequence Is Most Likely to Occur?

Series-A   H H H H H T T T T T

Series-B   T H T H T H T H T H

Series A _____   or   Series B _____

FIGURE 8.2 Quick Sequence Quiz

Mental Magnets

The same phenomenon occurs in sports. For decades, fans, coaches, players, and sportswriters in basketball have talked about players being hot at shooting baskets and other players who are cold. In some cases players thought to have a hot hand receive more playing time. To test the validity of that thesis, researchers Gillovich, Vallone, and Tversky conducted extensive studies of professional basketball players, which they reviewed in their 1985 book, *The Hot Hand in Basket Ball: On the Misperception of Random Sequences*, published by Academic Press. Using statistical methods to analyze professional basketball shooting success the researchers determined that the hot hand in basketball is an illusion. The perceived hot runs or hot hands of players fell well within the expected normal range.

Sports fans just love to find patterns and streaks. They enjoy tracking, monitoring, comparing, and celebrating them. Here a few examples from sports:

- The New England Patriots' record-setting 21 game winning streak
- The L.A. Lakers' record streak, winning 33 games in a row (1971/72 season)
- The 2,131 consecutive games played by Cal Ripkin

As the thought-leading author Nassim Taleb points out in his outstanding 2004 book *Fooled By Randomness*, published by TEXERE, "We humans are pattern-seeking machines" and "The world is much more random than we realize." His comments are absolutely critical for investors to fully understand. Ignoring the implications of his observations as they relate to the investment world can lead to frustration, disappointment, and trouble.

We can frequently see any number of what appear to be patterns, and assume that they provide real information that we can then turn into a profit. In fact, what we interpret as a pattern in very many cases is simply randomness successfully fooling us into thinking we are seeing something that isn't there.

Do you know what randomness looks like? Let's pause a moment and see very simply what randomness looks like by conducting a short visual exercise. Using a visual example of what was cited by Nassim Taleb in the text of *Fooled by Randomness*, which was also referenced in the previous paragraph, we'll first build a square dartboard on which a 16-square grid system has been set up, as illustrated in Figure 8.3.

Next we'll put our dartboard up on the wall and ask some of our friends to throw 16 darts at the dartboard. Once everyone has thrown their darts we see that the darts hit the dartboard and formed a configuration like the one depicted in Figure 8.4.

What Does Randomness Look Like?
Dart Board Example

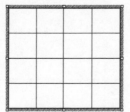

FIGURE 8.3 The Dart Board

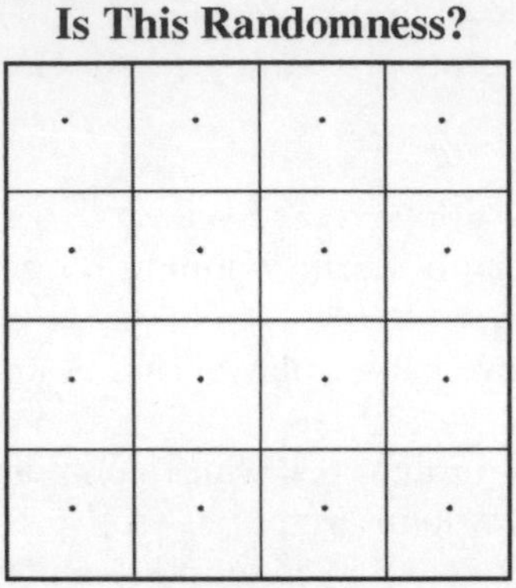

Is This Randomness?

FIGURE 8.4 What Does Randomness Look Like? Option 1

After viewing the locations of where the darts landed, ask yourself if the landing locations of those 16 darts look like a random pattern? Since every square contains a dart, and each dart landed in almost the exact center of each square, this example appears too even and too symmetrical to be random. The fact that this pattern is too even raises our concerns that some kind of collusion or planning was going on among our friends.

Now let's ask our friends to throw the darts again, and see what happens this time by looking at Figure 8.5.

Does Figure 8.5 look random to you? This pattern certainly looks more random than the previous example and one of the reasons is that in genuine randomness things have a tendency to cluster. That coupled with our brains bias to find patterns is one of the reasons it can be easy to see potential patterns in random distribution, when in fact there are none.

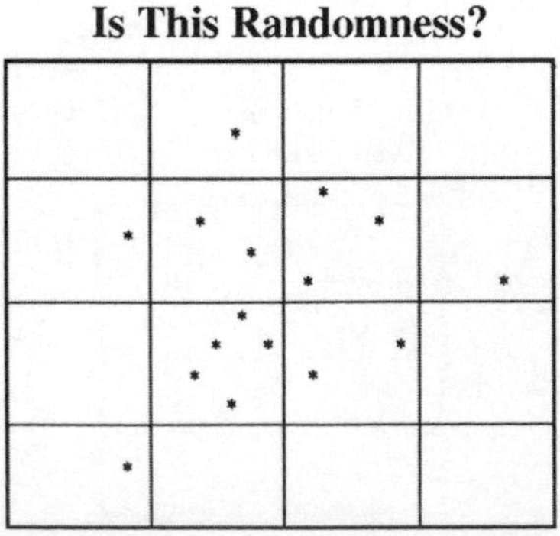

Is This Randomness?

FIGURE 8.5 What Does Randomness Look Like? Option 2

Luck, Smarts, or Both

A very common way randomness can trick us is through the methods many investors use and misuse in relying on investment track records in selecting money managers. Long and excellent investment track records have been traditionally viewed as one of the most important and best ways to evaluate and select investment managers. In fact, the longer and the better the track record the more appealing a manger can become to people in search of a money manager. There are, however, potential flaws in that assumption. That is why prospectuses and performance information always carry the admonition, required by securities regulators, that past performance is no indication of future results. Those potential flaws include whether a manager, his team, and his methods have been consistent over the time period being referenced, and whether the managers in question have been smart, lucky or both. If both, it is even more important to determine to what degree skill or luck contributed to the manager's superior returns. As nice as it is to have money with an investment manager who has luck on his side, luck is not something an investor should count on or use in selecting a manager. There are certainly a number of qualitative and quantitative tools investment analysts use to sort though these many factors in making their determinations, but the very nature of those methods relies on backward-looking, historical data, which can prove to be a fragile foundation on which to build one's future. Even the well-known mutual fund rating firm Morningstar, in explaining how to use their famous star ranking system (which is based on risk-adjusted, historical returns) says their star ratings are a good starting point in your fund selection process, not a summary recommendation.

A critical point to appreciate in using past performance as your primary selection criteria is how easily randomness can make luck look very much like skill. One excellent example of this phenomenon is presented by Nassim Taleb in *Fooled by Randomness*, where he reviews a powerful example using a thought experiment to construct a scenario where 10,000 fictional money managers, with $10,000 each, participate in a theoretical investment market. Annually, the participants in this market have an equal 50/50 chance, based on the flip of a coin, either to make $10,000 and continue to participate the next year or lose $10,000 and leave the market. The annual progress and the end results of Mr.Taleb's example are presented in Table 8.1.

In Table 8.1, you can see the following:

Year 1. The coin flip has eliminated 5,000 (50 percent) of the original 10,000 investors, and left 5,000 winning investors remaining, each with $10,000 more.

TABLE 8.1 How Can Luck Be Mistaken for Skill? 10,000 Investors Participate in Annual Coin Toss Market

Year 1	5,000 investors	5,000 investors
	+$10,000	−$10,000 and out
Year 2	2,500 investors	2,500 investors
	+$20,000	−$10,000 and out
Year 3	1,250 investors	1,250 investors
	+$30,000	−$10,000 and out
Year 4	625 investors	625 investors
	+$40,000	−$10,000 and out
Year 5	313 Investors	312 Investors
	+$50,000	−$10,000 and out

5th Year Results: 313 investors left (3.313% of total). Incisive investors or pure luck?

Year 2. The coin is flipped again and 2500 (50 percent) of the remaining investors are eliminated and 2500 remain, now up a total of $20,000 each.

Year 3. The 1,250 (50 percent) coin flip losers are eliminated and 1,250 investors who remain are now up $30,000.

Year 4. The coin flip eliminates 625 (50 percent) investors and the 625 remaining winners are each up $40,000.

Year 5 sees 312 investors (50 percent) eliminated and 313 investors winning, who are now each up $50,000.

So at the end of 5 years, there are 313 (3.13 percent) of the original 10,000 participants who have made money 5 years in a row by the pure luck of a coin toss. Now, were those same results to occur in the actual investment world, and the source of those remaining investors performance not divulged, those managers would be lauded and praised as standout investors. Because humans perceive randomness selectively we call randomness that works against us bad luck, and randomness that works for us skill. Of course, in the real world there are thousands of variables that impact money managers' returns. However, this exercise does show how easily pure luck can look very much like skill. Just keep in mind that top investment performers one year are often subpar performers the next and that the strategy of a consistently midlevel-performing money manager over the long term often outperforms the more compelling performance of the short-term stars.

It's important to remember and refer to these key points when you find yourself being attracted by patterns or making decisions based on patterns that appear to jump out at you, because those situations may be setting you up to fall into a classic decision making trap. Consider the following points.

- Randomness is much more prevalent than we realize.
- We consistently underestimate the level of randomness in everything.
- Our brains are hard-wired, pattern-seeking mechanisms.
- We look for patterns instinctively, to help simplify our decision making.
- Most patterns we see just don't hold up to statistical analysis.
- What any prospectus says about past performance is true: Past performance is no indication of future results.

Following the Herd

Humans share many biological functions, characteristics, and reactions with other animals. We have many common, deeply ingrained, hard-wired behaviors. Although we don't consider ourselves to be herd animals, we certainly have a lot in common with them. One of the most basic of those behaviors is the fact that humans are very social animals. Although we tend to focus on ourselves and our individual needs a great deal, social interaction, being accepted by and belonging to both small and large groups is a key motivator and driver of human behavior. None of us like to feel like an outsider. We all want to be insiders, and we find attractive advantages to being on the inside of groups. For some animal species, the norm is to live individual, solitary lives. They are almost totally solitary except for very temporary periods of interaction when they mate or rear their offspring. Humans are the exact opposite. We are not at all inclined to live solitary lives. In fact, people who choose to live alone or avoid social interaction are considered to have something wrong with them. They are viewed as being different, weird or antisocial, and are often characterized by the negative term "loner." We call people who don't socialize, antisocial, and that term carries a clearly negative connotation. In fact, socializing is so normal for us that some antisocial behavior is considered a mental illness. Based on a number of studies of the life expectancies of single people, married couples, and extended families living together, living alone also has a negative impact on our very life expectancy. Taken to its most extreme, the form of punishment that is considered even more grievous than death is solitary confinement. People in solitary conditions long enough can even go crazy and literally lose their minds because of lack of interaction with others.

Humans like and need to belong. We gain comfort and validation in conforming to the group. When we are uncertain as to what to do in almost any situation, we will look around and do what everyone else is doing, even when it may not make sense to us. Many bird and fish species exhibit the same behavior when as a defensive behavior they *flock* or *school* in the presence of threats. We humans would rather fit in with the crowd and be wrong, than be different and right. A fascinating and amusing example of this basic human need to not be different was demonstrated by the old TV show *Candid Camera* with Allen Funt, in a segment called "The Elevator." In that segment an unsuspecting individual is faced with the uncomfortable fact that all the others in an elevator (who were all in on the joke) were all facing the back of the elevator rather than facing the front. The big question, and the fun, was watching to see how each victim reacted to the internal conflict between logic (which was to face forward, toward the doors) and the instinct to do what everyone else was doing. What do you think the victims did in that situation? Which factor, logic or instinct, had greater influence in directing the victim's behavior? What do you think you would do in a similar situation? If you bet they would rather fit in with the others and be wrong, than be different from the others and be right, you'd be right.

This basic need to belong, this herding and social validation instinct, is so strong because of the survival advantages it offered to our early ancestors. Just imagine if you were an early human on the hunt with your tribe and you saw the majority of your group running back toward and then by you at full speed, with fear in their eyes, in the direction you had come from earlier in the day. Would you join them in running away and ask questions later or hold your ground to see what they were running from? This instinctual behavior is particularly visible in fashion, apparel, and fads of all sorts. It manifests itself in almost everything we do, including investments. In most of those situations fad and trend following is enjoyable, fun, and works in our favor because it helps us fit in, become part of the group, and stay current with the times. The only risk is that when a new trend or fad emerges we have to shelve our out-of-date items and stock up on the new fad or opt out entirely from participating in fads.

In the investment world a totally different effect occurs. If everyone else already has invested in a company, industry, investment theme, or market, the price has already been driven up by increased demand. As a result, the investment has an attractive and very compelling track record of success. Everyone likes it, is enthusiastic about it, and is making money on the investment. People start talking about it as a money-making machine, and assuming it will never go down in price, which is a fatal misjudgment.

The Greater Fool

Even though the risks in these types of situations are extreme, most investors perceive them as low to non-existent. To make matters even worse, some investors because of the buying frenzy even begin using borrowed money, or leverage, to buy more. As it nears its inevitable price peak, investors begin operating on the Greater Fool Theory. People using Greater Fool Thinking say to themselves that even though they know they're being foolish investing in this highly appreciated asset, they're counting on an even greater fool to buy it from them at an even higher price. Inevitably, the number of new buyers slows because there are just fewer and fewer people who haven't already bought. Soon the supply of all those owners who want to sell, and lock in their profits, overwhelms the demand of a diminishing number of new buyers, and prices begin to drop, and many times plunge precipitously. Then, the whole buying frenzy on the way up turns very quickly into a panic to get out on the way down, before prices go even lower and the entire situation gets ugly—which it does.

This phenomenon has occurred throughout human history so many times it's almost hard to believe. (Remember our historical overview of the history of risk in Chapter 3?) These herd instinct–driven panics and crashes have involved assets as diverse as tulip bulbs, agricultural and industrial commodities, railroad and canal shares, raw land, single-family homes, golf courses, commercial office buildings, and Sunbelt condominiums. They have also included the shares of CB radio companies, high technology companies, emerging markets, our own stock markets, and most recently U.S. single-family homes.

When investing, it's not just your own assessment of the future that matters, but also the combined sentiment and assessment of all market participants. An accurate reading of overall market sentiment can also provide important insights into your investment decision making and cues as to the best action for you individually to take. Typically equity markets will anticipate the business environment six to nine months into the future, with those assessments built into the price of stocks. In fact, the equity markets are good enough at predicting future business conditions that academic, corporate, and government economists view them as leading economic indicators. It's also very important to keep in mind that often, because of changes in business circumstances, business cycles and/or investor psychology, those market assessments of the broad universe of investors can be accurate, overly optimistic or overly pessimistic.

Trees Growing to the Sky

As we become more familiar with investing and investments in general one of the colorful phrases we'll hear is "trees don't grow to the sky." This particular saying refers to the tendency of some investors to fall in love with an investment that is doing well and to start believing that it will keep performing well indefinitely. Although there are some dramatic examples of investors who've seen enormous appreciation and become wealthy as a result of buying a stock and holding it for 10, 20, or 30 years and longer, those examples are very much the exception rather than the rule. In fact, there have been some spectacular business and investment successes, like Enron, that looked as though they could defy gravity and literally grow to the moon, but ended up on the ash heap of market history while decimating their investors and their employees' hopes, dreams, and net worth in the process. There have also been other, great firms and investments like IBM that temporarily lost their strong business and investment momentum, as well as investors' faith and loyal following. That loss of momentum then led to a change agent or catalyst like Lou Gerstner, Jr., being brought in at IBM, who then led the company to new business and investment success. These examples all share the common thread of another, slightly different, yet classic investor pitfall. This trap is alternatively called the Extension or Extrapolation Bias. It is based on the fact that we humans have a strong underlying propensity to assume that what is happening right now will be extended into the future, and that the longer any business, asset, or investment trend has been in place the more likely that trend will continue. An understanding of the nature of reversion to the mean, and the observable facts, show this is not the case. History also demonstrates over and over again that extended periods of substandard market performance are not followed by more of the same. They are consistently followed by periods of above-average returns. Most investors become more enthusiastic the longer the market is performing well, when they should be becoming more careful and cautious. These same investors become overly careful and cautious after major market declines because they fall into the trap of expecting the weak environment to continue, when, in fact, they should become enthusiastic and positive about the market's inevitable reversal. Rather than getting more comfortable the longer any trend is in place, investors should actually be more suspicious of a trend continuing. Remember, trees don't grow to the sky, and the longer a trend lasts outside the norm (positive or negative), the more likely it will shift in the opposite direction.

How can investors avoid these common and potentially devastating investment pitfalls? First, recognize they happen all the time, and can be very challenging to resist, and second, avoid trend following and performance chasing. If anything, look in the opposite direction of the trend or conventional wisdom. Third, stick to the investment wisdom of someone like Sir John Templeton who said, "The time of maximum pessimism is the time to buy. The time of maximum optimism is the time to sell." Fourth, if you ever consider the risky strategy of borrowing money to buy investments, (which is not recommended) only use it to buy assets that are underpriced and be certain you can comfortably bear the debt servicing costs for at east twice as long as you think you may hold the asset. Also never use borrowed money to buy assets that have already appreciated dramatically in price.

As "Risk-Wise" investors, it is critically important for us to understand our herd instincts and the Greater Fool and extrapolation traps in terms of how they apply to us individually and how they impact investors at large in the mass psychology that drives the markets. Understanding how and why these instincts and human tendencies work can go a long way in helping us identify them when they happen. That familiarity and understanding will also help us avoid these potential traps, and take advantage of the regularly occurring opportunities they can create in the markets. Keep in mind that in the natural world the desire to belong, and to be doing what everyone else is doing can offer real advantages. However, in the cyclical and upside-down world of investing, following our herd instincts and expecting the immediate past to continue into the future are among the most consistent errors investors continuously make.

Common Hidden Traps

Behavioral scientist have discovered a number of other common decision-making traps, which are reviewed very effectively in "The Hidden Traps of Decision Making" by John Hammond, Ralph Keeney, and Howard Rafia, which appeared in the September-October 1998 issue of *The Harvard Business Review*. Although they address decision-making biases very broadly, their thoughts apply to every investor and concur with some of the basic issues we've been discussing. Let's take a look at the general traps they identify from the perspective of how they present themselves in the investment world, and what individual investors can do to avoid them.

The Anchoring Trap is giving extra significance to the information you receive first. Here's a very common and realistic example of how this trap can work. In a casual conversation, you hear from a friend or co-worker about an investment that has a remarkable track record. Then based on their enthusiasm about their personal success and the outstanding track record they mention, with little or no additional information, you decide you will buy it, too. You can avoid this trap by first establishing a personal standard that before making any investment you must examine the details of all potential investments, including their potential risks before you make your final decision. You can also do some additional homework to verify the accuracy of the track record info you received, compare its performance to comparable benchmarks, determine if it's risk/reward characteristics are right for you and if it fits into your overall portfolio and is not duplicating an investment you already own. You can also check with other sources, including your financial advisor, who may already be familiar with the advantages and disadvantages of the particular alternative and save you a lot of time trouble and aggravation.

The Status Quo Trap occurs when we are attached to continuing to do what we've been doing, instead of objectively comparing it to potentially better alternatives. This trap often occurs when for various reasons an investment may have gained or carries a sentimental value that has little to do with its investment value. The key to avoiding this trap is to consider whether you'd buy this investment today, independent of its sentimental value. If not, then you probably should replace it with something you would buy. If yes, then continue to hold on and buy more if you like it so much.

The Sunk Cost Trap often happens when we resist doing something because it will verify that we made an incorrect decision in the first place. This trap most frequently occurs when investors see an investment drop in value after they buy it, and because it didn't work out as well and as rapidly as they anticipated they decide to sell it once it gets back up the price they originally paid for it and then get out even. The best way to avoid this trap is to recognize the fact that even the most savvy and sophisticated investors make investment mistakes all the time, and the best strategy to follow once you've made a mistake is to admit it, reposition the assets into a new opportunity, and then take a moment to determine what you can learn from that mistake so you can avoid repeating it in the future.

The Confirming Evidence Trap is one of the most difficult to control because of our strong natural tendency to want to be right and not be wrong. Once we are attracted by an idea, a person, a cause or an investment, we have a strong tendency to notice and embrace only the evidence that confirms our initial decisions and to ignore or disregard evidence that refutes our decision. One of the best ways to avoid this trap is to deliberately and consciously assemble and objectively evaluate, side by side, both the positive and negative evidence of the investment you're considering. Another method is to seek out the perspective and counsel of your trusted financial advisor in helping you objectively evaluate both the positive and negative evidence surrounding the investment decision you're considering.

The Estimating and Forecasting Trap occurs when intense or recent experiences or impressions can prejudice your forecasts and estimates positively or negatively. This trap appears quite regularly near the extremes of the investment markets' cycles. During particularly deep or extended bear markets when investor nerves are on edge, they're emotionally drained, generally depressed, and fearful that their forecasts and estimates for the future are abnormally low because of their recent unpleasant experiences. Not only are their forecasts in such conditions low, they are typically low and wrong by a wide margin, since over the last hundred years periods of outsized positive returns regularly follow periods of negative returns. The opposite occurs after extended market advances. In these cheerful times, investors' experiences have been very encouraging, and their attitudes are positive and optimistic. Since they've enjoyed consistent, positive returns, and it has been years since a serious market decline raised its ugly head, their forecasts for the future are for more of the same, generally proving to be high and wrong. Avoiding this trap can be accomplished by becoming more familiar with and knowledgeable about investment history, the psychology of investors during the various stages of the typical market cycle, and the reality of regression to the mean.

Guarding Against Decision-Making Traps

In the process of becoming "Risk-Wise" Investors it's not so critical to remember the details of every single potential decision-making pitfall as it is to understand that risks don't just exist in the world around us; they exist inside us as well. In guarding against those internal risks, we can apply the same process that has proven effective in guarding against external risks. Ultimately, the fundamental principle of successful risk management is understanding and appreciating the power of one simple statement. Risks that are predictable (meaning we know they can happen, we just don't know when) can be avoided, prevented, or managed. Now that you're aware of these internal decision-making risks and can predict them, you are in a much better position to prevent or minimize them, and become more and more effective "Risk-Wise" Investors.

CHAPTER 9

The Advantages of Managing Risk Categories

Our life is frittered away by detail. Simplify. Simply."

Henry David Thoreau

O nce risks have been identified and understood, the next step in our "Risk-Wise" risk management process is to determine the range of options that are available to either entirely avoid those risks we've identified or accept and manage them. Once that fundamental decision has been made, the next step is to decide to either accept the risks outright, with no risk management, or opt to accept the risks while also implementing risk management strategies. This process is very straightforward, uncomplicated, and relatively easy, when you are focusing on only few risks. However, as you begin incorporating more risks into your risk management planning, the process can become more challenging. In committing to truly, enterprise-wide, comprehensive risk management planning, the complexity of the process can become overwhelming and seem daunting to the point of frustration. That's exactly why so many large and successful firms have created chief risk officer positions and staffs. Effectively managing the multidimensional risks of an international enterprise is a critically important and time-consuming job. Even though, as individual investors, our risk management activities are not nearly as widespread and complex as those of international enterprises, there are still many benefits to considering ways to streamline the risk management process to simplify and reduce the time, energy, effort, and attention we need to dedicate to the effort. The purpose of this chapter is to review a very effective way to accomplish that objective while still honoring the advice and admonition of Albert Einstein, who said "Everything should be made as simple as possible, but not simpler."

Managing Specific Portfolio Risks

By focusing on specific risks and understanding each of them in detail we gain an enormous advantage in managing them. Great generals throughout history have used the same concept and benefited enormously by studying the detail about the armies they faced, including the personal backgrounds of the senior officers of their adversaries, their preferred tactics, biggest combat successes, worst defeats, and many other factors. Even today, a critical part of modern firefighters' training is studying, understanding, and personally experiencing the physics of fire, smoke, intense heat, and the burning characteristics of different classes of combustibles. All this studying is conducted for the key purpose of better understanding the nature and characteristics of their enemies. The same concepts and methods work well in managing investment risks, too. So let's highlight some of the risks that we can expect to face in our ever-changing business environment over the normal course of regular business and market cycles. Remember as you review these risks that every single one of them has happened many times in the past. This is not just an academic exercise. These risks are real, should be expected, and planned for.

> **Special Note 1:** Please note that although many investment resources include volatility as a risk, I deliberately chose not include volatility in this list of risks. My conviction is that categorizing volatility as a risk is both misleading and a grave misnomer. Volatility is simply a fact of life and a characteristic of any liquid market. It is neither good nor bad because it can both work in our favor (which it does most of the time) as well as work against us. Market price volatility is just the ongoing, momentary imbalance between current buyers and sellers, which many times has little to do with a company's intrinsic value for long-term investors. In my view, price volatility is an inseparable, sometimes convenient, sometimes inconvenient side effect of liquid markets. Spending time, energy, and resources to manage volatility seems to me like selecting a pet dog that you don't have to feed or clean up after. If you want to enjoy the many benefits of owning a dog, feeding it and cleaning up after it are basic facts of life for any dog owner. You can't have one without the other. So if you don't like volatility or feeding and cleaning up after a dog, don't get a dog or invest in liquid securities.

> **FYI:** There are a number of illiquid, low volatility investments you can choose from. Some have little or no price volatility but provide lower returns. Others can offer higher potential returns but can be more complicated, difficult to value, challenging to operate, plus cumbersome to buy and sell. It's your choice.

Special Note 2: In general, fixed-income investments are considered to carry less risk than equity investments. They are viewed as having less risk because they have a fixed repayment date for the face value of the bond, are sometimes backed by collateral, pay regular interest along the way, and bond debt service is paid before net earnings are determined for a company, and before any stock dividends can be paid. Although they share some risks with stocks they have their own forms of risk as well. Plus, bond prices change and market values (which are dependent on the rate of inflation, current interest rate levels, and the bond's credit rating) can at times be just as volatile as or even more volatile than stocks.

Common Risks of Equity (Stock) Investing

Below is a list of risks common to investing in stocks:

Company Risk	Operational Risk
Management Risk	Industry Risk
Economic Risk	Reputation Risk
Competition Risk	Product Obsolescence Risk
Regulatory Risk Legal Risk	Environmental Risk
Corruption Risk	Financial Risk
Inflation Risk	Liquidity Risk
Disaster and Catastrophic Risk	Currency Risk
*Market Risk	Liability Risk

*Overall market risk is generally recognized as the only risk that diversification cannot reduce. Market risk is, however, significantly reduced by time. The longer the portfolio holding period, the lower market risk becomes, until beyond 20 years market risk becomes statistically negligible.

Common Risk Management Strategies for Equity Portfolios

These risk management strategies are among those commonly used to reduce the risk of investing in stocks:

- Diversifying among a number of different-sized companies and industries
- Diversifying among both domestic and international companies
- Diversifying among fast-growing, younger firms and slower-growing, larger firms
- Investing in both value and growth stock categories
- Investing for at least a 5-year time horizon, since investing in equities for less than a *5-year* time horizon (does not allow for the time necessary to complete a typical complete business and market cycle)

SOME COMMON RISKS OF FIXED-INCOME INVESTING These are common risks encountered in bond investing:

Default Risk	Credit Quality
Downgrade Risk	Currency Risk
Inflation Risk	Interest Rate Risk
Liquidity Risk	Tax Risk
Call Risk (Call protection expires)	

COMMON RISK MANAGEMENT STRATEGIES FOR BOND PORTFOLIOS These strategies have proven their effectiveness at reducing the risks associated with investing in portfolios of bonds:

- Diversify among investment-grade corporate and government bonds or municipal bonds, if appropriate
- Diversify among various maturities from short and intermediate to long term (Shortening maturities in rising interest rate environments and extending them in falling interest rate environments)
- Matching bond credit quality with your desired risk level
- Diversify an appropriate portion of bond portfolio into inflation-adjusted bonds
- Diversify into quality convertible bonds and international bonds

Some Common Risks of Balanced (Stock and Bond Portfolios) Portfolios

Although balanced portfolios are among the most conservative strategies, these risks are associated with that type of investing:

- Asset allocation mix
- Inappropriate value/growth mix
- Inappropriate domestic/international mix market risk
- No regular rebalancing plan

Common Portfolio Level Risk Management Strategies

Below is a quick review of risk management methods that can reduce the risks of even well diversified portfolios:

- Conduct a regular asset allocation review (at least annually)
- Diversifying among different-sized companies, investment styles, and global geographies
- Implement portfolio rebalancing plan (at least annually)
- Maintain long-term investment holding periods

- Monitor ongoing decisions, additions, and deletions to insure that desired portfolio risk levels are not increased unintentionally

Making the Job Easier

Just remembering all the different types of risk we reviewed may at this point seem overwhelming. It can start to become intimidating if you begin thinking about the time, energy, and effort involved in developing a risk management plan and monitoring process for each and every one of them. In fact, if you're feeling that way now, and are wondering if all that effort will be worth it, I have some good news for you. It doesn't have to be that complicated, and in truth there are some practical ways to simplify the process.

The first consideration is to remember that risk management is a very personal process. Specific risks that are important or relevant to you may be unimportant and irrelevant to your neighbor for a variety of factors. So you should only focus on risks that can impact you, and eliminate all the others from consideration. As a result, the first simplification step in our process is to eliminate any risks that don't directly apply to you or your particular situation. For example, if you live in the western United Sates and hurricanes never occur there, you don't really need to be concerned about them, unless you have property, business, or investments interests in Florida. Conversely, if you live in California and don't need to think about hurricanes at all, you do need to think about earthquakes and their potential impact on you and your portfolio. Using this example, it's straightforward to see how you can easily and quickly discard risks that you aren't exposed to from consideration.

The next step is to recognize that many risks have similarities in the way they behave, their physical and financial impacts, the way they affect the various investment types, investment markets, and the components of the economy. For risk management planning purposes, by using their common characteristics you can group risks with similar characteristics together to simplify your risk management planning process. Here are a few examples.

One way to simplify your risk management efforts is to consider grouping the risks you face based on your ability to control the likelihood of a risk impacting you and then controlling its impact, should it occur. For example, there are some risks you can avoid entirely by not engaging in any actions that expose you to those risks in the first place. There are also risks that you just cannot avoid, but where you do have some control through your direct preventative actions, over the likelihood of those risks occurring at all. Then there are a category of risks that you cannot avoid, and cannot control by reducing their likelihood, but can, should they occur, reduce their impact through advance preparation. Since you can't avoid the risks in this group, and you can't control their likelihood, the only practical risk management alternative left is to implement strategies that will limit the impact of these risk types when they occur.

Another major category of risks are the ones that you may knowingly seek, because of the substantial rewards offered by the activities they're associated with. With these types of situations, the best strategy is to take the initiative to aggressively implement your risk management actions in advance, to reduce both the likelihood and the impact of any of the potential risks occurring. To help you become more familiar with these groupings let's review each of them in more detail, as well as some specific, real-life examples that demonstrate how these strategies work.

Risks You Can Avoid Completely

The easiest, most basic, efficient, and effective risk management strategy is to entirely avoid exposure to risks you are concerned about. Whether in your everyday life or your investments, if you can avoid exposing yourself to a risk it cannot directly harm you. That approach can be a very attractive alternative, but there is a downside to consider. The downside of avoiding exposing yourself to a risk or set of risks is that you'll also avoid exposing yourself to potential rewards as well. Like many things in life, to get one thing you many times have to give up something else. However, it doesn't have to be a totally all-or-nothing situation. You can avoid some risks selectively and accept others so that you end up with a balanced approach, which has still reduced your overall risk exposure. I'm sure you can think of any number of alternatives in the financial world where you can avoid risk of capital; all the same, you already also know the returns they provide reflect their lower risk. Whether what's best for us is to avoid risk entirely, or use a more balanced approach to our investment risk and reward exposure is ultimately our responsibility and opportunity. The key test in our decision process is whether we can live with the consequences should our decision prove to be wrong.

Internal Risks You Can Avoid

The risks that reside within us would logically seem to be the easiest risks to avoid. Nevertheless, they can present a considerable challenge. These insidious and self-generated risks can be more difficult to detect because they sneak up on us so gradually and quietly that they can be hard to notice. Yet they can easily turn us into out own worst enemies, if we don't develop appropriate safeguards. The first and most important step in controlling them is recognizing them in their multiple forms. Although we have already reviewed them in detail in chapter 6 (How Your Body Can Work Against You), they are important enough to highlight again from the perspective of the market situations that tend to draw out our internal risks. The environments where these internal risks are most common and when we need to elevate our guard against them the most include:

- Periods of overall market or asset class underperformance (elevates perceived risk/reduces real risk)
- Periods of overall market or asset class outperformance (reduces perceived risk/elevates real risk)
- Outperformance of select asset classes (makes us feel left out)
- Opportunities that are too good to be true (reduced perceived risk/elevated real risk)
- Losing our long-term focus to short-term anomalies (e.g., fear or greed)
- Overmanaging investments
- Our herd instinct (it can be very difficult to avoid doing what everyone else is doing)
- Temptation to modify investment philosophy to justify potential short-term opportunities
- Pattern finding in randomness (make sure to control the natural inclination to find patterns where none exist, and then apply meaning to them)
- Cognitive reflection decision-making errors (going with the fast, first, easy answers, rather than taking the time to double-check them)
- Common subliminal decision-making traps

Risks You Can't Avoid But Can Manage

There are a number of life and investment risks that are so much a part of the fabric of our modern lives that, as much as we'd like to, they just can't be avoided. We know that negative surprises will happen in these areas and that risk will materialize. We just don't know when. Economic, market, safety, health, environmental, accident, and career risks are just a few of the many risks that fall into this category. Although we can't avoid them, we can manage them at two different levels and in the process reduce their overall potential to harm us. Our first level of defense is to implement strategies to reduce the probability of situations carrying these risks from impacting us. In our investments we can accomplish this through asset allocation and through well thought-out investment diversification. In our daily lives we can do it by being selective about where we live, where we work, how we take care of ourselves. We can then go one step further by having plans and resources in place to reduce the impact of risks that may occur, in case our best efforts don't work. In the investment world that can be as simple as having a cash reserve ready to put to work when (not if) surprise market drops present a unique buying opportunity. In our everyday lives it can be as simple as having insurance in place to protect our health, lives, and property in case of negative surprises in those areas.

Risks You Can't Avoid and Can't Control

One of the most challenging categories of risk to deal with are those risks you can't avoid and you can't personally control. These risks include economic slowdowns, broad-based financial and credit crises, wars, accidents, natural disasters, serious medical or physical problems—to name a few. When they happen, it seems that the only thing we can do is just react to them. What's most frustrating about these risks is the feeling of helplessness when they hit and there's little or nothing we can do to prevent or control them. Since many of these risks do not give us advance notice before they strike, the best strategy for dealing with them is to put initiatives in place before they occur, which will minimize their impact and damage. Rather than hope they won't happen, the more effective and proactive strategy is to assume they will happen, and be prepared for them. In the investment world, since recessions and economic slowdowns are a regular feature of the economic and market cycles and should be expected, one answer is preparing a well-thought-out risk management or recession investment strategy plan. Such plans not only significantly reduce the emotional impact of these events, they can also serve as a guide in helping you make the right moves at the right time, and turn a potential problem into a potential opportunity. In our daily lives one example can be planning ahead for the fact that in the event of a widespread natural disaster in our area, we very well could be totally on our own for five or six days before government officials can mount a comprehensive relief effort. So setting aside enough food, water, first aid materials, necessary supplies, and communications equipment for such a contingency can turn a potential disaster into an inconvenience for those who are prepared in advance.

Risks and Rewards You Knowingly Seek and Can Control

Of course seeking risk alone, without potential rewards is very destructive and unstable personal behavior and not a subject we'll be addressing here. However, seeking rewards that carry known risks is the foundation of human progress and what innovation and growth is all about. It's what skydivers, hang gliders, wilderness skiers and snow boarders, scuba divers, private pilots, and rock and ice climbers do all the time. They receive enormous satisfaction and psychic rewards from these activities while taking what can at times seem like significant risks. In reality, if you ever have the opportunity to talk with any participants in these high-risk sports you'll learn how meticulous they are about risk management: how much attention they pay to proper training, preparation, planning, technique, proper and well maintained equipment, evaluation of conditions, emergency preparedness, and contingency planning. It works the same with the more aggressive investment strategies. They offer higher returns and carry higher risks. If you know what you are doing, are fully prepared, and understand the risks and how to manage them, they can be an attractive way to improve your overall investment returns. However, if you engage in these advanced strategies without knowledge, preparation, and experience in the discipline, and you lack a comprehensive understanding of the risks involved, it's a form of financial suicide.

A Closer Look at Crisis Events

Now that we've addressed a number of ways to group risks, let's turn our attention to risks that can have a very strong emotional effect on us and on our markets. Crisis events, both natural and manmade, have been a characteristic of human existence throughout history. They have included floods, fires, earthquakes, famines, hurricanes, tornadoes, land and rock slides, massive explosions, accidents, bombs, financial collapses, tsunamis, defaults, regime shifts, coup d'états, business slowdowns (recessions), business collapses (depressions), sudden deaths and assassinations of key leaders, disease epidemics, surprise attacks, wars—in addition to international crises, sudden and devastating asset price collapses of all kinds, and more common in recent decades, terrorist attacks.

Psychologists have proven that some of these dramatic, high impact events and situations can generate feelings of risk and uncertainty that are even greater than their real risks. For a number of reasons, our perception of the risks associated with these emotionally impacting events are magnified by our internal risk management systems so we perceive these risks as greater than they really are. This elevation of our perception of risk occurs when a risk occurs that has one or more of the following factors: (1) It has large-scale consequences, (2) It is new or unfamiliar to us, (3) It is beyond our ability to control or influence, (4) It occurs suddenly and without warning. Because of the elevated emotional impact and higher risk perception these particular risks carry, as opposed to their actual risk, it is critical that we prepare in advance for them. The simple act of becoming familiar with these risks and developing advance risk management plans of action for when they do occur will help us keep our heads clear and emotions in check when (not if) they do happen. That advance preparation will pay big dividends when any of these risks occur. People who are not as prepared as we are will be surprised, anxious, emotional, uncertain, and reactive. We on the other hand, as a result of our knowledge and advance preparation will not be surprised, will keep out wits about us, and will be in a better position to survive, stay level-headed, be proactive, and potentially benefit from the situation.

Crisis Event Categories

There are various crisis event categories, including:

Natural Disasters: Earthquakes, Floods, Fires, Hurricanes, Tornadoes, Tsunamis, Fires, Landslides, and So on. Although these events can have severe impact for those directly involved and often receive a great deal of sensational media coverage, the majority of these events have a local or, at most, regional impact. Even if they cause extensive local damage, except in rare instances these incidents will have no to little impact on the national markets or economy or on broadly diversified investment portfolios.

Manmade Crisis Events: Terrorist Attacks, Explosions, Nuclear Power Accidents, Wars, Assassinations, Political Crises, and So On. Although these events can be spectacular and generate perceived risks that are greater than their real risks, they tend to have only local or regional impact (unless the event exposes a broader vulnerability) and only short-term impact on the national markets or diversified portfolios. September 11, 2001, is a classic example in which all of the four risk perception amplification factors discussed earlier, occurred simultaneously. On opening a few days after 9/11, the initial reaction of the markets was a dramatic drop in the equity markets and an enormous increase in demand for the safety of government bonds. However, within just a few weeks the stock market had recovered all its losses related to the event. The even bigger issues putting downward pressure on the equity markets from early 2000 to well after 9/11 were the recession at the time and the downward adjustment still going on after the breaking of the Internet bubble. Although a nuclear power accident would be an initial shock to the markets, which would recover quickly, it would also likely have its biggest effect in its geographic area and in the nuclear power industry itself. A large and sustainable impact on our geographically and functionally diverse national economy and markets would likely not occur.

Financial Crises: Recessions; Sudden Market Collapses; Bankruptcies/Defaults; and Financial, Credit, Liquidity, Currency, and International Crises. The individual bankruptcy of a well known firm would, of course, have a devastating effect on the shareholders, bondholders, employees, and creditors of that firm and likely negatively affect the share prices of firms in the same industry. However, it would be unlikely to affect the entire economy and market. Recessions and financial crises are another matter entirely. Because of their impact across the depth and breadth of the whole economy, they can have a profound impact on the equity and bond markets as well as interest rates and monetary policy. Recessions are a regular part of economic cycle. In fact we are currently in the eighth recession since 1960. So we've had a lot of experience with them. A common action we have historically seen is the equity markets beginning to retreat six to nine months before economic activity visibly slows and a recession becomes obvious. The same phenomenon occurs on the way out of recessionary bottoms. The equity markets begin rising many months in advance of improving economic news. This advanced anticipation of future business activity slowdowns and pickups frustrates many investors, particularly coming off recessionary market bottoms. Then investors are very skeptical of a rising market without it being confirmed by rising business activity and rising earnings. Once the business news and earnings pick up again and finally confirm the market advance, investors buy back into the market with confidence, just about the time the stock market is ready to drop back and consolidate its previous advance from the recessionary markets lows. Although these types of corrections only last a few weeks to a few months, they often cause investors to throw up their arms in utter frustration, and once again question their understanding of what drives markets and their own investment judgment.

The bond prices are a totally different story, in that they do not typically anticipate market moves as much as they react almost instantaneously to changes in interest rates inflation rates, and credit quality.

Simple Is Better

With our attention as investors being pulled moment by moment, from event to event by our worldwide, 24/7 news services, there are some real benefits to stepping back and taking a big picture view of the risks we face. Since many types of investment-related risks have a number of physical, financial, and behavioral characteristics in common with one another, managing those risks within general risk categories can simplify the many complexities of managing them individually. Grouping these risks with common characteristics and managing them with common risk mitigation strategies can leverage our time and our risk management resources, and help us become more effective risk managers in the process. It doesn't mean that we should ever relax or let our guard down when it comes to the ever-evolving nature of old and new risks. It does offer a way to organize our thinking about risk and help make the job of managing risks less complex.

CHAPTER 10

Understanding and Prioritizing Risks

Before a problem can be solved, it must be clearly stated and defined.
William Feather

With the pace of change in the world continuing to accelerate while showing no signs of slowing down any time soon, and risks seeming to be coming at us faster and faster with increasing ferocity and impact, how do we even begin to get our arms around the challenges of managing all these potential risks. Where do we even start? With so many possible risks at so many levels, how can we even begin to decide which risks to avoid entirely, which risks to manage, and which risks to just accept with no risk management, and live with their consequences?

These issues become even more challenging when we realize that risk management also has a cost. Since, in this world at least, there's no such thing as a free lunch and everything has a cost, risk management does too. As we discussed before, to obtain any one thing, we generally have to give up something else, and risk management is no exception. The costs of risk management include our time for risk management planning and monitoring, lost opportunity (remember lower risk also means lower returns), and the financial costs of implementing risk management strategies. Insurance, professional asset management, diversification, professional advice, developing and staying current on our knowledge of recent developments and risk reduction methodologies all have costs associated with them. Some investors have even become so extreme in their risk management efforts to fully neutralize all their risks that they also unknowingly limit their potential upside to a point where they would have been better served by placing all their investments in CDs, and saving themselves a lot of unnecessary time and trouble.

The "Risk-Wise" Personal Risk Assessment

So with a full range of risks to manage and finite risk management resources that don't allow us the luxury of managing every single risk we face, even if we wanted to, what can we do? The answer is to refer back to the "Risk-Wise" Investor–Risk Management Process outlined in the second chapter of this book. If you recall, the first step of that process is the Personal Risk Assessment, which includes four distinct and sequential substeps. The first element of the assessment process is defining risk, the second is identifying risks, the third element is understanding risk, and the fourth is determining which risks to avoid, accept, and/or manage. For our purposes in this chapter we'll be focusing on the "Risk-Wise" process of understanding risks. We'll then use that understanding to rank and prioritize the risks we each personally face, so that our risk management resources are most focused on the most important risks we face, and less focused on the lower priority risks.

Understanding Risks

The process of understanding risks has three principal elements. The first is the likelihood or probability of each risk occurring, the second is the personal impact of each risk, should it occur, and the third is learning as much about the characteristics of each risk as possible (factors that influence its behavior, ability to manifest, character, necessary precursor situations, factors to manage it once it occurs, plus a number of other considerations).

A risk's likelihood is important to know because it gives us a good sense of how often to expect it will occur. The likelihood of risks can range from being highly likely to very unlikely, with additional possibilities between the two extremes. Each individual risk's likelihood will sit somewhere along that spectrum of probabilities, and typically remain relatively stable, unless or until something happens to increase or decrease its chances of coming about.

The potential impact of risks is even more important to our understanding, knowledge, and effective management of risks. Although the severity of a risk's impact can vary a great deal from person to person, its probability does not. For an example, consider the annual probability of a hurricane hitting the U.S. mainland, which is virtually certain. That probability is the same for everyone, however its impact is highly subjective. A hurricane hitting Florida will have a high and potentially devastating impact on someone living where it hits, while someone living in Colorado, which is never impacted by hurricanes, will not be directly impacted at all. Although, our Colorado resident may still be *indirectly* impacted by the hurricane, if she has friends, relatives, or financial interests in Florida.

The relationship between a risk's likelihood and impact work very much the same way in the investment world. Just as an individual company or even an industry may experience a negative business or regulatory development that adversely impacts their business, reduces their profitability, and sinks their stock price, that development's impact may have little or no effect on other companies in other industries or the markets.

Step 1: Identify Each Risk of Concern

Our first step in the process of understanding risk is to identify the risks we're most concerned about and the risks we'll face, and then write them down to begin the risk management process.

Since you can't manage a risk you can't identify, writing them down on your list is the first step in managing them. You can include any risk you're concerned about on your risk list. If you're working with a financial advisor, you should to ask him to take a look at your list and suggest adding risks that you may have overlooked. Remember that the risks you are concerned about and that you choose to list and identify may be totally different from the examples I provide. That's perfectly fine, because the whole purpose of this process is to help you better manage the risk you're personally concerned about.

Here are a just few examples of possible risks of personal concern.

- Outliving my money
- Not meeting my investment objectives
- Terrorism
- Recessions
- Inflation
- Deflation
- Liquidity
- Industry
- Market
- Retirement income level

Once you've thought through the risks you're concerned about and the written them all down you're ready to move to the next step in understanding your risk.

Step 2: Rate Each Risk's Likelihood

Your second step in understanding a risk is to rate the probability or likelihood of each of these risks occurring over the next five years (our minimum investment time horizon) The risk likelihood categories we'll use are: high, moderate, and low. You can certainly look out longer than five years for this exercise, but since the world is changing so rapidly, even projecting what it will be like in five years is a challenge. Plus, investors should revisit their risk management plans and adjust these ranking at least every couple of years, just to make any necessary adjustments because of changing conditions.

Remember these are examples only. You should use your own judgments coupled with your advisor(s) as the ones you should rely on.

Rating the Probability of Risk Occurring: High, Moderate, Low

- Terrorism (moderate)
- Recessions (high)
- Inflation (low)
- Deflation (moderate)
- Liquidity (low)
- Industry (high)
- Market (high)
- Retirement income level (moderate)
- Outliving my money (moderate)
- Meeting my investment objectives (moderate)

Now that you've rated the likelihood of each of your risks you are ready to move to the next step.

Step 3: Rate Each Risk's Potential Impact

Step 3 involves rating the potential impact on your own personal situation were these risks to occur. In other words, were these risks to happen would they have a low, moderate, or high negative impact on your personal situation. (The previous likelihood ratings have been included for convenience purposes.)

Sample Rating of Risk Likelihood and Impact

Risk	Likelihood			Personal Impact		
	(Low/Moderate/High)			**(Low/Moderate/High)**		
	Low	Moderate	High	Low	Moderate	High
Terrorism	X					X
Recession		X			X	
Inflation			X			X
Deflation		X				X
Liquidity	X					X
Industry		X		X		
Market		X			X	
Retire Income Level		X				X
Outliving My Money		X				X
Meeting Invest. Object.		X				X

Once you have identified and recorded your risks, and then rated them as to the individual probability of them occurring, and their potential personal impact, you are ready to prioritize them.

Prioritizing Risks

The *big* question and *big* potential pitfall is still how you go about effectively prioritizing risks. Many investors give their highest risk management priority to the highest likelihood risks. Their logic is that since these risks are showing up and attacking us so frequently, it only makes sense to deal with them first and neutralize them. Even though that logic sounds reasonable, and it's gratifying to swat down some of those nuisance risks that can drive us crazy, it's actually a trap. Dealing with those frequent and irritating, lower-impact risks can consume valuable risk management time and resources, leaving us even more vulnerable to the less frequent, and more harmful, higher-impact risks. Although, in the heat of the investment marketplace it can seem counterintuitive to disregard those more frequent, smaller-impact risks, it can pay off when the infrequent, high-impact, heavyweight risks arrive. So the most effective method to use in prioritizing risks is to *prioritize risks by their impact first*, not their likelihood. In doing so, we can focus our risk management attention on the all-important, high-impact risks rather than be distracted by the frequent, low-impact risks, which we may even decide to just accept or ignore altogether. In addition, this method also exemplifies, and makes actionable, one of the basic principles of "Risk-Wise" Investing, which is to honestly recognize risks and then directly face them. As uncomfortable as that initial encounter may feel, it's the only way to gain real power over risks, as opposed to the unacceptable alternative of allowing them to have power over us. Finally, this impact-based priority ranking adheres to the venerable adage of traditional wisdom, which asserts to always hope for the best, but plan for the worst.

Risk Management Priority Rankings

Here, in descending order from the most important to the least, is an example of how the various risk impact and risk likelihood combinations should be prioritized.

9. ***High impact/high probability.*** These risks will happen and must be addressed as imminent, with immediate measures implemented to reduce their likelihood, limit their impact, and recover as fast as possible after they occur.

8. ***High impact/moderate probability.*** Although the likelihood of these risks is moderate, their high potential impact requires measures to immediately reduce their probability further, prepare to mitigate their impact when they occur, and recover from their effects as soon as possible.

7. ***High impact/low probability.*** Irrespective of the lower likelihood of these risks, their high potential negative impact requires the same level of preparation, risk reduction, and risk mitigation as any high-impact imminent risk. This type of risk may be an excellent candidate for automated risk mitigation systems to overcome inevitable assumptions that events of this type are so rare that they won't happen.

6. ***Moderate impact/high probability.*** These risks are serious enough and happen frequently enough that they must be addressed in any risk management effort. They are top of the mind risks as well, because they occur so frequently.

5. ***Moderate impact/moderate probability.*** This level of risk represents a transition point where investors who will not be seriously impacted or can recover quickly from moderate impact risks may want to consider accepting these risks with little or no specific risk management initiatives. Otherwise, implementing risk management initiatives makes sense with these types of risk.

4. ***Moderate impact/low probability.*** Any investor who cannot easily tolerate a moderate impact risk occurring should protect against this type of risk.

3. ***Low impact/high probability.*** If the impact of these risks occurring will have no intermediate or longer-term effects on an investor or investors can recover from the impact of these risks quickly, then there is little reason to be concerned by them. There may, in fact, be ways to convert their frequent occurrence into opportunities.

2- ***Low Impact/moderate probability-*** Because of their low impact these risks can be accepted by all but conservative, risk averse investors. The occurrence of these risks can also offer opportunities to more venturesome investors.

1. ***Low impact/low probability.*** These risks are the easiest to accept without any risk management initiatives because such initiatives provide little benefit for the effort. They can best be dealt with by just building their likelihood and impact into normal expectations.

This, impact-based, priority ranking system has proven its effectiveness in dealing with risks big and small in every human endeavor from science, medicine, aviation, construction, farming, and warfare all the way to firefighting, police work, childcare, film making, and sports. Where this methodology really shines in the investment world is in how you can adapt it for your own investment purposes and priorities. Depending on your own preferences, you may want to concentrate your risk management on only the high-impact risks, or on both the high and moderate risk categories. You may also decide that you want to prevent being exposed to a specific risk by totally avoiding activities that expose you to that risk and move a portion of your assets into investment alternatives offering guarantees against that risk, or you can consider alternatives, like hedging, that can offset the negative impact of that risk occurring. With all its flexibility, the key consideration to the success of your efforts is what's right for you. The acid test is your level of comfort with your plans, and whether they will they provide you the peace of mind that allows you to sleep better at night. Since life is too short to do anything with your money you're not comfortable doing, make sure that your risk management planning and initiatives meet that standard.

Special New Risk Management Priority Category

There's another category of risk we haven't yet mentioned in our discussion about prioritizing risks. These particular risks are very rare, high-impact events, which are totally unexpected, typically have extreme, widespread impact, and are logically explained after the fact. You may have already guessed that I'm talking about the black swan events, which have become so much better understood after Nassim Taleb's best-selling book of the same name.

Because the pace of change in the world is accelerating and our globe is so interconnected that we now live in a truly global economy, these black swan events are increasing in frequency and growing in their impact. Examples over the last 10 years include the worldwide explosion of the Internet and information revolution, the incredible revolution in biotechnology and genetics that is just getting started, the terrorist attacks of 9/11, the global housing boom and subsequent mortgage mess, and most recently the historic stock market volatility of the fall of 2008. Given their increasing frequency we need to plan for these black swans as well. The challenge is, that by definition, black swans are both unpredictable and unexpected in terms of their timing and magnitude. So, what's the answer? The answer, which is both simple and complex at the same time, is to expect the unexpected. So here's a supplementary risk management category for your consideration:

Uncertain Impact/Totally Unexpected and Rare Events

Since humans like to be in control, and don't much care for surprises unless they're the pleasant kind, these totally unexpected events often create a dramatic increase in our perception of risk. Remember the four situations psychologists have proven to create perceived risk greater that the real risks are:

1. Large-scale consequences
2. Beyond our control or influence
3. New or unfamiliar
4. Sudden occurrence

So it's very important to plan on these types of sudden unexpected events occurring and to expect and prepare for our risk perception to shoot off the charts. It's then crucial to determine, as quickly as possible, their potential, personal impact on each of us. Most likely these events' impact will have a high direct impact on some people and little or no direct impact on the majority. The key point, from an investment perspective, is to recognize that they can and will happen, and that all investors should expect and prepare for them in advance. As part of your planning and preparation, also remember the higher perceived risks associated with these types of events and the fact that the markets abhor surprises and usually react to negative surprises very negatively. This combination of factors will likely lead to dramatic sell-offs in the stock markets and a rush to quality and government bonds in the debt markets. (Remember what happened on and just after 9/11?) The important thing to keep in mind in your planning is that these market overreactions to rare, chance events are usually short-lived. So the reaction of some investors to sell, sell, sell is almost always a mistake (witness 9/11 again). The other way to look at any sharp surprise-driven sell-offs is as a potential opportunity to buy well-run businesses at an emotionally discounted price.

You may want to consider dedicating (in advance) a small portion of your portfolio, a separate pool of funds, or a call option purchase plan to opportunistically take advantage of these temporary, deeply oversold conditions. That way, because you have a plan in place to take advantage of them, you'll actually look forward to surprise market drops. Just remember to be patient, since these kinds of opportunities are by definition, rare events. In the mean time, you might get some valuable experience and practice by taking advantage of the deeply oversold conditions that typically occur once or twice a year as part of the normal overbought/oversold cycles of the markets. Either way, it's important to think ahead and prepare for these types of totally unexpected, surprise rare events. At a minimum, a well thought out plan of what to do when these black swans do occur will insure better control of the normally strong emotional reactions they generate.

Instability Is the Norm

As we've reviewed in this books several times already, it is absolutely critical that we recognize that the old model of looking at the world—that stability is the normal state of things and instability is a temporary exception—is a dysfunctional model of how our modern, rapidly changing world works. Our world today is actually functioning in the exact opposite way, where instability is the norm and stability is the exception. In such a world understanding and managing the risks and rewards, and living with rapid change and uncertainty will become more and more important skills.

How we each choose to allocate our risk management attention and resources is ultimately our own responsibility and as individual as each one of us. Taking a risk management priority ranking off the shelf and implementing it without first adjusting it to your own unique situation, personal preferences, and priorities can be a big mistake The more time you spend studying and understanding the risks you face and determining which risks to avoid entirely, which to accept and manage, and which to accept outright, the more successful risk manager you'll become.

CHAPTER 11

The "Risk-Wise" Risk Management Planning Process

Expect the best, plan for the worst, and prepare to be surprised.
Dennis Waitley

Now that we've reviewed a full lineup of diverse, risk related topics, it's time to explore how to apply all those insights and information into a practical, user-friendly, nontechnical method to manage risk. Of course, having all that knowledge about the fundamental nature of risk, how it works, its history, various approaches to managing it—all the way to how our bodies can both help and harm us in our risk management efforts—is totally useless, unless we can put it to work for our personal benefit. Most investors tend to complicate their efforts in this regard by addressing risks individually, sequentially or as they pop up over time, rather than via a comprehensive, well thought out, and proactive risk management plan. To that end, this chapter is dedicated to helping you become familiar and completely comfortable with an easy-to-use, very effective, and holistic risk management planning process. It's a system that you can put to work right away in preparing for and effectively managing the risks you'll face. One of its big additional advantages is the program's adaptability in dealing with risks well beyond those in the investment world. When you think about it, that really shouldn't be surprising, given that the method is patterned on the highly adaptable risk management process we use in our daily lives. Ultimately, the multifunctionality and flexibility of this approach allows anyone who uses it to also manage the full range of risks she faces every day. Let's begin with a brief review of the steps in "Risk-Wise" Investor risk management process.

Outlined below are the basic steps of the "Risk-Wise" Investor risk management planning process:

1. **Personal risk assessment**
   - Define risk
   - Identify risks
   - Understand risks
   - Determine which risks to avoid, accept, and/or manage
2. **Review risk reduction/management strategies available**
3. **Evaluate your risk/reward trade-offs**
4. **Make your decision to act or not act—then implement**
5. **Ongoing, effective risk monitoring and decision making**

In this chapter, we will conduct an in-depth examination of the details of each step in the "Risk-Wise" Investor risk management process.

Step 1: Personal Risk Assessment

The personal risk assessment is focused on five key steps that must be addressed before proceeding with the rest of the risk management planning process Those risk assessment steps include defining, identifying, understanding, prioritizing, and then finally deciding which risks to avoid entirely, which risks to accept and manage, and which risks to accept outright, with no risk management effort.

Define Risk

You are certainly free to use any definition of risk you desire. However, one thing we know is that our definition or risk has enormous influence on how easy and effective or difficult and ineffective our risk management efforts will be. The right definition will empower us and make our job easier, the wrong definition will weaken us and make the job much tougher and much less effective.

The definition I personally use, and recommend that you use and embrace as well is this: *The degree to which an outcome differs from your expectations*. Since we have full responsibility for our financial futures and full and total control over what we expect, this definition fits our needs directly by perfectly balancing our responsibility and our control. Should you, however, decide to use another definition of risk, I'm giving you fair warning that not using the definition provided above will dramatically reduce the effectiveness of the "Risk-Wise" risk management planning process. Its effectiveness will be reduced because the entire "Risk-Wise" system is based on our individual ability to control our own expectations with total responsibility for what happens to us. The balance between having full control of and full responsibility for our expectations is the foundation, strength, and power of this approach. Any other definition of risk will unbalance the system and deliver disappointing results.

What to Expect

Given that risk is the degree to which an outcome differs from expectations, what we expect is very, very important. The more accurate our expectations, the fewer risks we'll experience, the better prepared we'll be, and the fewer negative surprises we'll have. So, the really big question of risk management becomes this: What should we expect when investing? Of course, legions of well paid analysts, economists, pundits, prognosticators, and so-called experts (not to mention, friends and neighbors) have very strong opinions and guesses they love to share with us, that unfortunately turn out to be wrong, much more than they are right. The uncomfortable fact is that not only do they *not* know what to expect, no one else really knows or ever has known what to expect. The world is just too random and recursive. So where can we look for some guidance? One of the best places to start is to review, and then re-review again, the brief history of risk presented in Chapter 3 of this book. As you journey through the centuries, you'll begin to see patterns. Those patterns link together and show regular, continuous, relentless progress, growth, and improvement in our economic, social, and physical conditions, overall well-being and enormous advancement in the quality of our lives. Sure, our increasing prosperity has suffered the periodic setbacks of wars, economic slumps, market crashes, and financial panics. As serious and frightening as these episodes have been, they have always proved to be temporary downward blips in the continuously upward march of progress. The many, sometimes hard-to-believe asset bubbles where we humans get carried away by our emotions, herd mentality, and greed have also proved to be short-lived. These extreme events have happened almost too many times to count, all around the world in the last four centuries, but the victims pick themselves up, dust themselves off, and within a year or two the past is forgotten, and it's off to the races again. We can also expect human nature to fundamentally remain the same, whether when interacting with one another directly or in the international financial markets. Warren Buffett may have said it best in commenting about what to expect from human nature in the investment world when he said, "The fact that people will be full of greed, fear, or folly is predictable. The sequence is not predictable."

The last 100 years have been the most remarkable in human history. In that relatively brief period, we have seen unbelievable changes. Those developments, which have included everything from the spectacular and uplifting achievements of space flight to the absolutely horrific events of nuclear war, would have been totally incomprehensible (or at least considered magic) to people living 100 years ago who would have been granted a glimpse of our world today. People a 100 years from now, at the turn of the twenty-second century will be saying the same thing about us and our current limited view of the incredible opportunities, progress, and unbelievably bright future that lies ahead for us. Since we don't have crystal balls, and so much has been packed into the last 100 years, it can be very instructive to look back at the events and markets of that period to gain insights into of the range of possibilities we can expect going forward.

Considering that history tends to repeat itself but always with a difference, please take a few moments to review some of the following examples of how the markets have behaved in the past, in order to gain a better idea of what we can expect in the future. Please also keep in mind what Warren Buffett said about how predictable human behavior patterns are but that "the sequence is not predictable."

HISTORY OF U.S BUSINESS CONTRACTIONS   Let's start with Table 11.1, which outlines the duration of every one of the 33 business slowdowns in the United States since 1857. That frequency averages out to a business slowdown approximately every 4.5 years, and reaffirms the fact that business slowdowns and recessions are a regular part of the economic landscape that must be planned for and expected.

It's interesting to note that prior to the 1920s business slowdowns were generally called "panics" because of their violent drops and the strong emotional reactions their volatility generated in the people they affected. The great business slowdown and deflation of the 1930s was called a Depression, a term that since those days has been reserved for business contractions greater than 10 percent of Gross National Product (there has been only one). We now call business contractions recessions, and their starts are only declared by the NBER after the contraction has begun, and are declared ended only well after a sustainable recovery has begun.

As you can see in Table 11.1, the longest recorded business contraction lasted 65 months, back in the 1870s, long before the founding of the U.S Federal Reserve Bank in 1913. Since 1913 the longest contraction took 43 months to bottom out and start recovering. As the table indicates, since the 1940s the average business slump has lasted about 10 months. When you look at the average numbers, it's clear that the length of business slowdowns have been getting shorter over time. In addition, the average length of the business expansions between contractions has been lengthening. From 1854 to 1919 the average expansion period lasted four years. From 1919 to 1945 the average expansion length stayed about the same at four years, while in the period from 1945 to 2008 it lengthened by 50 percent to an average of

TABLE 11.1 U.S. Business Contractions and Expansions 1857–2008

Contractions (recessions) Start at the Peak of a Business Cycle and End at the Trough

Business Cycle Reference Dates		Duration in Months			
Peak	Trough	Contraction	Expansion	Cycle	
		Peak to Trough	Previous Trough to This Peak	Trough from Previous Trough	Peak from Previous Peak
	December 1854(IV)	—	—	—	—
June 1857(II)	December 1858(IV)	18	30	48	—
October 1860(III)	June 1861 (III)	8	22	30	40
April 19865(I)	December 1867(I)	32	46	78	54
June 1869(II)	December 1870(IV)	18	18	36	50
October 1873(III)	March 1879(I)	65	34	99	52
March 1872(I)	May 1885(II)	38	36	74	101
March 1887(II)	April 1888(I)	13	22	35	60
July 1890(III)	May 1891(II)	10	27	37	40
January 1893(I)	June 1894(II)	17	20	37	30
December 1895(IV)	June 1897(II)	18	18	36	35
June 1899(III)	December 1900(IV)	18	24	42	42
September 1902(IV)	August 1904(III)	23	21	44	39
May 1907(II)	June 1908(II)	13	33	46	56
January 1910(I)	January 1912(IV)	24	19	43	32
January 1913(I)	December 1914(IV)	23	12	35	36
August 1918(III)	March 1919(I)	7	44	51	67
January 1920(I)	July 1921(III)	18	10	28	17
May 1923(II)	July 1924(III)	14	22	36	40
October 1926(III)	November 1927(IV)	13	27	40	41
August 1929(III)	March 1933(I)	43	21	64	34
May 1937(II)	June 1938(II)	13	50	63	93
February 1945(I)	October 1945(IV)	8	80	88	93
November 1948(IV)	October 1949(IV)	11	37	48	45
July 1953(II)	May 1954(II)	10	45	55	56
August 1957(III)	April 1958(II)	8	39	47	49
April 1960(II)	February 1961(I)	10	24	34	32
December 1969(IV)	November 1970(IV)	10	106	117	116
November 1973(IV)	March 1975(I)	16	36	52	47
January 1980(I)	July 1980(III)	6	58	64	74
July 1981(III)	November 1982(IV)	16	12	28	18
July 1990(III)	March 1991(I)	8	92	100	108
March 2001(I)	November 2001(IV)	8	120	128	128
December 2007(IV)			73		81
Average, all cycles:					
1854–2001 (32 cycles)		17	38	55	56*
1854–1919 (16 cycles)		22	27	48	49†
1919–1945 (6 cycles)		18	35	53	53
1945–2001 (10 cycles)		10	57	67	67

Quarterly dates are in parentheses.

*31 cycles.

†15 cycles.

Source: National Bureau of Economic Research (NBER), www.nber.org.

about six years. Some interpret that extension in the length of more recent business expansions to be the result of the Federal Reserve Bank's becoming more skilled at managing the economic intricacies of growth and inflation. Nevertheless, as the National Bureau of Economic Research's table dramatically points out, up and down business cycles have been around for a long time, and are likely to be around for a long time to come. They are a fact of life that every business person and investor must factor into their business, investment, and risk management plans.

DISCOUNTING FUNCTION OF THE EQUITY MARKETS   The stock market's unusual and prognostic ability to move three, six, or nine months in advance of as-yet unseen developments actually occurring is one of the most unnatural and difficult investment concepts to grasp and apply. Although, this ability to discount, factor in, or take into account the future is puzzling, it's also a fascinating business fact that all investors need to understand. The market regularly moves up in the face of current negative news because it's already anticipating the positive news to follow. Conversely, with good news all round, the market can begin to drop for no clear reason, in anticipation of weakening business conditions that won't become recognized for many months. The key is to recognize that this phenomenon exists and to factor it into your investment thinking.

When making investment decisions, what's most important is, as much as possible, to minimize your focus on current events in favor of what you believe business conditions will be like at least six months in the future. There's a great deal of speculation about why this discounting occurs, with the most plausible explanation being that current equity market price levels represent the cumulative best thinking about future business conditions. So if market participants generally have a positive feel for future business conditions, sellers of stocks will defer their sales in anticipation of higher prices in the future that in turn will lower the supply of stock currently for sale. That lower supply coupled with the same or increased demand by buyers who want to buy before potentially improving business conditions materialize, creates additional demand for the more limited supply, which causes prices to rise. The markets' discounting function is the basis behind the old Wall Street adage: Don't fight the tape, meaning that the markets may know something you don't, so be very careful or very confident if you are investing against the conventional wisdom. In the spirit of one picture being worth a thousand words, take a look at Figure 11.1 for an example of the equity markets' discounting ability around recessions. As you study the chart of the S&P 500 Index over the last 50 years, with recessions shaded in grey (note the most recent recessions which started in December 2007, is not shaded in), see if you can see how the S & P 500 Index behaves before, during, and after recessions.

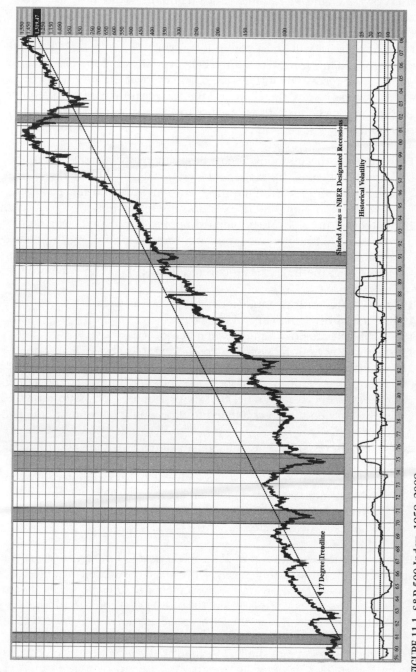

FIGURE 11.1 S&P 500 Index, 1958–2008

Source: Chart Courtesy of Scott Gray.

135

In reviewing Figure 11.1, you'll notice that in most cases the index displays very similar behavioral patterns, around each of the eight recessions we can observe in this figure's timeframe.

The following list will assist you in identifying those typical behavioral patterns (depicted in Figure 11.1) of the S&P 500 Index before, during, and after each of the recessions in the U.S. economy over the fifty years from 1959–2008. As you review the chart and the list, please remember the grey shaded bars on the chart represent each of the recessions also addressed in the following list.

1960 Recession. The index begins dropping many months before the recession begins, bottoms, and starts rising in the middle of the recession, and by the time the recession ends and the economic news is improving, the index is up substantially.

1970 Recession. The index starts dropping about one year before the recession begins, bottoms, and starts rising during the recession midpoint. By the end of the recession when business news is improving, the index has recovered to its general level before the recession.

1974–1975 Recession. Same general behavior as above.

1980 Recession. Same general behavior as above.

1981–1982 Recession. Same general behavior as above.

1990–1991 Recession. Same general behavior as above.

2001 Recession: A pattern anomaly. The index started dropping well in advance of the recession, bottomed, and began rising during the recession, was significantly above its recession bottom by the recession's end, then continued to drop until bottoming in the fall of 2003.

2007–2009 Recession. The index hit an all-time high in October 2007, and began dropping in advance of the start of the recession, which was later determined to be December 2007. It continued to drop until November 2008. As of this writing in early 2009, the November 2008 bottom for the index has been broken, and the economic news continues to deteriorate.

Figures 11.2 through 11.8 provide a more detailed perspective on the investment impact of the historic business cycle data presented in Table 11.1. Figure 11.2 leads off by showing the movements of Dow Jones Industrial Averages over the period of time from 1901 to 2008. Then the subsequent charts, Figures 11.3–11.8, review the DJIA's price movements every 20 years, through the end of 2008.

From the perspective of the 107 years of DJIA monthly price changes shown in Figure 11.2, it's easy to see that the period of time from 1982

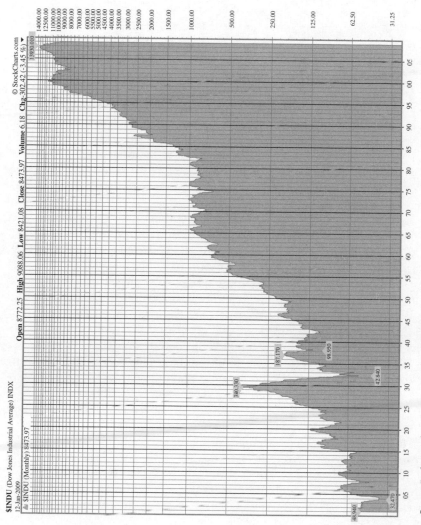

FIGURE 11.2 Dow Jones Industrial Averages, 1901–2008

Source: Chart Courtesy of StockCharts.com.

through 2000 was one of the smoother, and least volatile bull market advances in history (with the one exception of the historic market crash on October of 1987).

Figure 11.3 shows the Dow Jones Industrial Averages from 1901 to 1919 What is quite interesting in reviewing this figure is that the Panic of 1907 occurred as a result of a major banking crisis. We saw the same phenomenon again in the great market drops of 1930, 1931, 1932, and 2008 that were all also connected with banking crises. According to www.ChartoftheDay.com, these four market corrections, associated with banking crises are also ranked as the four largest annual percent decline market drops in the last 112 years. In every case however, the economy and the markets rebounded.

Figure 11.4 clearly shows the great bull market of the Roaring Twenties, and the dramatic three-year market drop from the 1929 peak to the ultimate market bottom in 1932. It also demonstrates, even during the depths of the Great Depression, the great power of the market coming off a major bottom. During that challenging economic period the Dow Jones Industrial Average increased almost fivefold, in just five years, from a low of around 40 in 1932, to a high near 200 in early 1937.

Figure 11.5 illustrates the discounting function of the stock market during the darkest days of World War II, when the DJIA bottomed and began rising. In spite of the consistently negative and depressing news at the time, the DJIA began climbing. Well before U.S. battlefield victories began, the market began rallying in anticipation of the overwhelming strength and commitment of the Allies turning the tide and eventually winning World War II.

The 1960s and 1970s were a volatile period socially, politically, economically, and in the markets. Although the DJIA could not seem to break above and hold the 1,000 level for very long, the large up, down, and generally sideways overall market direction were a dream come true for dollar-cost-averaging aficionados (see Figure 11.6). There were also areas including the energy and natural resources industries that prospered in the high inflation environment of the 1970s.

This market environment taught investors the benefits of, for a least a portion of their investment portfolios, the advantages and risk management benefits of buying on dips when the market was oversold. During these drops, investors were deeply depressed and fear was palpable. They then learned to take profits when the market moved to the opposite extreme of being overbought and too optimistic.

Figure 11.7 is an excellent example of what a great bull market looks like. Granted there were trouble spots and nervous stomachs in 1982, 1984, the recession of 1990, and again with the Asian Contagion of 1997, and the Russian Crisis, and the spectacular collapse of the Long-term Capital Management hedge fund in 1998. The big shake-up of that long bull market

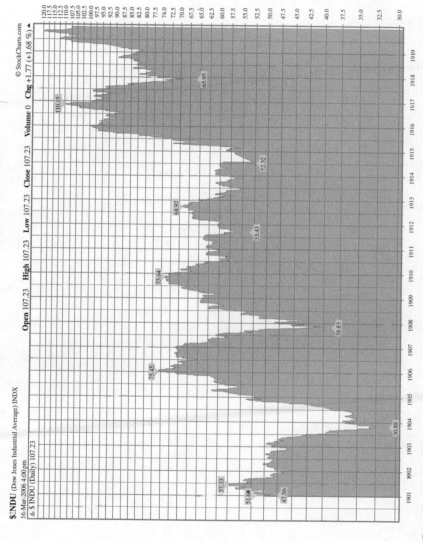

FIGURE 11.3 Dow Jones Industrial Averages, 1901–1919

Source: Chart Courtesy of StockCharts.com.

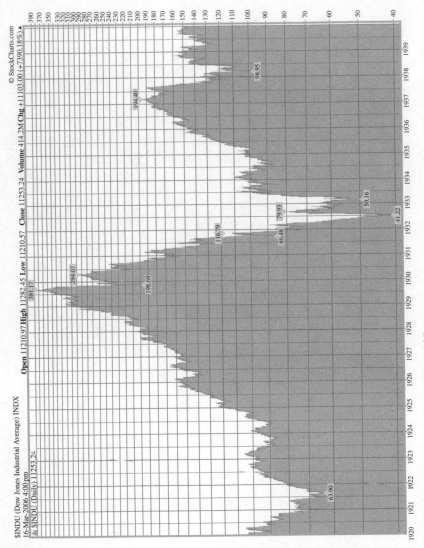

FIGURE 11.4 Dow Jones Industrial Averages, 1920–1939

Source: Chart Courtesy of StockCharts.com.

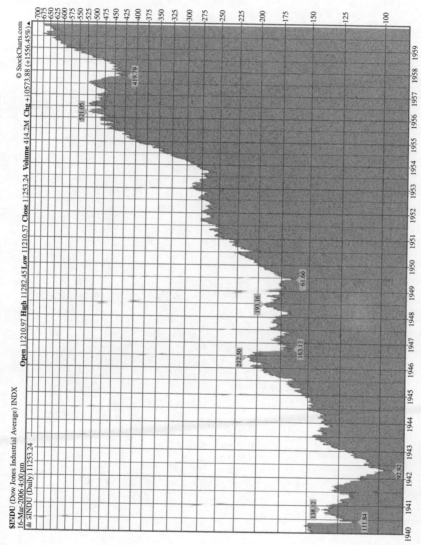

FIGURE 11.5 Dow Jones Industrial Averages, 1940–1959

Source: Chart Courtesy of StockCharts.com.

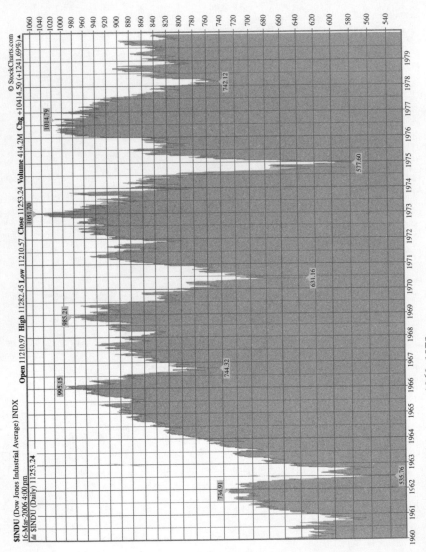

FIGURE 11.6 Dow Jones Industrial Averages, 1960–1979

Source: Chart Courtesy of StockCharts.com

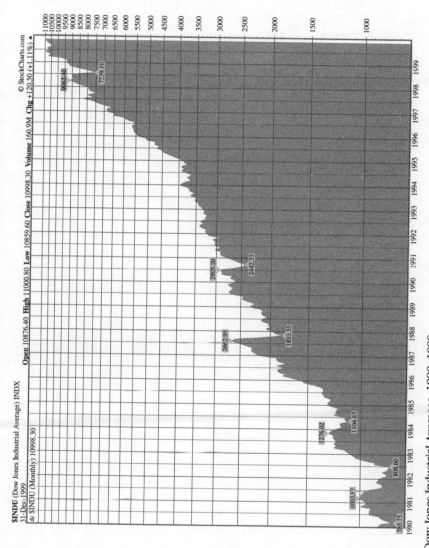

FIGURE 11.7 Dow Jones Industrial Averages, 1980–1999

Source: Chart Courtesy of StockCharts.com.

143

was October 19, 1987, when the DJIA dropped 21 percent in one day on record volume. It was the biggest, single-day percent drop in market history, before or since. Although that market crash shook both novice and professional investors to their core, within a few months the indices had recovered much of what had been lost in the crash. It also taught the generation of investors who experienced it, both the dangers and risks of panic selling and the benefits of buy-and-hold investing.

Market movements in this decade are not unlike those that we've seen previously from 1901 to 1919, 1920 to 1939, and 1960 to 1979 (see Figure 11.8). The market crash of 2008 with the DJIA down over 30 percent in one year was certainly a shock to investors. However, the one-year drop in 1931 of over 50 percent and the crash of 1907, down almost 40 percent, from both of which the market eventually recovered, helped put 2008 into a historical perspective and give investors in 2008 some hope. Those market crashes also help us to understand that big market drops are to be expected from time to time, and as painful as they can be for short-term investors, long-term investors view them as opportunities to buy quality companies at bargain prices. As the old Wall Street maxim says: In time of crisis money moves from weak hands to strong hands.

WHAT SHOULD WE EXPECT? After reviewing the market movements of the last 107 years, we should expect more of the same but at a faster and faster rate in the future. Our world's continuously accelerating pace of change will drive more uncertainty and also drive more opportunity than ever before. We should expect the quality of our lives to continue to improve and stock prices to significantly increase over time. Of course, we'll continue to experience continued economic and market corrections and the favorite dance of Wall Street, The Wall Street Shuffle. It's an easy dance to learn out once you become familiar with it's always changing steps; like two steps forward, then one step back, then three steps forward, then two steps back . . . and so on. As economic and business activity, innovation, and profitability grow over time, so will corporate earnings and stock prices. There will be robust business expansions interspersed with tough, sometimes frightening business contractions and market setbacks. There will be crisis events of every sort, some will be expected and some will be complete surprises. There will be booms, bubbles, busts, wars, panics and crashes, rising and falling interest rates, scandals, scallywags, demoralizing violations of our trust, and heroes of all types. Numerous times, investors will see their herd instinct, to do what everyone else is doing, lead legions of them to the financial slaughterhouses, just as they've been doing for centuries. We'll have incredible opportunities and, because we can sometimes be our own worst enemies, we'll also become victims of painful, self-inflicted blunders. All in all, directly facing, understanding, and effectively managing our risks will become even

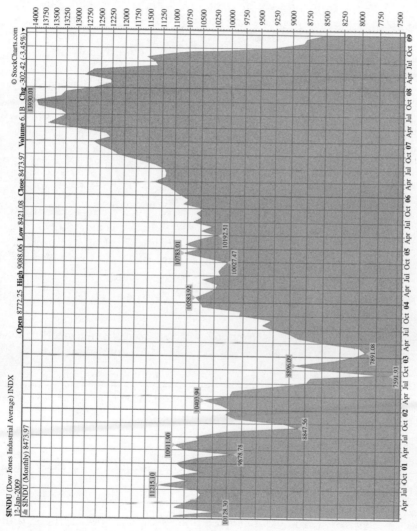

FIGURE 11.8 Dow Jones Industrial Averages, 2000–2008

Source: Chart Courtesy of StockCharts.com.

more important to our investment and life success and to accomplishing our dreams and objectives.

Identify Risks

Since it's impossible to manage any risk you haven't identified, our next step is to list all the risks you face or are concerned about in writing. Please remember to be as specific as possible. Don't worry about categorizing them or listing them in any specific sequences; just get them down on paper for now, and we'll categorize them later. Although a few examples are provided below, it is very important to develop your own personal list that flows directly from your own thinking. Although in this book we're focusing on investment risks, and indirectly on economic risks, add anything to your list you like, even if it doesn't have anything to do with economics or investing, because we'll touch on how to begin managing those other risks a little later. Just start asking yourself what are you most concerned about? What makes you nervous, upset, or keeps you up at night? What are you most afraid of? What do you have too much or too little of? Whatever subjects or possibilities cause you concern, write them down. A key reason the "Risk-Wise" Risk Management Planning method is so effective is that it focuses in the risks of concern specific to you. Here are a few examples of possible risks, but please remember, do not use these particular risks in your risk list unless they are real concerns to you.

Sample Risks of Personal Concern

Outlined below are samples of risks of personal concern that need to be addressed as part of any personal financial planning and implementation process.

Outliving my money	Meeting my investment objectives	Inflation
Terrorism risk	Recessions	Industry
Deflation	Liquidity risk	Underperformance
Market risk	Retirement income	
Security asset	Victim of graft/fraud	

Understand Risks

As we discussed in the previous chapter, understanding risk has three main elements. First is determining the likelihood or probability of a risk occurring. The answer to this question doesn't have to be an exact statistic; in fact it can work better just using one of three general likelihood categories (such as frequent—high, moderate, or infrequent, rare—low).

The second element in understanding risk is each specific risk's potential personal impact, should it occur. Each risk's impact can be ranked using a term from one of these three categories, devastating or severe, moderate, mild or low. It is very important to rate a risk's impact based on its personal impact on you if it should occur. When making that impact determination it's very important to understand the subjective nature of impact, since two people experiencing the same risk occurring at the same time can experience a very different impact from that same risk. For example, the stock market drops 20 percent in a week. To a 25-year-old investor who is just beginning to invest toward his retirement and has $5,000 invested in his 401(k), a 20 percent drop, means he's down $1,000, and additional contributions to the 401(k) plan will buy more shares of stock because the stock price is now lower. For a retired 80-year-old widow with a $300,000 portfolio, making no new contributions and living off the income from the portfolio, her impact is –20 percent or minus $60,000, plus her portfolio's income-generating ability has been slashed 20 percent as well. Clearly there is a very big difference in impact on two different people from an event that occurs at the same time.

Now that you've identified your risks, and have them each ranked for high, moderate, or low likelihood, and ranked for severe, moderate, or mild impact, the next step to prioritize your risks. Since all risks are not created equal and some can affect us more than others, it is extremely important to determine which risks should cause us the most concern and which ones to focus our risk management efforts on first. Most individuals and investors have a strong tendency to address risks as they appear, by thinking that they don't have to worry about a risk until they actually occur, or by preparing for them based on their frequency of occurrence. Although this approach can be easy and convenient, it doesn't allow them any advance preparation or time to put risk reduction or risk management initiatives in place to address the bigger, high-impact risks. This frequently places these people who take things as they come at a serious disadvantage in effectively managing the big risks when they happen. Since risks can occur so rapidly, the followers of this thinking are many times left with the worst option of all, which is to do their best to recover from these big risks' negative effects. A better way is to plan for all risks in advance in a well-thought-out comprehensive fashion. Experience has also taught us that even if a risk has a low probability of occurring, if it has a high potential impact, the high potential impact must take priority. So it is a crucial next step, once risks have been identified and classified as to their probability and impact, to rank them based on their impact. Using this approach the priority ranking will then run in descending risk order from high probability/high impact risks to low probability/low impact risk. Here is an example of this risk priority ranking system.

Risk Management Priority Ranking (Highest Impact to Lowest)

9. High impact/high probability
8. High impact/moderate probability
7. High impact/low probability
6. Moderate impact/high probability
5. Moderate impact/moderate probability
4. Moderate impact/low probability
3. Low impact/high probability
2. Low impact/moderate probability
1. Low impact/low probability

DETERMINE RISKS TO AVOID, PREVENT, ACCEPT, AND MANAGE   Now that all the identified risks have been prioritized, it's time to personally determine which risks must be managed, which can be accepted as is, without any special risk management considerations, and which can or should be avoided entirely or prevented, if at all possible. Since it's one of the easiest and most effective risk management methods, clearly any risk which can avoided or prevented, without sacrificing a desirable or necessary reward or benefit, should be prevented. Sometimes, however, that's just not either possible, desirable, or worth giving up the pursuit of potential rewards. So, in order to attain the benefits we seek, we have to accept their associated risks, and those risks must then be managed accordingly. The last decision at this level of the process is then to determine which risks to accept outright. Recognizing that each of us is different, and everyone must make these decisions for herself, the low-impact category in general represents the best candidates for this option, with the low-impact and low-probability risk being the easiest choice. Now that we've completed our risk assessment process and we know which risks we want to prevent or avoid, the ones we want to accept and manage, and the risks we'll accept outright, we're ready to move to the next step in the "Risk-Wise" Investor Risk Management Planning Process.

Step 2: Risk Management Strategies Review and Selection

Once the risks to be managed have been identified, the next step is to explore the various risk management options that are appropriate for each particular risk.

Your Risk Management Strategy Foundation

Before proceeding with this review of risk management strategies, it's crucial to emphasize the importance of having a well-thought-out, personal financial plan in order to maximize the benefits of the risk management methods reviewed in this book. To do otherwise is definitely placing the cart before the horse. All the information and recommendations in this book are based on the foundation of you having a thoughtful, written financial plan. Your overall financial plan, if not yet in place, should be developed and put into place as soon as possible. At a minimum, it should document your present financial situation; your specific financial goals, objectives, and time frames; and how you plan to achieve those goals within that time frame. Having, and actively using, your financial plan as a reference guide and working document in tracking your progress toward reaching your goals is also the foundation of any successful risk management strategy.

In today's rapidly changing world, achieving your financial goals requires both well-thought-out financial planning and sound risk management planning with both being properly executed and regularly monitored. The "Risk-Wise" Investor Risk Management Planning process will be most effective when used in concert with your financial plan. Using just one without the other is a disservice to your own best interests.

Risk Management Strategies

We'll be covering risk management strategies from three different levels and two functional areas. To begin we'll review what each of us can personally do to enhance our risk management effectiveness, then examine professional resources that can help in the cause, and finally discuss risk management strategies at the portfolio level. As part of that portfolio-level discussion, we'll also examine both passive and active risk management strategies you'll want to consider.

PERSONAL STRATEGIES Since each of us have control over and ultimate responsibility for the effectiveness of our investment success and risk management efforts, focusing on the individual contributions we can make to our own success seems like a good place to start. Although everyone seems to have less and less free time these days, a strategy that has proven its effectiveness is to *become a true student of risk management*. You can start by creating your own personal risk management education course, and begin reading and studying books and material on subjects related to practical risk management that interest you. (Hopefully you've already embarked on that course of action, and that's why you're reading this book.) Risk and risk management are such a rich, multidisciplinary subject area, are so vast, and offer so many directions to follow from market history to behavioral finance, to physiology, mass psychology, decision science, investment dynamics, and beyond that it really doesn't matter where you begin, just start. After all, Louis Pasteur said "Chance favors the prepared mind," and any investment we make in improving our knowledge of risk and risk management will better prepare us for the chance to use that knowledge for our own benefit. There are also numerous professional risk management organizations and institutions of higher learning that offer courses of study, conferences, programs, and educational opportunities on risk and risk management to anyone who has an interest in improving his knowledge of the subject. They'll all welcome your interest.

Another easy to implement step, which can pay big risk management rewards is to *develop a personal risk manager's view of the world*. Begin noticing and thinking more actively about not just the positive rewards or benefits of actions and decisions, but also their potential negative consequences and risks. Become a little suspicious of decisions that come too easily or quickly rather than trust them totally. Make sure you're looking at both the potential positive and negative results of actions or decisions, and that the classic bias of relying too much on information that supports your initial position, doesn't trap you. Because it's a change from our normal behavior, consciously thinking differently will take some work and may initially make us feel a little awkward or weird. Nevertheless, if you continue to work at dispassionately considering both the potential rewards and potential risks, you will gradually rewire your thought patterns. Your new "Risk-Wise" thinking process will become more and more automatic, and you'll soon start experiencing fewer missteps and nightmares as you advance toward your goals.

A third personal strategy is to conduct scenarios based thought experiments, research, and planning on a range of possible situations where different risks or crisis events, and their secondary and tertiary risks, might occur. You can then develop game plans on how you could protect against, avoid, manage, neutralize or even take advantage of those risk events and their impact, should they actually occur. These types of scenario-based exercises are exactly the kind of thing military planners, every member of the armed forces, professional emergency responders, commercial airline pilots and crews, and even scuba divers do on a regular basis. They are continuously preparing and training so that they are literally preprogrammed to be ready to respond automatically for any eventuality. In the investment world we tend to focus so much on portfolio-related issues that we neglect preparing ourselves mentally—planning and thinking ahead, developing prevention and response plans, and practicing those responses to help us respond properly and quickly when there may be little or no time to think or when fear hijacks our logic.

With the uncertainty in our world continuing to increase, and the stakes we have at risk never higher, anything we can do to better prepare for unpleasant surprises and crisis situations will pay us handsome returns when we need them the most. Given that reality, the best and most "Risk-Wise" approach would be to implement all three of the personal risk management strategies we just reviewed.

PROFESSIONAL STRATEGIES   With the increasing speed of change, the incredible growth in communications, information, and the pace of life itself, knowledge is becoming more and more specialized. With the same thing happening in the financial services world, professional financial advisors, tax advisors, business advisors, consultants, and investment managers can provide information, insight, perspective, and value that would be nearly impossible to obtain on our own.

Full-service financial advisors can help us beyond building a financial plan. Through their personal knowledge of us, and our needs, they can also help us implement, manage, and adapt our personal plans to meet our changing circumstances over time. In addition, they can serve as experienced and knowledgeable sounding boards for our ideas or questions, information resources, and to double-check actions we're contemplating that may be common investor pitfalls or not be in our own best interests.

Tax advisors, business advisors, attorneys, and consultants, although not formally considered risk managers per se, can help us within their specialties, to leverage our opportunities, and protect our interests. They can also save us time, trouble, and money, plus reduce the likelihood and minimize the impact of potential problems.

Although there are many investors who prefer to manage their own investments themselves, packaged investment products developed over the last 30 years have been a boon to many other individual investors. These vehicles provide individuals access to *professional investment managers and institutional money management expertise*, worldwide diversification, a full range of investment options, tremendous flexibility, and transparency. They have also enlarged the assortment of investment opportunities for individual investors enormously, with less risk than if these investors were to implement these strategies on their own. For investors interested in more custom, individualized programs, there's also a full selection of professionally managed alternatives for them as well.

PORTFOLIO-LEVEL STRATEGIES (EXAMINE STRENGTHS AND WEAKNESSES)   There are a number of portfolio-level risk management strategies to choose from. Some are tried and true methods that have proven their value in all types of market and investment conditions and have become stalwarts of sound portfolio management. Others are newer and innovative, and offer additional advantages. We'll review both types as we explore these risk management strategies from the functional perspective of whether they are passive or active risk management strategies.

Regardless of how we categorize them, all these portfolio-level risk management methods offer both advantages and disadvantages that need to be considered and balanced when deciding which one to use to address the specific high-impact risks that need to be managed.

PASSIVE RISK MANAGEMENT STRATEGIES   Once these strategies are in place, they require little extra attention or work other than occasional rebalancing. Below is a list of the passive risk management strategies you will implore:

Time in the market is the first of these passive strategies. There are numerous academic studies that demonstrate that time in the market reduces market risk. These studies demonstrate that the longer the holding period for a well-diversified investment portfolio of stocks, the less risk there is of a negative long-term return. In fact the studies show that beyond a 20-year holding period, so far there are no historic periods where a long-term investor did not have a positive return on investment.

Broad diversification is frequently used to reduce portfolio risk, reduce portfolio volatility, and to improve returns. This passive strategy, starting at the highest level is *overall asset allocation* that establishes the basic risk/reward characteristics of the portfolio. Next the optimal *domestic/international* allocation within each of the equity and fixed-income allocations is determined. Then on the equity side the appropriate diversification between *value and growth* investment styles and *large-, mid-, and small-sized companies* is made. On the fixed-income side, the overall fixed-income percentage allocation decisions need to be made between *government, municipal, corporate,* and *high yield bonds*, as well as the *average duration* (interest rate volatility) appropriate for the portfolio. Once those higher-level decisions are made, the final decisions as to which investment managers, mutual funds, exchange-traded funds, or other investments to use to actually invest and manage the monies risk are made. On an ongoing basis, the investment portfolio is then monitored and periodically (generally annually) rebalanced. Sometimes a rules-based method is used to rebalance any portion of the portfolio that exceeds a prespecified percentage of the total portfolio, regardless of the timeframe. Rebalancing occurs when funds from areas of the portfolio that have become overweighted, because of their investment success, are rebalanced into areas of the portfolio, which have become underweighted. This rebalancing reduces the risk of the portfolio becoming overweighted in some areas and underweighted in others that adversely affects returns.

Guaranteed and stable value investments also fall into the passive category and can be attractive alternatives for investors who want
or need principal guarantees for at least a portion of their portfolios. Certificates of deposits offer guarantee of principal with a
slightly higher yield the longer you're willing to commit your funds.
Deferred, fixed annuities can be a viable option as well, since they
offer guarantee of principal, a guaranteed fixed return for a period
of time, tax deferral on earnings, as long as they are not withdraw
from the annuity, and the ability to convert to a life income if you
want to annuitize your investment. Some insurance companies and
investment managers also offer stable value investments that do
not fluctuate in principal value yet offer returns based on indexes
or interest rates. With the choices within each of these categories
varying significantly, it's important to evaluate all the various factors
before deciding which alternative best fits your individual needs.

ACTIVE RISK MANAGEMENT STRATEGIES   Active risk management methods vary
dramatically from conservative active strategies that simply rebalance an
asset allocated portfolio more frequently than usual to very aggressive, high
risk, strategies involving timing market moves and using borrowed money
to finance trading activities. Between these extremes there are hundreds of
different approaches that can sound very compelling but are often challenging to implement effectively over time. Here are few active strategies you
should be aware of.

Technical analysis is based on the concept that investment prices move
in both short- and long-term trends and that trends, once established tend to continue, until they are broken. Advocates of this
method believe that the price movement of a stock or index provides all the information one needs to know about a company.
Technical analysis focuses on the charts of stock price movements,
and identification of underlying trends, and price support and resis-
tance levels. Based on reading these charts, technical analysts will
attempt to capitalize on stock price movement trends to reduce risks
and improve returns.

Market timing is the term to describe various systems that attempt to
sell stocks, indexes, or other securities when they are high and buy
them when they are low ranging over periods of days, weeks, or
months, depending on the timer and the timing system they use.
Timers want to take advantage of rising stock prices and avoiding,
falling stock prices and increase their returns and reduce their risk
as a result.

Variable annuities offer the opportunity to build an investment portfolio of mutual fund–like accounts within an insurance policy, which allows the deferral of income taxes on gains until funds are withdrawn. For a cost, they can also offer optional riders that guarantee your principal and/or your principal and minimum return level when you either die or elect to annuitize your investments. Just be sure to compare their advantages and disadvantages with all the other alternatives you may be considering before you make your decision. *Special note*: Fixed or variable annuity contract gurantees should be scrutinized so you are familiar with any exceptions that may invalidate the contract gurantees.

Hedging strategies allow investors to implement various security positions, which can reduce a portfolio's risk exposure. A hedge offsets losses in the investor's portfolio if the markets drops, but also offsets gains if the market rises. If the market drops, the hedge will go up offsetting the investor's loss. Conversely, if the market goes up, the hedge will drop in value and will offset the gains on the investor's portfolio. Hedges are most often used by investors who want to hold onto their portfolio, but also want to protect themselves, in part or entirely, from the possibility of an adverse market move. Because of their complexity and the sometimes daily rebalancing that's necessary to keep hedges in balance, only sophisticated investors should even consider these strategies.

Options hedging strategies can also be an attractive and effective way to reduce volatility risk and risk exposure. However, like all securities some options strategies are low risk and conservative while others are very high risk and aggressive. Before you engage in the options market be certain that you know what you're doing and that you are working with an advisor who's very knowledgeable and experienced in using options as hedging tools. You may also want to consider using an investment manager or mutual fund that uses option strategies to help manage risk. *(Options offer a number of hedging strategies from writing and buying options to establishing collars, spreads, straddles and straps. Writing call options, against established stock positions, has been used for decades by investors who want to increase the income from their existing equity portfolios and provide a modest cushion against lower market prices. However like other hedging strategies, writing call options also limits appreciation potential. Buying call options can provide the upside potential of stock ownership at only a fraction of the cost of full stock ownership. However, since once options expire they become worthless, close attention must be paid to the relationship between the market price of the underling stock, the option's strike price, and its expiration date.)*

Cash hedging (not to be confused with timing) is a semiactive risk management strategy used by investors who believe in the advantages and benefits of long-term investing but also recognize that markets periodically become dramatically overvalued and undervalued. They want to use these periodic valuation extremes to their advantage. These investors are realists who are familiar with market history, economic history, and the fact that our economy is cyclical and regularly experiences recessions and significant market drops of 20 percent plus, approximately every four to five years. They also believe in not taking unnecessary risks, and would rather protect against their downside risk and have greater peace of mind, even if it means missing some upside potential. Cash hedgers also recognize that the best time to have cash on hand and buy stocks is when the markets are low and investors are fearful. So, once a market advance has extended over three or four years, they start to become more cautious and begin monitoring the economy and markets more closely. If they begin to feel uncomfortable about the economy or think the market is becoming overextended, they gradually reduce their exposure to the stock market and start to raise cash. Should things begin to look even more troubling in either the markets or the economy, they'll sell more, move the proceeds to money funds, eventually taking their equity holdings down to no lower then 50 percent of normal (because they never want to be totally out of the market) and then they wait to see what happens. Once the markets are down significantly, the business news is consistently negative, and most investors feel negatively about stocks, these cash hedgers start putting money back into stocks again. They begin investing the roughly half of their investment funds, which are now temporarily in money funds, back into the market again over a two-to-four-month period. They are then ready to ride the next bull market cycle when it comes.

Gold and Precious Metals have been used as hedges against financial instability and inflation throughout history. If owning gold or other precious metals, shares of companies that mine and refine those metals makes you feel more comfortable, then by all means do so. Please keep in mind that because of the often counter cyclical nature of their price moves, when the economy is humming along normally they tend to underperform and when the economy is weak they tend to do better. In any case, unless you expect a catastrophe of biblical proportions or extremely high inflation you should limit your holding in this area to no more than 5 to 10 percent of your investment portfolio.

ACTIVE AND PASSIVE STRATEGIES Working together, these active and passive risk management strategies can all help in various ways to better manage and reduce risks. The passive strategies are quite effective over longer time frames and are also relatively easy to implement. The various active risk management strategies we reviewed can be helpful as well. It is important to remember that because they are active strategies requiring ongoing, accurate decision making, and in some cases strong conviction about future market moves, they are also more subject to human error. It's also important to keep in mind that any weakness in the implementation of these more complex strategies can lead to breakdowns in our risk management effectiveness. Since active risk management strategies also tend to be more complex, their success requires that only knowledgeable and experienced investors who are familiar with their operations, weaknesses, and strengths use them.

Step 3: Evaluate Your Risk Reward Trade-offs

Once our investment objectives are set, our risks identified and prioritized, and our risk management strategies determined, it's time to perform one final predecision check. Do the potential rewards justify the risks? Are our risk management plans in place? Are we following the herd, doing what everyone else is doing, letting our emotions override our logic, or is our logic managing our emotions? If you can answer those questions properly you're good to go.

Step 4: Make Your Decision to Act or Not Act—Then Implement

By this stage your decision should be straightforward and relatively easy. If for some reason it's neither straightforward nor easy, or if you're uncomfortable about your options in any way, it's time to pause and give yourself more time or more information. Always keep in mind that one of the most basic rules of investing is to only do things you are totally comfortable doing. Life is just too short to make decisions to do things that make you uncomfortable or that keep you awake at night. So if you are uncomfortable for any reason, make an effort to identify what element of your contemplated action is bothering you. Once you've identified that element, consider the implication of just discarding it. If those implications are small or nonexistent, how to proceed will be quite obvious. Should the implications be significant, it's time to go back and consider other, different, or creative solutions. Either way you're ahead because you've learned one more alternative that won't work for you in this situation.

Step 5: Ongoing Risk Monitoring and Decision Making

Once you make your decision to proceed and put your plan into action, the new risk-monitoring phase begins. The purpose of the monitoring phase is to regularly check on your progress toward your planned goal and, if anything goes awry, to make the adjustments necessary to get back on course. It also an opportunity reconfirm that your circumstance and priorities are the same and that no developments or risks have popped up that may require a re-evaluation of your plan. For this phase to be effective, you must set up a regular monitoring process where you can review what's working, what's not working, and what adjustments need to be made to your plan. It's also important to be continuously on guard for new potential risk and threats, as well as for older, more comfortable risks, which have evolved into new threats. It's also critical to create an ongoing, risk managed decision-making checklist.

Decision-Making Checklist

Just as commercial airline pilots who have thousands of takeoffs and landing under their belt, always go through a preflight checklist to minimize their risks before leaving the ground, it's critical to create your own risk managed decision-making checklist to use every time you're considering an addition, deletion, or change to your investment portfolio, financial plan, or risk management plan. Your checklist can then help you make sure that you are not falling into any common decision-making or risk management traps or increasing the risks of your portfolio unintentionally.

Reviewing the "Risk-Wise" Investor Risk Management Process Steps

In closing this chapter let's review the steps in the Risk-Wise Investor risk management process one more time.

1. Personal risk assessment
   - Define risk
   - Identify risks
   - Understand risks
   - Determine which risks to avoid, accept, and/or manage
2. Review risk reduction/management strategies available
3. Evaluate your risk/reward trade-offs
4. Make your decision to act or not act—then implement
5. Ongoing, effective risk monitoring and decision making

Once this "Risk-Wise" Investor risk management planning process has been completed, you'll have a much better understanding of the risks you expect to face, and a comprehensive plan in place to manage them. Then with your regular, ongoing monitoring and use of a risk managed decision-making checklist, you'll be a more knowledgeable, less emotional, more informed, and better prepared "Risk-Wise" Investor. You'll also have more realistic expectations, make fewer mis-steps, experience fewer negative surprises and improve the likelihood of reaching your long-term investment goals.

CHAPTER 12

Models of Outstanding Risk Management

We were just doing what we were trained to do.
Captain Chesley "Sully" Sullenberger
Pilot, U.S. Air Flight 1549

Effective risk management does not happen by accident. First and foremost, it goes well beyond just planning for positive outcomes, but more importantly it faces the reality that surprises happen all the time, and things frequently go wrong when we least expect them to. In addition, efficacious risk management is all about embracing full responsibility for what happens to us with the knowledge that we have the ability to avoid or prevent many risks, and to minimize the impact of those risks that can't be avoided or prevented. Implicit in that conviction is total confidence that knowledge and understanding of risks combined with thoughtful planning, preparation, training, vigilance, and continuous improvement can reduce the likelihood of risks occurring, and minimize their impact if they nevertheless do occur. Risk management success isn't the result of hope, luck, blind faith, or mysticism. It is the result of hard work, dedicated effort, thoughtful planning, realistic training, extensive preparation, excellent execution, continuous improvement, and the rewards for all that effort can be massive.

Real-World Risk Management Examples

There are countless examples of the success of this proactive approach all around us. Think of all the enormous payoffs in lives, limbs, and disfigurements saved when automobile manufacturers began to focus on auto accident safety and risk management. For decades cars were all about style, and safety was a low priority consideration. One of the auto industry's first risk management innovations was auto safety glass that didn't shatter in accidents, then came soft dashboards, followed sequentially by collapsing steering wheels, seat belts, shoulder belts, shock-absorbing bumpers, head restraints to protect against whiplash from rear-end collisions, crumple zones, front airbags, antilock brakes that don't skid, and side airbags. Now new safety innovations continue almost every year.

Once automakers accepted, identified, and understood the various risks of auto accidents and then began to manage them, the risks of driving improved. As a result, we can now routinely walk away from auto accidents that would have killed us just 20 years ago. Individuals and entire families, that before might have been obliterated by car accidents, now live long, happy, and productive lives together. We enjoy all these benefits today because 40 years ago carmakers began working on ways to reduce the risk and minimize the impact of auto accidents.

The same increasing focus on reducing the probability and minimizing the potential impact of risks has occurred in numerous other areas of our lives. We now see tamper-proof food and medicine bottles, the FDA overseeing rigorous and lengthy testing and approval processes on the safety and efficacy of new drugs, and even removing drugs from the marketplace that demonstrate risks greater than their benefits. Sports have even been impacted by this trend of improving risk management. Forty years ago, about the only sports using helmets were football and racecar driving. Now hockey, lacrosse, baseball, bicycling, skiing, snowboarding, skate boarding and others do the same. We've also seen a dramatic and simultaneous increase in the use of face, mouth, and teeth protection systems, even in sports where protective helmets aren't used.

Improved risk management has even impacted the workplace. According to the U. S. Department of Labor's OSHA (Occupational Safety and Health Administration), whose mission is to prevent workplace-related illnesses, injuries, and deaths, workplace deaths/year have dropped 62 percent and injuries 42 percent since OSHA's founding in 1971.

For some reason, over the last 40 years investing has lagged behind this broad-based, international trend of dramatic risk management improvements in so many other areas of life. Yes, asset allocation among stocks, bonds, and cash, as well as diversification has become much easier to access and more commonly used by investors over the last 25 years. However, as the devastating and broad-based market collapses of 2008 demonstrated, when no asset classes were spared the pain of major price declines, even thorough asset allocation and diversification didn't significantly reduce risk in 2008. This lag may be a result of the complacency generated by the almost two-decade bull market in stocks, which started in 1982. Also contributing to the good feelings and limited concerns about risk was the remarkable, three-decade decline of inflation and interest rates, which started in 1982. That combination of factors created a historic and exceptionally long bull market in bond prices as well. In such extended bull markets, investors have a tendency to perceive downside risks as temporary or negligible and view as much bigger the risk of missing out on the upside. They become complacent about downside risk, when in truth those potentially devastating risks are lying in wait, just as potentially harmful as ever. Investors may further get so caught up and distracted by the media sirens ever-changing best performer lists, and become so distracted by their frenzied efforts to find the best investment to buy, that they don't think about risk at all. It may also be that many investors just don't believe that beyond asset allocation and diversification, there's much else they can do to reduce the downside risk of investing. Whatever the reason, there is a great deal that we can learn about improving effective investment risk management. However, the insights we seek are not going to be found by looking in the investment world more intensely. Instead we need to expand our horizons totally outside the confines of the world of investments to organizations that deal successfully with life-threatening risks on a daily basis. Because of the nature of their work, each day workers in these professions go about their business approaching everything they do expecting and preparing for things to go wrong, and accomplishing their missions anyway. As a result they can teach us a great deal about becoming better managers of investment risk.

Lessons from Everyday Risk Managers

Fortunately, because of the specialization of our modern society we don't all have to engage in activities that expose us to life-threatening risks. However, for that very reason there are a number of career fields where engaging in activities with either the high probability of risks occurring or the presence of risks with high potential impact, or both, are just part of the job. As a result of the prevalence of high likelihood risks or the low likelihood/high impact risks occurring in these career fields, the practitioners of these trades take risk and risk management very seriously. They know that the more effort they invest in preparing for and managing risks, the more successful they'll be. As a result of their ongoing investment of time, energy, and effort to manage the risks they face every day, they have learned a great deal about managing risk and uncertainty that can help us in our management of investment risks.

Although there's a wide range of fields we could choose from, we'll be directing our attention toward a select four. Just becoming familiar with the risk management methods used by these four "Risk-Wise" disciplines should give us an enormous leg-up in our personal investment risk management efforts. These four fields are:

1. Commercial aviation
2. The armed services
3. Fire fighting
4. Law enforcement

Commercial Aviation

Commercial aviation is the safest and most efficient form of transportation in the world. It certainly didn't start that way, however. Gaining insights into how commercial airline travel made the transition from its early checkered safety record to the safest form of transportation the world has ever known can help us manage the risk we face more effectively as well.

Brief History of Passenger Airlines[1]

In 1903 the aviation industry got its start with the Wright brothers' first flight at Kitty Hawk, North Carolina. Initially the public was very skeptical of air travel as an option because of their concern that it was too dangerous, very unreliable, and uncomfortable. What really energized the industry was the United States participation in World War I. The government funded research and development, and manufacturing efforts accelerated improvements in aircraft reliability and safety. After the war the industry stagnated except for efforts to establish airmail service, the airplane's novelty appeal, and early initiatives to explore other uses for this new technology, including carrying paying passengers. The first successful solo transatlantic flight by Charles Lindberg in 1927 ignited a surge in the public interest in aviation.

During this period the U.S. Government gave private airlines, through a competitive bidding system, the opportunity to function as mail carriers. The combination of mail and cargo revenue then made carrying passengers economically viable and the precursors of today's American Airlines and United Airlines began passenger operations. Initially passengers were considered as just an augment to airmail revenues, and because of the common perception of a poor safety record and expensive ticket costs, passenger traffic grew very slowly.

To counter the great deal of disorganization in the industry, in 1938 the young industry's first independent regulatory bureau, The Civil Aeronautics Authority was created.

That same year many airline companies began flying the new DC-3 aircraft. These new planes were a huge improvement over their predecessors because they were specifically designed to carry both mail and passengers and could seat up to 21 passengers.

When the United States entered World War II, commercial airline fleets and pilots were moved to England to assist in the war effort. The war also stimulated a major aircraft research and development effort, which subsequently extended beyond the war to commercial aircraft. A very important postwar innovative development for commercial aviation was the four-engine passenger plane. This one innovation dramatically cut the time to cross both continents and oceans, making airlines a serious competitor for the traditional passengers of ocean liners and trains.

Enormous improvements in the comfort and passenger capacity of commercial aircraft occurred in the 1950s, and the first jet flights were started in 1959, shortening coast-to-coast travel times even further. However, during the 1950s there were some major in-air collisions that led to the Federal Aviation Act being passed in 1958, and the creation of the Federal Aviation Administration or FAA. The FAA was then charged with creating a national air traffic control system to reduce the likelihood of disastrous midair collisions. In an expanding effort to improve safety, the National Transportation and Safety Board was created in 1967 as an independent agency chartered by Congress. It was charged to investigate every civil aviation accident in the United States and significant accidents in the other modes of transportation—railroad, highway, marine and pipeline—and issuing safety recommendations aimed at preventing future accidents.

The 1970s saw enormous increases in costs for aviation, particularly in fuels costs, and the introduction of new more fuel-efficient and quieter engines. Deregulation came to the commercial airline industry in the 1980s leading the proliferation of regional airlines. There was then an enormous increase in the number of passengers and more geographic areas served by commercial airlines when big price decreases took place in the 1990s. Then, as a result of the events of 9/11 security issues related to commercial travel became a critical issue for both the airlines and the traveling public.

Risk Management Methods

The responsibility for aviation safety is not the responsibility of one group of people. It is the responsibility of a working partnership between every participant in this vital industry, from aircraft manufactures, maintenance firms, and regulatory agencies, to airlines and their staffs all over the world, all dedicated to safety industry wide. They are all focused on identifying risks, understanding those risks (including exhaustive postaccident investigations, reporting, and industry-wide recommendations by the NTSB) designing and implementing risk control systems and even backup systems, to training and preparing for all manner of negative surprises and decision-making errors. Following are some examples:

- The National Transportation Safety Board[2] in its own materials states, "Since its inception in 1967, the NTSB has investigated more than 124,000 aviation accidents and over 10,000 surface transportation accidents. In so doing, it has become one of the world's premier accident investigation agencies. On call 24 hours a day, 365 days a year, NTSB investigators travel throughout the country and to every corner of the world to investigate significant accidents and develop factual records and safety recommendations.

  The NTSB has issued more than 12,000 recommendations in all transportation modes to more than 2,200 recipients. Although the NTSB does not regulate transportation equipment, personnel, or operations, and the NTSB does not initiate enforcement action, its reputation for impartiality and thoroughness has enabled the NTSB to achieve such success in shaping transportation safety improvements that more than 82 percent of its recommendations have been adopted by those in a position to effect change. Many safety features currently incorporated into airplanes, automobiles, trains, pipelines and marine vessels had their genesis in NTSB recommendations."

  Following are the NTSB's six "Most Wanted" Transportation Safety Improvements in aviation issue areas, as of January 2009:

  1. Reduce danger to aircraft flying in icing conditions
  2. Improve runway safety
  3. Require crash-protected image recorders in cockpits
  4. Reduce accidents and incidents caused by human fatigue
  5. Improve crew resource management for on-demand and air taxi flight crews
  6. Improve safety of emergency medical services flights

- The Federal Aviation Administration-Air Traffic Control System celebrated its fiftieth anniversary in 2008:[3] As the FAA says on its web site, "since President Eisenhower signed the Federal Aviation Act of 1958, the world of air travel has changed in ways even the most farsighted pundit could not have foreseen. For example, in 1958 about 53 million passengers boarded airplanes, compared to the 776 million expected in 2008. In 1958, FAA air traffic controllers handled about 26.6 million takeoffs and landings, a figure expected to be around 44.1 million in 2008. Even as the U.S. aviation system has grown tremendously, the FAA has made sure it runs safely as well as efficiently. In 1958, there were nine fatal commercial air accidents in the United States resulting in 145 fatalities. For the two years 2007 and 2008, there have been no fatal passenger airline accidents and no fatalities among the more than 1.5 billion passengers who have flown during that time. The FAA has become the 'gold standard' for safety, and our regulations and best practices are copied by much of the rest of the world."

FAA Lesson Learned From Transport Plane Accidents

FAA Accident Threat Categories. These include bird hazards, cabin safety/hazardous cargo, flight deck layout/avionics confusion, crew resource management, fuel exhaustion, fuel tank ignition, inclement weather/icing, incorrect piloting techniques, in-flight upsets, landing/takeoff incursions, midair/ground incursions, pressurization/decompression failures, structural failures, uncommanded thrust reversal, uncontrolled fire, wind shear.

FAA Common Accident Themes. These include flawed assumptions, human error (the most common of all aviation accident themes), organizational lapses, pre-existing failures, unintended consequences, jetliner safety.[4]

Aircraft manufacturers have done a remarkable job in not just making our new, modern aircraft of today more comfortable, entertaining, quieter, faster, and more convenient; they've even, and most importantly, made them much safer too.

Aircraft maintenance is a critical element to risk management. U.S. Airlines spend more than $10 billion per year to keep their aircraft safe and in top working order. Airline maintenance programs specify the timeframes in which specific aircraft and engine parts must be inspected and repaired or replaced as necessary by FAA-certified specialists. Plus careful records of these inspections and repairs must be maintained and always available for FAA inspection. For each hour that a plane flies, maintenance crews spend about three-and-one-half hours working to maintain it. Between a series of increasingly thorough scheduled maintenance procedures, computers on the planes monitor the performance of its systems and record any abnormal temperatures, fuel, or oil consumption. In newer aircraft, that data is transmitted to ground stations while the plane is in flight.

Aircraft operations. Everyone working on a plane and those who fly them must be personally licensed by the FAA, and achieve certain levels of specific experience and training. Pilots, flight engineers, flight navigators, aircraft mechanics, aircraft dispatchers, and flight attendants all must meet FAA licensing requirements.

Pilots. To apply for a job with an airline, a pilot must have a minimum of 1,500 hours of flight time, including at least 250 hours flying as a pilot in command of an aircraft. The average newly hired pilot has almost 4,000 flight hours. Pilots also must fly with an FAA flight examiner to demonstrate their skill at takeoffs, landings, in-flight maneuvers, and emergency procedures in either an airplane or a sophisticated simulator. They also must pass exams that test their knowledge of radio communications, navigation, meteorology, aircraft operations, and other subjects necessary to conduct commercial air services. Finally, pilots must also pass psychological and aptitude tests and a comprehensive physical exam. Only about 10 to 15 percent of applicants applying for the position of pilot are accepted into the training programs.

Once they enter training, they are involved in classroom, simulator, hands-on equipment training as well as self-testing, and computerized video training. All training exercises are followed up with flight checks, drills, and exams to insure thorough understanding and competence in the subjects covered. In addition, pilots and flight engineers are required to participate in regular, recurring training each year. This training typically requires two to four days in an advanced simulator. These highly sophisticated simulators allow pilots to practice emergency procedures for situations like wind shear and engine fires that cannot be practiced safely aboard a real plane. Captains are required to complete some training elements every six months. Although their duty schedules may require spending 250 hours away from their home base each month, a pilot is only permitted 75 to 85 hours of flying time/month. Pilots also have mandated rest period of a minimum of eight hours between assignments.

Before boarding their planes, pilots are required to file a flight plan and are briefed on weather conditions all along their planned route of travel. Once on their planes, pilots are also required to perform a physical inspection of the exterior of their aircraft to check for any abnormalities or potential problems in addition to a complete and extensive pre-flight checklist before they even roll out of their gate. They also use pre-landing checklists and carry easy to find and read emergency procedure checklists for every conceivable emergency situation. Pilots also assume full responsibility for the safety of everyone on the aircraft as well as the aircraft itself, until it safely arrives at their destination and all passengers have off loaded.

Flight attendants, in addition to insuring that passengers are comfortable, are responsible for the in-flight safety of all passengers. Initial training for a new flight attendant is usually around six weeks and is designed to familiarize them with the aircraft, emergency procedures, and in-flight service. Flight attendants are also trained to assist passengers with medical difficulties and medical emergencies. Crewmembers who will be working on flights that travel higher than 25,000 feet in altitude are also required to undergo special training in respiration, hypoxia, and additional altitude-related situations.

Air traffic delays, although very frustrating to most airline passengers, are actually physical manifestations of the high priority placed on risk management by our air traffic control system. In fact, 66 percent of all air traffic delays back in 2007 were due to weather-related events. This occurs because as weather deteriorates, visibility is reduced and the maximum number of take-offs and landings at affected airports is reduced, which creates flight delays and cancellations. These are inconveniences to be sure, but inconveniences are much preferable to the alternative of increasing the risk of disasters. Controllers learned a long time ago that bad weather complicates flight operations and raises the risks of negative surprises. So rather than accepting those increased risks, controllers' high priority on risk management and aircraft safety compels them to adapt to changing conditions and slow down operations to counteract and manage the temporary, increased risks. So the next time you become frustrated by a flight delay or cancellation, just take a moment to remember that the inconvenience is due to the high priority commercial aviation places on your personal safety. Would you want it any other way?[5]

Commercial Aviation Summary

Clearly, the outstanding safety record of modern commercial aviation is due to an intense, comprehensive, and ongoing focus on risk management planning and execution at all levels. As proud as everyone in the commercial aviation field is of their track record of success, one of the most impressive things about them is that they are not resting on their laurels. Instead, their success has made them even more passionate about the importance of continuing to work at making their risk management efforts better and better, every single day. They certainly serve as a fine model to pattern ourselves after, in our own efforts to better understand and manage investment risks we face.

The Armed Services

There is no more uncertain or risk-filled endeavor in the long and often violent history of mankind than armed combat. Wars, battles and even skirmishes are notorious for their unpredictability, life and death risks, surprises, and developments that defy prediction. As a result, the members of the armed services (army, navy air force, marines, and coast guard) have more and longer continuous experience than anyone else in dealing with enormous levels of risks and uncertainty that are difficult to imagine, in incredibly volatile environments. Dealing with those challenging issues has clearly taught them a great deal of what works and what doesn't work in understanding and managing risk and uncertainty. With our time constraints, we unfortunately don't have the luxury to study the detail of how every armed service approaches their unique set of risk challenges. Instead we'll review a few examples from several branches of the military that are representative of the basic approaches they use in addressing many of the risks they face, and that can be instructive and of benefit to us.

The U.S. Navy

One of the navy's biggest risks for their ships at sea is something you may at first find surprising. With all that water around, many people not familiar with shipboard life are often surprised to learn that the navy considers the risk of fire so big a risk. Of course there are many other risks captains and crews at sea are concerned about. Nevertheless, when you think about it for a moment it becomes crystal clear why the navy gives managing the risk of fire such a high priority. First, nowhere is the fearsome destructive power of fire more formidable than onboard navy ships designed to wage war. Not only are they self-contained communities of people, which also carry bombs, missiles, ammunition, fuel, and numerous other combustibles that could easily explode if exposed to fire, there's also nowhere to get away from a fire when you're hundreds of mile at sea. Although steel construction and water-tight doors reduce the threat, all those flammables coupled with steel's ability to transfer heat rapidly means it's a three-dimensional threat that, if its gets going, can move in six directions at once. The navy and ships crew have a great respect for fire, and since they don't have any other options at sea, they must immediately attack any fire, go right to its source, and get it under control fast. The navy spends a lot of time, energy, and effort on prevention of all sorts, including regular preventative maintenance on literally every piece of equipment, and fire prevention to minimize the chance of onboard fires is just one part of that very important process. Navy warships also have built in fire suppression systems and fire-fighting equipment located around the vessel and specifically trained damage control experts to help minimize the risk and to fight fires when they occur. However, their risk management efforts don't stop there. They go multiple steps further by providing hands-on training to every crew member in fighting various types of fire, from common wood and paper fires, to fuel fires, electrical fires, and chemical fires. They even teach crewmembers special techniques for removing ordinance from damaged aircraft, rescuing airmen and fellow crewmembers, as well as preventative maintenance services for damage control equipment. Then to reinforce that training, regular drills are held frequently enough that the crews preprogram their brains and fire-fighting procedures so well that they automatically kick when a fire actually occurs. All members of the crew, no matter what their regular job, are aware that one day they may have to enter an incredibly hot, smoke-filled space, with no visibility, fight a fire, and put it out. So they take their ongoing training and drills very seriously, because their lives and the lives of the shipmates are on the line. All crewmembers have a pre-assigned fire-fighting task and fire station that they are required to man whenever the ship's fire alarm sounds. Although drills in general are less frequent when a ship is in port, when underway at sea, both planned and surprise fire and emergency drills happen quite frequently to insure that everyone is prepared to deal with emergencies and surprises. To add additional realism and give them the confidence that comes with thorough advance preparation, even navy basic training requires that recruits be signed off on a controlled burn fire-fighting exercise where they must enter a mock-up of a ship's interior filled with acrid smoke which severely blocks their vision find the fire, put it out, then find their way back out successfully.

The unique demands of the submarine service, and its smaller crew sizes require advanced levels in cross training. Over the course of a year of service, every submarine crewmember is typically required to cross-train on every other crewmember's job functions, so in an emergency situation they can quickly jump in where they are needed to get the job done.[6]

The U.S. Air Force

The air force faces a different yet similar set of challenges. As former F-15 fighter pilot James D. Murphy points out in his book *Flawless Execution*, published in 2005 by ReganBooks, the U.S. Air Force had a major risk management problem back in 1952. That year their aircraft accident rate had increased to the worst ever since 1947 when the air force was established as independent armed service. With 1,214 airmen killed in accidents in just that one year, there was something terribly wrong. It was determined that training was the core problem behind this high accident rate. Pilots were not provided with a way to think through their problems before they metamorphosed into costly accidents. The air force began studying the problem and identified human factors as the central cause. They focused intensely on these human factors, including the way aircraft were designed and how the pilot and the machine interacted. They studied cockpit layout, instrument and control locations, and how that might be reconfigured to optimize pilot efficiency and effectiveness. They also focused on all the numerous elements of pilot training and how those areas could be improved. The air force even studied how pilots and flight crews integrated all the processes, communications, and details in the cockpit to manage the data and accomplish the mission. As a result, training was modified and updated, then again, and again. The air force elevated training to a science, and increased their efforts to the point where training became an integral part of every pilot's daily life. Rather than just fly, pilots began to view being a pilot and continuously training as almost synonymous. The progress since those early days when they started directly facing the accident problem has been outstanding. By 2002, the air force was flying many more missions than before with an accident rate that plummeted to a total of only nine airmen being lost that year. That single-digit statistic represented the remarkable achievement of an over 99 percent drop in accident-related losses. Clearly those kind of results are not an accident. They are the result of facing risk directly and realistically, identifying, understanding, prioritizing, and directly addressing them, while practicing using numerous checklists, and preparing for them over and over again.

Fire and Law Enforcement Services

Fire fighting and police work are two other fields where risk is a routine fact of life and the potential for catastrophic risk and uncertainty are considered a normal part of the job. Traditionally the top priorities of fire fighters have been to save lives and limit fires from spreading. Over time fire fighters have built a well-deserved reputation for their heroism in risking their own lives to save others at almost any cost. Historically fire-fighting practices were based on fire fighters' individual intuition and experiences or insights passed down from one generation of fire fighters to the next. These priorities began to shift in the 1960s and 1970s when fire activity began to increase for a variety of reasons. That period also saw significant efforts expended and advances resulting from extensively studying the nature of fire and how it behaves. That knowledge and understanding of the physical properties and behavior of fire have helped fire fighters control it more effectively while simultaneously reducing the risks for fighting it. During this timeframe early fire detection and warning devices started to become more commonplace when municipalities stared requiring the use of smoke detectors and alarm and sprinkler systems in commercial buildings and eventually residential properties. At this time another curious trend developed with the civilian death rate from fires dropping while fire fighter deaths did not. This then led to the introduction of new high tech protective clothing and breathing apparatus to help firemen reduce the risk of injuries, burns, smoke inhalation, and worse. It also prompted some shifts and rethinking in basic fire-fighting philosophy. The traditional mission of saving lives at any cost led to situations where firemen actually lost their lives in efforts to save people in burning structures who were never there or in danger in the first place. A new more thoughtful philosophy and priority emerged as the mission became "Risk A Lot, To Save A Lot ... Risk A Little To Save a Little." The concept of incident priority evolved out of that new updated mission. Incident priority is a method fire chiefs can use to analyze a fire incident situation within 30 seconds of their arrival, in terms of what can be saved, versus what are they willing to risk to save it. The steps of the Incident Priority Protocol are:

> *Priority 1* is life safety (with civilian life being #1 and fire fighter's life being #2).
> Priority 2 is incident stabilization (insuring that the damage does not spread).
> Priority 3 is property conservation and the environment.

Some fire fighters also use another protocol or checklist of steps when fighting fires. This prioritized checklist helps them sequentially address and prioritze numerous fire-fighting factors in the order of their importance. They call this the "shirtsleeves" method, since the mnemonic SSLEEVES is used to easily remember the priorities. Here's a quick review:

S Size-up.
S Sufficient help for the job.
L Life Safety.
E Entry: Can you gain entry to the fire area to fight it?
E Exposure: Determine if any structures or property exposed to the fire may begin to burn without defensive measures. If so, then implement a defense.
V Ventilation. Is the fire properly ventilated?
E Extinguishment.
S Salvage.

Actually organizing fire-fighting operations against these priorities is where the fire-fighting effort becomes most effective.

These improvements in the strategies for managing fires have also been paralleled in the increased understanding of the importance of training in improving and maintaining the full range of fire-fighting skills. Simulation is becoming a more widely used training tool in the fire-fighting world, just as it has in civil aviation, and the military. Videos and computer enhancements along with the sounds, smells, and touch of real fire-fighting environments not only add to the realism of this type of training but help its impact make a more indelible imprint on the brains of the fire professionals. In order to gain maximum proficiency, even these modern training tools need to be supplemented with critical, real hands-on training that firemen get from fighting real fires in safe and realistic fire-training facilities like professional fire academies. Just as checklists are important for aircraft pilots, they have also been independently developed and used by fire fighters and the military. The fact that checklists have been independently developed and commonly used as risk management tools in such widely varied fields is a testament to their value and a strong statement that we should consider using them in our own investment risk management.

We are all familiar with the important work of law enforcement, and the positive impact police have on the safety of our communities. They also go through extensive training and preparation for the risks they face as well as opportunities they have to make a positive difference in the lives of the people they serve. In addition to their traditional law enforcement skills training, police officers are also often trained and drilled in emergency and disaster response, certified in emergency medical skills.. They are even trained in conflict resolution where they learn to de-escalate situations with aggressive or emotionally out-of-control individuals with just the sound and tone of their voice.

Common Lessons Learned From Outstanding Risk Managers

In reviewing the many ways professionals in these diverse fields approach the unique risk management challenges they face, a few lessons common to all of them are apparent. They are:

- Expect and plan for negative surprises
- Face risks directly
- Acknowledge and identify risks
- Study and understand the nature and behavior of risks as thoroughly as they can (Including debriefing after every incident or mission to understand what worked, what didn't work, what can be done better in the future, and what lessons were learned.)
- Prioritize risks in advance
- Develop, implement, and practice risk management initiatives
- Prepare for risks in advance because they know that it is much more efficient and cost effective than recovering after them
- Use checklists to help avoid the risks of missing something important

Those very same lessons can also benefit each one of us in improving our more and more important personal risk management skills.

CHAPTER 13

The Value of Knowledgeable and Trusted Financial Advice

To accept good advice is to increase ones own ability.
Johann Wolfgang Goethe

Today's faster moving and more complex world has more opportunities and more potential pitfalls than ever before. The investment environment and financial services world is no different. The continuing explosion of information and flow of communications about the economy, business, and investing has become so overwhelming that it's almost impossible to keep up with it all. At the same time, we're becoming more individually responsible for planning, funding, and managing our own long-term financial goals. The array of investment alternatives to choose from is mushrooming, too.

Not only do we need to decide between how to best allocate our financial resources to maximize returns and minimize risk, we also need to determine which type of investment vehicles to use, and the best options for us within each of those vehicle categories. Even straightforward questions can be challenging to answer. For instance: Is it better to invest in prepackaged, "set it and forget it" investment solutions or to build your own customized portfolios? The pure number and variety of investment alternatives are both a blessing and a curse. Fortunately, the number of financial advisors available to help us sort through all these issues has been expanding as well. Unfortunately, the large number advisors to select from; the variety of advisor types; the designations some carry; and their wide-ranging levels of expertise, interests, and personal and business styles can make it very confusing just trying to find the right advisor to meet our particular needs. It's definitely worth the effort because selecting the right investment advisor(s) for you can make an enormous difference in your ultimate investment success.

Our purpose in this chapter is to make that job a little easier for you by applying our "Risk-Wise" Investor approach to financial advice, meaning the more you know and understand while considering both the rewards and the risks, the better decisions you'll make and the more successful investor you'll become. First we'll provide you with background information on what financial advice is, what it's not, and what services advisors typically offer. Then we'll review the types of advisors you can choose from, discuss their professional designations, the price of advice, how to select and then work with your advisor, and finally red flags to look out for that may be an indication that you should be looking for another advisor.

The following review of the types of professional financial advisors, financial planning, professional designations, pricing methods, and finding a financial advisor includes information from these sources:

Path to Investing.org, an educational resource of the Securities Industry Association, now known as the Securities and Financial Markets Association

Find a Planner, Financial Planning Association, wwww.fpa.org

Finding a Financial Advisor, Senior Magazine.com

Finding a Financial Advisor, About.com

Choosing a Financial Advisor, cfainstitute.org/aboutus/investors/tools/index.html

Professional Financial Advice

The single most important thought to keep in mind when considering financial advice is as valuable as good advice can be: Each one of us alone has full personal responsibility for our long-term investment success, not anyone else. We have full control and full responsibility for every decision we make, every success, and every disappointment. The purpose of advice is to provide us with better quality information in making our decisions. We can then accept the advice or discard it, but it is always our decision. As temping as it may be to allow advisors to make decisions for us, advisors cannot and should not make our decisions. To do otherwise is to abdicate our decision-making power. We are the ones who will live with the results of our decisions, both positive and negative ones, and we are the only ones who should be making them. Over many decades in the investment business I've come to learn one of the best tests of the rightness or wrongness of any decision, after analyzing the viable options, the rewards, and the risks, and after factoring in advice from knowledgeable and trusted advisors, is the touchstone of our own personal comfort level with the decision. If you are comfortable with a particular decision, then proceed. If uncomfortable, defer your decision and work at determining what aspects of the potential action are making you uncomfortable, while you also gather additional information or advice on those discomforting aspects. Once you have enough time and information to comfortably make your decision you are set to proceed. My observation is that life is just too short and precious to do things we are not comfortable doing.

Faux Advice

What masquerades as financial advice is just about everywhere today. From people we interact with on a regular basis, such as personal friends and business associates to barbers, hairdressers, neighbors, casual conversations often evolve into discussions about the economy, markets, investments, and peoples' favorite investment picks. The media is now packed with pundits, soothsayers, economic forecasters, and the like who pound the table and our ears with their fearless forecasts of what to buy, own, or sell today. The fact that they are frequently wrong and many times promote the exact opposite of what they were saying a day or two before never seems to diminish their enthusiasm. They aren't talking about investing; they're talking about trading and gambling, which have very similar and unpleasant outcomes. Please do not view their comments as advice or pay any attention at all to them, except for the potential entertainment value they offer. They are not real financial advisors, and their opinions are not advice. They are entertainers trying to get and keep your attention so their ratings stay high enough that they get to keep their entertainment jobs. True financial advice is very different. It has a several characteristics that set it dramatically apart from opinions shared with a general audience.

True Advice

True financial advice can only be offered by people who meet the three following criteria. First, they are knowledgeable about and experienced in the subject for which you are seeking their advice. Second, they are thoroughly familiar with your particular personal financial situation. Third, their advice is specifically directed to you and your situation alone, and not to anyone else. As a general rule and corollary to the criteria mentioned above, any recommendations you hear to a broad audience or recommendations by someone who doesn't know you and the details of your situation extremely well, even if they come from an expert source, should be immediately dismissed.

Working with a financial advisor should be a real partnering, collaborative relationship. You bring unparalleled knowledge of yourself, your financial goals and needs, likes, dislikes, and tolerance for risk taking. Your financial advisor brings extensive knowledge of the investment markets and expertise in helping investors plan for and then achieve their financial goals. Advisors normally have access to a wide range of investment alternatives to choose from in helping you create the right mix of investments for your particular situation. For your joint relationship to work its best, honest and open communications between the two of you are the key. The more your advisor knows about where you are financially and where you want to go, the better resource she'll be in helping you reach your objective. So be as open honest and direct as possible. On the flip side of the coin, your advisor has an obligation to respect your desires and priorities and to be as open, transparent, and direct as possible in making you aware of the rewards, risks, uncertainties, and the fees or charges involved the investments they recommend and in you compensating them for their services. Sometimes, early in a relationship, investors will withhold information from their advisor because they are unsure whether their advisor can be trusted. But, in fact, when investors tell an advisor they are placing their full faith and trust for their financial future in their advisor's hands it makes the advisor want to work even harder at doing the best possible job for the investor. Just remember that your ultimate success in achieving your goals is based on the level of trust and openness between you and your advisor.

Basic Financial Plan Elements

The power of a written financial plan cannot be emphasized too much. The difference between just thinking about plans and making them tangible, by putting them in black and white, is enormous. Although financial plans can vary enormously in style, flow, detail, and the unique difference of every individual, they all contain the same seven standard elements of a good financial plan:

1. Your specific goals or objectives
2. Your time frame for reaching that goal
3. Your current financial and tax situation
4. Summary of all financial holdings
5. Your risk tolerance
6. Your liquidity or cash needs
7. Special issues that may affect you investment selection

Working closely with your financial advisor, and being as specific and precise as possible in completing the details of you financial plan, will insure a clear and open communication between you and your advisor, a strong working relationship, and a better plan.

Once you've completed your written financial plan and your goals are established, you're ready to go to work with you advisor in putting your plan into action. Helping you make your asset allocation decisions and specific investment decisions within each asset class and then purchasing the investments you select is all part of the advisor's service. Once you're up and running, your advisor can also help you schedule regular portfolio reviews to make sure you're on track to meet your goals. If you're an active investor, your financial consultant can also help you develop, buy, and sell decision criteria, keep you updated on new investment opportunities that meet your selection criteria, and be available to update your market moves. Many firms also offer educational and investment seminars where you can learn about a range of topics and investments.

Questions Are Good

Advisors will ask lots of question of their clients in order to understand their situation as thoroughly as possible, and investors should ask lots of questions of their advisor. Financial advisors also recognize how important it is that investors understand what they are doing and why, and they encourage questions from their investors. Remember, there is no such thing as a dumb question, so never hold back asking any question of your advisor. Also, sometime advisors unintentionally will slip into investment techno speak and use terms and phraseology you may not understand. Should that ever happen, stop them right away and ask them to explain what the term means, or what they were just talking about in plain English. They'll be glad you asked, and you will be, too. In fact, if any advisor you ever work with dismisses your questions, seems reluctant to answer them, doesn't seem to have time to provide you the answers you seek, or becomes exasperated by your requests to explain investment terminology, it may be time for you to look for a new investment advisor.

Financial Advisor Services

Your financial advisor can provide a range of services, from helping assessing your current financial situation, making financial decisions, creating and implementing comprehensive financial plans and retirement plans, to helping rebalance your portfolio as your plans or market conditions change. Your adviser can help you determine how well you are doing toward reaching your financial goals, provide advice on specific investments, help you better understand and manage the risks you're concerned about, develop investment decision-making and risk management strategies, and alert you to particular investment opportunities that may interest you. Advisors can also serve as sounding boards for investment ideas you're considering and as a double check in helping you avoid potential investment mistakes and decision-making traps common to many investors. Your advisor can also be very helpful in coordinating your investment allocations and risk exposure across all your accounts, from single and joint accounts to retirement plan accounts and more. Because many advisors are active in their local business community, your advisor may also be a good resource when you are looking for other professional services. Usually when you ask for a professional referral, most advisors will give you at least three names, so that you have a range of options to choose from.

Types of Financial Advisors

With more providers of financial advice available today than ever before, it can be very helpful to have a understanding of some of the more commonly found types of financial advisors. Familiarity with some of their similarities and differences can help you decide on the best type of financial advisor for your particular needs and preferences.

Financial Advisors/Financial Consultants/Stockbrokers. These financial advisors work for national or regional brokerage firms and provide advice based on overall financial plans or specific investments based on a client's interests or particular needs. They will buy and sell stocks, bonds, exchange-traded funds, mutual funds, options and the full range of investment, retirement, 529 college savings plans, and financial products including alternative investments and separately managed accounts on clients' behalf. Many of these advisors are also insurance licensed and can help clients interested in life insurance, fixed annuities, and variable annuities. They may be paid commissions based on trade volume or annual fees based on account size or some of both.

Financial Planners. These financial advisors work for large nationwide firms, regional or local firms, or individually. They provide investment advice, financial planning, ongoing investment analysis, and general advice. Plus, many also offer life insurance and both fixed and variable insurance products in conjunction with their financial planning. Depending on the nature of the practice they are typically compensated by fees, commissions, or both.

Financial Institution (Bank) Representative. These financial advisors work in bank branches and banks. They offer financial planning and a range of investment alternatives including insured and guaranteed bank products like CDs as well as retirement and college savings funds, mutual funds and other uninsured products, including fixed and variable annuities. Sometimes they also offer assistance with banking. They often receive a salary and sometimes commissions on the sale of mutual funds and annuities.

Registered Investment Advisors. RIA firms and individual RIAs are money managers. They manage portfolios of investments on behalf of their clients. Those portfolios can range from individual stocks and bonds to exchange-traded funds and mutual funds and combinations of all three. Some RIAs also offer insurance. These advisors are compensated by receiving investment management fees on the assets they have under their management.

Certified Public Accountants (CPAs). In addition to their tax planning and tax preparation work they offer financial planning and investment advice for a fee, and also sell mutual funds and annuities.

Professional Designations

Although professional designations demonstrate advisors' commitment to continuing their professional studies and adherence to a code of professional responsibility, these designations are just one of the factors to consider when selecting an advisor. However, if you have a particular interest in more specialized financial advice and services, these designations will help make your selection job easier. Next you'll find a brief overview of some of the more common designations. Since these particular descriptions are very cursory, I'd encourage you learn more about these designations by researching them individually on the Internet. Should you find an advisor with a designation on her business card that's not included in this review or that you don't recognize, be sure to ask about it. I'm confident the adviser will be most pleased to explain what it means, what she had to study in order to qualify for it, and how she uses that advanced knowledge in her practice.

CFA (Certified Financial Analyst). This distinction is granted by the Institute of Chartered Financial Analysts to financial professionals who complete a broad three-part, three-year graduate-level course of study, with a six-hour exam at the end of each part, along with other requirements.

CFP (Certified Financial Planner). Granted by the Certified Financial Planner Board of Standards to those investment advisors successfully completing a comprehensive course of study, 10 hours of exams, and adherence to a code of ethics.

ChFC (Chartered Financial Consultant). The designation granted by the American College, Bryn Mawr, Pennsylvania, primarily to insurance agents who have completed a course of study and exams and then have been accredited in financial planning.

CIMA (Certified Investment Management Analyst). These investment professionals provide investment advice to individuals and institutions. This designation is granted by the Investment Management Consultants Association to financial advisors who meet minimum educational and experience requirements and then complete two levels of study and testing on subjects including asset allocation, investment manager search and selection, investment policy, and performance measurement.

PFS (Personal Financial Specialist). This is the designation awarded to certified public accountants by the American Institute of Certified Public Accountants who successfully complete their course of study and examinations on financial planning.

CAIA (Chartered Alternative Investment Analyst). This is the professional designation granted by the CAIA Association to investment professionals who complete a broad-based course of study on alternative investments that can include hedge funds, private equity, venture capital, managed futures, derivatives and foreign exchange investments, and adhere to professional and ethical standards.

Financial Advice Pricing

Financial advisor are compensated for their expertise, time, and services in a number of ways. Some advisors use an approach where their compensation is built into the price of the investments they offer. Some will add their fees to the cost of the investments, and others you'll pay separately. You'll also find advisors who just charge you for their time to complete a financial plan, which you can invest through them or take to another advisor, at your option. In addition, it's very important that you request a written statement of cost or fee overview from any advisors who don't immediately provide you with one. Be sure you understand the costs, how the advisor is compensated, the services the advisor will provide, and how long they expect it will take to complete your plan, before you officially engage an advisor. Here's a quick review of advisor compensation methods:

Hourly Charges. These advisors charge an hourly rate, very similar to the method used by attorneys. You only pay them for the time they spend on your case.

Salary. These advisors receive a salary from their firm and are not paid commissions or fees.

Commissions. These advisors receive commissions on the investments they sell that are a percentage of the amount being invested. The sales charges built into many investment products like mutual funds are set and fully disclosed in the fund's prospectus. Different investments and different funds often vary in the commission levels they pay.

Fee Based. Advisors using this compensation method charge a fee for their services and in addition can earn commission on the products they sell.

Fee Only. These advisors only charge a fee and do not charge or receive commissions on investments you purchase through them. As a result, many of them will only use investments that do not have a sales charge. The fees they charge are generally a small percent of the value of the total amount of assets you invest with them, charged on a monthly or quarterly basis.

Since advisors can be paid in many different ways, it is critical to keep in mind that the way they are paid is less important than the quality of their advice. The key is to understand how they are paid. Some investors will use an hourly paid advisor to help create their financial plan and then ask a commission-based advisor to invest it. Other investors prefer to have a commission-based advisor help them prepare their plan for free, so they can see the completed plan first. Then have that advisor invest the funds and get paid for creating the plan from the commissions. How your advisor is compensated is like many things in life, in that there's really no one right way or wrong way; what matters is what works best for you. In the great scheme of things the quality of your advisor and his advice is a much more important consideration than how he is paid. So be sure the advice you are getting is right for you and that your advisor has thoroughly reviewed both the rewards and the risks of the initiatives you're planning.

Finding Your Financial Advisor

For many people, finding a financial advisor seems like a time consuming, complicated, and potentially frustrating process. So they are tremendously relieved when a financial advisor who's working at growing her client base finds them. This can happen through a mail introduction, when you're attending a financial seminar, reading an article by a financial advisor in your local newspaper, or a number of other ways, and can work very well for both you and the advisor. However, rarely do the timing of our need for financial advice and a well-qualified advisor reaching out to contact us, match in real life. It's very similar to what it's like with police officers. With them it seems they are never right there when you need them, but always right there when you don't.

What's Your Ideal Advisor Look Like?

So here are some ideas that may help you get started in making the process of finding a good financial advisor less challenging and frustrating.

First is the very important step of evaluating yourself, your needs, and your preferences, so that you'll have a better idea of what you need in an advisor. By reviewing not only your financial situation and needs, but also your personality and communications style, likes, dislikes, preferences, and interests, including the importance you place on meeting face to face with your advisor, you'll know more about what you need in an advisor. Even making the decision right up front as to how far you are willing to travel to meet with an advisor can simplify your selection process dramatically. Now you may think that ease of meeting with your advisor is a small point. But given the importance of excellent communications and trust in advisor/investor relationships, easily meeting with your advisor face to face when you need to can make an enormous difference in the mutual trust and quality of the relationship. You may also want to think about the age, experience level, and gender you may prefer in your ideal advisor. Would you feel more comfortable with someone close to you own age, older, or younger? Thinking these general issues through first will help you develop a better idea of what you want, which will help you find an advisor more easily. Remember, unless know what you're looking for, you won't even know when you've found it.

Where Do You Begin Looking for an Advisor?

Once you've identified the general characteristics you're looking for in your advisor, the next natural step is to be talking with your family, friends, colleagues, and employer to learn if they can recommend someone with the characteristics you've already identified. Some of them may be able to refer you to an advisor who fits your description perfectly; others may have excellent referral ideas to advisors who don't quite meet you ideal profile. (That's okay too, and you may at want to interview them anyway just for comparison purposes.) Next consult your accountant, tax preparer, or attorney to learn if they have any recommendations. You can also attend events in your community about managing your investments and other financial affairs along with classes, professional meetings, and investments seminars offered. It's also easy to contact brokerage firms, banks, and financial planning firms in your community and ask for recommendations of people on their staffs who fit your criteria and have the qualifications you're looking for in your advisor.

Evaluating Advisors

Assessing financial advisors and determining the right one for you is a very subjective exercise. In that process here are a few general areas on which to focus your thinking.

Investment industry experience is one of the real benefits an advisor offers. Since normal business cycles take four to six years to complete, if you have the choice, it's better to work with an advisor with at least that much experience.

Personal reputation means a lot, so the fact that you have already been referred by one of your contacts to an advisor is a big plus; any additional references the advisor can provide should add to your comfort level. Should you wish, you can also access the Financial Industry Regulatory Authority or FINRA broker check services to learn the background and check the credentials of all advisors currently securities licensed by Googling "FINRA Broker Check" or going to this web address: www.finra.org/Investors/ToolsCalculators/Broker Check/index.htm'

Capabilities and expertise Some financial advisors are generalists, while others have special interests or expertise in specific areas. So be sure the advisors interests, skills and expertise match your own.

Personal compatibility As important as all the above factors are, your compatibility with you financial advisor is even more important. You will hopefully be working together for a long time, so it's critical that you feel totally comfortable with your advisor and are confident that you can build an open and mutually trusting relationship.

How Will You Know Which One Is the One for You?

As an initial screen you can call the advisors who your friends and contacts have referred you to, for a preliminary screening interview. When you call, let them know why you called and what you're looking for, and conduct a brief preliminary telephone interview. Just the way you and your initial call are handled, how you are treated, and the tone of the conversation will tell you a lot about who you'd like to meet and interview in person. If you like the way they sound, it can be the perfect time to set up a personal meeting.

When you initially interview the advisors on the phone, you can start with general questions about their professional background, training, designations, experience in the financial business, how they go about the financial planning and investment process, the address of their web site, if they have one, the range of services they offer, how they work with their clients, and how many clients they already serve with the same type of background and needs as you. Once you meet in person, plan on having no more than a 30 minute meeting. That should give you enough time to get a solid impression while respecting their time. Also have a few clear objectives as to what you want to find out before you conclude the meeting. Start the meeting by giving the advisor a very brief overview of both your current financial position, and long-term investment goal and timeframe. Then begin asking you questions. Here are eight samples questions you may want to consider:

1. What is the process you follow when beginning to work with a new client?
2. What types of investment do you recommend and use or sell the most?
3. How often do you communicate with your clients?
4. How do you update your clients on their investments?
5. Who backs you up if you are sick, on vacation, or incapacitated?
6. How do you help your investors manage risk?
7. How do you get compensated?
8. Are any of you current clients available for me to call as references?

Generally speaking, with the answers you get to these questions plus your gut feelings at least one will stand out as your best choice.

Working with Your Advisor

Once you decide with whom you want to work, be certain to schedule a meeting to start your relationship with a thorough review of all your current investment, legal, and tax information, along with your insurance advisors, and a detailed conversation about your long-term goals and the timeframe within which you wan to achieve them.

Some investors strongly prefer working with one financial advisor who oversees all the client's investment accounts and financial assets, making the advisor's job easier and the investor's record-keeping easier as well. Other investors prefer to spread their investment portfolio around among two or three different advisors. They do so because they like using different advisors with different expertise. These investors sometimes also feel that with several different advisors to choose from, they are keeping all their options open, can quickly obtain several different (and sometime conflicting) opinions from more than one advisor who know their personal circumstances well, and have diversified advice and portfolios. These different philosophies are one more example that demonstrates that what's best for an investor is totally up to each one of them.

Red Flags

Investment advisors provide an extremely valuable and critically important service to investors and their families throughout the world. These financial advisors take great pride in doing their very best for their clients, always placing their investors' interests before their own, and being fully committed to the highest levels of professional ethics and personalized service. Advisors also take tremendous pride in their own, their firms', and their industry's reputation. However, on rare occasions there are individuals that may not measure up to these high professional standards. As a result, the following list is provided to you as a heads-up. If you personally experience any of these red flags you'll know it's likely time to be looking for another financial advisor.

- Your phone calls to your advisor are not returned promptly.
- Your opinions and personal preferences are not respected.
- Your questions are not answered clearly or directly.
- Attempts are made to talk you into doing things you are not comfortable doing.
- You are talked down to or treated in a condescending manner.
- Risks and rewards are not both discussed thoroughly when making investment recommendations and/or decisions.
- You are rushed into making a decision.
- You are urged to be less conservative and more aggressive than your personal comfort level.
- You sense an advisor is placing his or her interests before your own.
- The BIG "red flag" of an advisor asking you to make investment checks out to them personally (*which is a violation of securities law*) rather than to the advisor's custodian firm or the investment entity. For additional security, always include your account number on your check.

Knowledgeable and Trusted Advice

The services of a knowledgeable and trusted financial advisor, who knows you and the details of your unique financial situation, and who respects you and your wishes can be priceless. Just as working with the right doctor, accountant, attorney, or tax professional can make a world of difference in those fields, working with the right financial advisor can make an enormous difference in helping you reach your long-term investment goals. Just remember that your relationship with your financial advisor must be an open partnership. Also of paramount importance is to keep in mind that although advisors provide professional advice and counsel the ultimate decision-making authority and the ultimate responsibility for your results resides with you.

CHAPTER 14

Navigating Crisis Events
and Bear Markets

Cash combined with courage in a crisis, is priceless.

Warren Buffett

I nvesting when the economy is solid, inflation is under control, interest rates are stable, surprises are few, budgets are balanced, the world is at peace, Congress is in recess, and markets are behaving themselves and moving higher is easy, pleasant, and even enjoyable. There's only one little problem with that scenario. That unique confluence of events is extremely rare, never sustainable for very long, and not at all an example of how our world or the markets really work over time. We love to believe that stability is the norm in our world and instability the exception. All the same, when you look back though history, reality shows us that the exact opposite is the truth. Instability, uncertainty and dynamic change are the norm, and stability is the exception. Even the Greek philosopher Plato observed over 2000 years ago that the only thing in life that remained the same is change. The incredible pace of worldwide change today does not favor stability. Instead, rapid change drives even more instability and uncertainty, which in turn drives more change, indicating that things are not likely to settle down and stabilize any time soon.

The skills for successful investing and decision making in the of face of crisis events, recessions, bear markets, and increase uncertainty have always been important for "Risk-Wise" Investors; however, in our current state of extreme uncertainty they are more important than ever. To that end, we'll work toward addressing those issues by applying the "Risk-Wise" Investor approach to risks associated with navigating crisis events, recessions and business slowdowns, bear markets, and increased levels of uncertainty. We'll identify them, understand and prioritize them, then review potential risk management methods for each of them, so that we can bring a knowledge and information-based approach to our decisions for dealing with these emotionally charged subjects that can so easily pull investors into common perception/reality and decision making traps.

Crisis Events

Crisis events are a regular part of human existence and have been for tens of thousands of years. While some are manmade and others occur naturally, because of their unexpected and sudden occurrence, large-scale consequences, inability to control, and newness or lack of familiarity, they share a common ability to generate extreme emotional responses in us. These extreme emotional responses frequently generate activation of our innate, freeze/flight/fight response, that causes increased heart and respiration rates; elevated blood pressure; digestion shutdown; increased perspiration; and heightened sensitivity to sound, sight, and smell; as well as high fear and anxiety levels. When these responses occur as the result of real physical threats, they can be of enormous help to our survival because responding to physical threats is exactly what our ingrained natural responses have evolved to do. When these physical fear responses occur because of a financial crisis (or other, nonphysical threat) those hard-wired instincts can actually work against our own best financial interests. Those physical world threat responses often create a negative financial effect because your body's instincts don't discriminate between a physical treat and a financial one. Our human body senses any threat, whether physical, financial, or even make believe (as in a horror or action movie) as physical and directs us to initiate a physical response. While physical responses work extremely well at readying us for action in dealing with physical risks, such actions have been frequently been proven to be the wrong things to do when dealing with generally short-lived financial threats. Almost the only way for us to comply with our body's strong instinct to flee and get away from a perceived financial threat is to sell and get out of the market. Unfortunately that's what many investors do when a sudden crisis strikes and emotions are running. Generally speaking, that action has been a mistake in the past, and one of the worst reasons and worst times to sell.

History shows us that even surprise crisis events that generate strong emotional reactions, generally result in short-lived and sometimes sharp market corrections that reverse themselves within a few weeks or months. Therefore these crisis events have historically demonstrated that they are more of a buying opportunity than a reason to sell out of the market. Please review Table 14.1 for the details. This data, courtesy of Ned Davis Research,

TABLE 14.1 Crisis Events, DJIA Declines and Subsequent Performance

Event	Reaction Dates	Reaction Date % Gain/Loss	DJIA Percentage Gain Days After Reaction Dates			
			22	63	126	253
Panic of 1907	02/15/1907–11/20/1907	−42.9	6.9	14.7	29.9	48.3
Exchange Closed WWI	07/22/1914–12/24/1914	−10.2	10.0	6.6	21.2	80.2
Woodrow Wilson Stroke	09/25/1919–09/26/1919	1.3	5.7	−4.5	−16.0	−21.8
Bombing at JP Morgan Office	09/15/1920–09/30/1920	−5.5	2.4	−14.9	−9.5	−17.3
Market Crash of 1929	10/11/1929–11/13/1929	−43.7	27.3	34.1	46.0	11.8
Germany invades France	05/09/1940–06/22/1940	−17.1	−0.5	8.4	7.0	−5.2
Pearl Harbor	12/06/1941–12/10/1941	−6.5	3.8	−2.9	−9.6	5.4
Truman Upset Victory	11/02/1948–11/10/1948	−4.9	1.6	3.5	1.9	6.1
Korean War	06/23/1950–07/13/1950	−12.0	9.1	15.3	19.2	26.3
Eisenhower Heart Attack	09/23/1955–09/26/1955	−6.5	0.0	6.6	11.7	5.7
Suez Canal Crisis	10/30/1956–10/31/1956	−1.4	0.3	−0.6	3.4	−9.5
Sputnik	10/03/1957–10/22/1957	−9.9	5.5	6.7	7.2	29.2
Cuban Missile Crisis	10/19/1962–10/27/1962	1.1	12.1	17.1	24.2	30.4
JFK Assassinated	11/21/1963–11/22/1963	−2.9	7.2	12.4	15.1	24.0
Martin Luther King Assassinated	04/03/1968–04/05/1968	−0.4	5.3	6.4	9.3	10.8
U.S. Bombs Cambodia	04/29/1970–05/14/1970	−7.1	0.4	3.8	13.5	36.7
Kent State Shooting	05/01/1970–05/26/1970	−14.0	9.9	20.3	20.7	43.7
Penn Central Bankruptcy	06/19/1970–07/07/1970	−7.1	8.0	16.0	24.9	33.8
Arab Oil Embargo	10/16/1973–12/05/1973	−18.5	9.3	10.2	7.2	−25.5
Nixon Resigns	08/07/1974–08/29/1974	−17.6	−7.9	−5.7	12.5	27.2
Iranian Hostage Crisis	11/02/1979–11/07/1979	−2.7	4.7	11.1	2.3	17.0
U.S.S.R. in Afghanistan	12/24/1979–01/03/1980	−2.2	6.7	−4.0	6.8	21.0
Hunt Silver Crash	02/13/1980–03/27/1980	−15.9	6.7	16.2	25.8	30.6
Falkland Islands War	04/01/1982–05/07/1982	4.3	−8.5	−9.8	20.8	41.8
Beirut Bombing	10/21/1983–10/23/1983	0.0	2.1	−0.5	−6.9-	−2.9
U.S. Invades Grenada	10/24/1983–11/07/1983	−2.7	3.9	−2.8	−3.2	2.4
Continental Illinois Bailout	05/08/1984–05/27/1984	−6.4	2.3	11.5	10.1	18.3
U.S. Bombs Libya	04/14/1986–04/21/1986	2.8	−4.3	−4.1	−1.0	25.9
Financial Panic '87	10/02/1987–10/19/1987	−34.2	11.5	11.4	15.0	24.2
Invasion of Panama	12/15/1989–12/20/1989	−1.9	−2.7	0.3	8.0	−2.2
Iraq invades Kuwait	08/02/1990–08/23/1990	−13.3	0.1	2.3	16.3	22.4

(Continued)

189

TABLE 14.1 (Continued)

Event	Reaction Dates	Reaction Date % Gain/Loss	DJIA Percentage Gain Days After Reaction Dates			
			22	63	126	253
Gulf War	01/16/1991–01/17/1991	4.6	11.8	14.3	15.0	24.5
Gorbachev Coup	08/16/1991–08/19/1991	-2.4	4.4	1.6	11.3	14.9
ERM U.K. Currency Crisis	09/15/1992–10/16/1992	-4.6	0.6	3.2	9.2	14.7
World Trade Center Bombing	02/25/1993–02/27/1993	-0.3	2.4	5.1	8.5	14.2
Oklahoma City Bombing	04/18/1995–04/20/1995	1.2	3.9	9.7	12.9	30.8
Asian Stock Market Crisis	10/07/1997–10/27/1997	-12.4	8.8	10.5	25.0	16.9
U.S. Embassy Bombings Africa	08/06/1998–08/14/1998	-1.8	-4.0	4.8	10.4	32.0
U.S.S. Cole Yemen Bombing	10/11/2000–10/18/2000	-4.2	6.6	6.1	6.1	-5.1
WTC and Pentagon Terrorist Attacks	09/10/2001–19/21/2001	-14.3	13.4	21.2	24.8	-6.7
War in Afghanistan	10/05/2001–10/09/2001	-0.7	5.9	11.5	12.4	-16.8
Bali Nightclub Bombing	10/11/2002–10/13/2002	0.3	6.6	12.3	6.7	24.4
Iraq War	03/19/2003–05/01/2003	2.3	5.5	9.2	15.6	22.0
Madrid Terrorist Attacks	03/10/2004–03/24/2004	-2.4	3.9	3.9	-0.1	4.4
London Train Bombing	07/06/2005–07/07/2005	0.3	2.3	0.1	5.6	7.8
India Israel and Lebanon Bombing	07/11/2006–07/18/2006	-3.0	5.0	10.9	16.4	28.3
Mean		-7.3	4.7	6.7	11.2	16.2
Median		-3.6	4.8	6.6	10.9	17.6

The 22, 63, 126 and 253 day rate-of-change is calculated from the last day in the reaction dates column. The first date in the reaction dates column indicates the start of the market reaction or the trading day prior to the event.

1914 data: In 1916 a new list of 20 stocks for the DJIA was adopted and computed back to the reopening of the exchange on 12/12/1914. NDR analysis for this study adjusted the DJIA index level prior to 12/12/1914 to reflect an accurate and consistent data set. From *The Dow Jones Averages 1985–1990*, edited by Phyllis S. Pierce.

Days = Market Days

Source: Permission by Ned Davis Research ©Ned Davis Research, Inc. Further distribution prohibited without prior permission. All Rights Reserved. Permission also granted by Dow Jones & Company, Inc. Dow Jones® and the Dow Jones Industrial Average are service marks of Dow Jones & Company, Inc. The Dow Jones Industrial Average and related data are proprietary to Dow Jones & Company, Inc.

reviews crisis events since 1907, and both the short- and long-term reaction of the Dow Jones Industrial average following the crisis event.

As you can see from Table 14.1 there have been a large number of crisis events since 1907. Although the surprise and emotions of the moment sometimes drive the equity market lower, crisis-related market drops of the past have *always* proved temporary. Of course, individual investors have to determine the potential impact of crisis risks they're exposed to, and whether they want to accept, manage, or avoid this type of risk. However, when considering crisis risk from a general perspective and using our "Risk-Wise" risk priority ranking system, crisis risk generally appears to have a moderate to high probability with a moderate short-tem impact and an almost nonexistent long-term impact.

The Unique Nature of Financial Crises

Financial crisis risk can be another mater entirely because it is literally a different kind of animal from natural, political, terrorist, or other manmade risks. The reason financial crises risk are different is that money and finance are so universal and so tied to investing and the investment markets. As a result, financial crisis risk has a greater impact on the markets and investing in general than other types of crisis risk. In reviewing the details of Table 14.1, you may have noticed that many of the crisis events on the list associated with money and finance were associated with some of the largest declines. In addition, financial crises associated with systemic banking crises have seen some of the biggest declines in the investment markets and the longest periods of time for the market to recover. Figure 14.1 displays the Dow Jones Industrial Average's worst 15 years since 1896. Over that 112 year period of time, the −33.8 percent drop in the DJIA in 2008 is the third worst.

What is of particular relevance to our current discussion is the fact that major systemic banking crises occurred in 1907, 1930,1931, and 2008, which were also the four worst-performing years in the DJIA in the past 112 years. So even though a financial crisis involving the banking system is a relatively rare event, and has a low probability of occurring, its potential impact on the economy and stock market is extremely high. Figure 14.1 also demonstrates an almost perfect correlation between years experiencing banking crises and the worst DJIA performance in over 100 years. As a result, any financial crisis associated with a systemic banking crises must be taken very seriously, and must be given the highest risk management priority. It is also interesting to note from Figure 14.2 that the loss of the DJIA in the first year for the banking crisis of 1930 was very similar in size to the DJIA loss in 2008. Potentially even more alarming for us in 2009 is the fact that 1931, the second year of

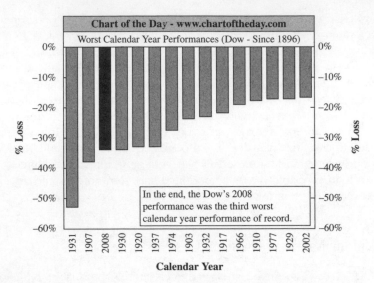

FIGURE 14.1 Worst Calendar Year Performance (Dow Jones Industrial Average 1896–2008)

Source: Used with permission from Chart of the Day, www.chartoftheday.com.

that banking crisis and of the Great Depression was an even worse year for the equity market than 1930. That year the DJIA was down for the second straight year with a crushing loss of over 50 percent, making it the single worst year for the index in the last 112 years.

Hopefully, the aggressive action of the Federal Reserve Bank, the historically gigantic economic stimulus package being launched by the federal government, and the fact that our legislators are resisting the kind of protectionist legislation that devastated foreign trade in the 1930s will avert a repeat of 1931 and get our current economy and psychology turned around. However, sound principles of risk management require that "Risk-Wise" investors with shorter investment time horizons who are also exposed to high impact risks err on the side of caution and preserve their principal. For longer-term investors, the gut wrenching market downturns of the past have proven to be outstanding long-term buying opportunities precisely because of all the negative business and economic news and higher perceived risk.

What to Do When You're Uncertain?

In uncertain times, these kinds of decisions are real balancing acts that we each must weigh from our own personal perspective. One of the safest and best options if you are truly uncertain as to what to do is to do nothing or shift to a totally defensive position and wait until the uncertainty clarifies. Moving to the investment sidelines in high quality, safe, liquid short-term cash investments and waiting for the market to drop back further or for the dark economic clouds to clear and blue skies return makes a great deal of sense in uncertain times. That strategy removes the risk of suffering further market downside, but also increases the risk of not participating when the market turns positive, as it typically does. In fact, equity markets are well known for beginning new market advances well before recessions end and business news begins to improve. The other alternative may be to remain fully invested and ride out the storm, however long it takes. The risk with that strategy is that although you'll participate when the markets move higher you'll also participate if they go lower too. There is a middle ground alternative as well that both reduces your downside risk and upside potential (your exposure), yet provides options and flexibility whether the stock market rises or falls. That alternative is to reduce your overall exposure and partially hedging your portfolio by moving a portion (10 to 50 percent) into cash equivalents. Once completed, you've reduced both your risk and return on your portfolio, and you're in a position to take advantage of any further market corrections by buying back into the holdings you like, only at a lower prices, which also lowers your cost basis and makes future market gains that much more profitable. It also helps avoid one of the most common investor mistakes of all, which is being fully invested as major market bottoms occur and not having any ready cash available to take advantage of historic, rock-bottom market prices and values. Should the opposite alternative occur, the stock market begins heading higher and the economic sunlight returns, you can buy back into your favorite holdings when you are comfortable. You'll know that your existing holdings have already increased in price from the market's improvement. Plus, additional investments you make then, when added to your previous holdings will lower your average overall cost basis. This method provides you with a lower average cost on your holdings than if you had previously fully liquidated your portfolio and were now putting your entire portfolio back into the markets at higher prices.

Of course, these decisions would be much easier if we had an idea of how much further, if at all, the markets may fall or how long the current period of market weakness may last. Although no one really knows, to aid in that effort you may want to examine the depth and duration of market corrections of the past. Figure 14.2 is a very useful chart that does just that in a way that is visually easy to see and understand. This chart depicts both the depth and the duration of 26 of the major corrections of 15 percent or greater of the Dow Jones Industrial Average since 1900, from their very peak to their ultimate bottom.

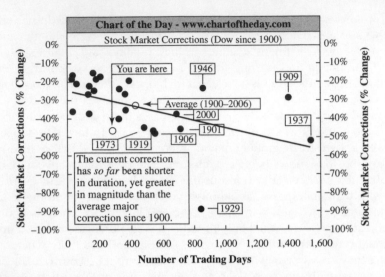

FIGURE 14.2 Stock Market Corrections (Dow Jones Industrial Average 1900–November 2008 Low)

Source: With permission from Chart of the Day, www.chartoftheday.com.

Each dot on Figure 14.2 represents a major correction in the DJIA with its magnitude on the vertical axis and its duration in days on the horizontal graph. For instance, the most recent correction started when the DJIA peaked at 14,155 on October 11, 2007. The 2008 bottom at 7392, was set on November 21, 2008, has held, with a total peak to trough correction of almost 48 percent.

The 2007–2008 market correction has proven to be slightly below average in duration and above average in magnitude. It is the fourth-deepest market correction in the last 108 years and is only exceeded in depth by the market drops in 1906, 1929, and 1937. The 2007–2008 DJIA decline is also the most severe market correction in that index since World War II.

Crisis Summary

The best way to deal with crisis events is to expect them and prepare a plan of action for how you will deal with them, well in advance. Commercial aviation, the military, fire fighters, and others use that technique very effectively, and you can too. Natural crisis events, like earthquakes, hurricanes, and floods that can impact us personally and physically must be taken very seriously and fully prepared for as well. From an investment perspective, their primarily local and regional impact combined with a low potential impact on the markets means they are a risk we can generally afford to accept (unless an investor has special circumstances) with no need for any extraordinary risk management initiatives.

If, however, a natural risk has the potential for broader impact, it would be imprudent to dismiss it without a risk assessment review first.

Political Crisis Risks

Political crises that have occurred in the past have demonstrated that even if the markets react negatively to them, those reactions are typically not severe and recoveries follow within a month. As a result, these types of risk, regardless of their frequency, can also be categorized as low impact risks, which can be accepted with no need for special proactive risk management.

Terrorist Risk

Terrorism is a highly emotional issue because it is designed to generate fear, surprise, terror, and emotional extremes. Rather than sit back and become worried and anxious or alternatively apathetic about terrorist risk, the best approach is to assume it will happen tomorrow and put a plan in place to deal with it head on. Once you have thought through a range of possibilities, from its directly affecting you to its indirect effect if it occurs at a distant location, you can then create plans to prepare for and deal with each scenario your envision. You'll have neutralized your fears and minimized the risks should they actually materialize. Again, the key is to face the risk directly, assume it will happen, and prepare for it now. Once you follow those steps, you'll control the risk rather than the risk controlling you.

Financial Crisis

Financial crisis risks should viewed seriously, in that they are moderately frequent and can have moderate to high impact on an investment portfolio. Beyond normal passive or semipassive portfolio asset allocation and diversification, it makes sense to consider implementing active defensive strategies if a potential financial crisis is looming. Such strategies may include raising cash positions, hedging with inverse or noncorrelating alternatives, reducing exposure to investments or moving funds to investments that may be less vulnerable to such problems.

Financial Crises Associated with Systemic Banking Crises

Banking-related crises have proven in the past to generate the biggest risks with the longest durations of any crisis events. As a result they should be taken extremely seriously, prepared for with caution, and be addressed with a strong emphasis on preservation of capital instead of risk-oriented investments. Because these types of crises tend to be more complicated and challenging to resolve than most economic problems, have the propensity for increased negative surprises occurring, and require significant time to overcome, the risk of being left behind by a major market move as one of these types of crises is ending is significantly less than the risk of being exposed to more market losses.

Bear Market Profile

Stock market corrections of 20 percent or more have been a regular feature of liquid markets as long as they have existed. At a fundamental level, these declining market periods are generally the result of the excesses that have developed in an expanding economy being corrected by either the economy itself slowing or conscious slowing being engineered by the Federal Reserve Bank. As Figure 14.2 demonstrates there have been 26 bear market in the last 108 years. So, on average they occur about every four years and last approximately one year, although there can be wide variation in their depth and duration around the average. Bear markets are generally characterized by steady drops in the price of stocks over an extended period of months and sometimes beyond a year. Once a normal market correction of 5 to 10 percent begins to deepen into the 15 to 20 percent range, its character begins to shift, particularly if it's accompanied by weakening economic news and negative corporate earnings surprises. Investor pessimism begins to increase, which increases selling pressure, which creates more pessimism and begins a vicious self-feeding downward spiral. Periodically short-term rallies within the overall downward trend develop, retrace a portion of previous loses, and entice some brave souls to buy back in. These short-term rallies within downward trending bear market, are often called "bear traps," or "sucker rallies" because after modest run-ups they fail to gain significant upward momentum, roll over, and take the market to even lower lows. Eventually bear markets bottom out after selling pressure is exhausted or price levels have dropped to such a low point that investors with funds to invest, in spite of the overwhelming negative news, just can't resist the incredible values. Near bear market lows it's not unusual to see some companies' stock prices drop to the point that their shares are so undervalued that they sell at levels lower the individual firm's asset values, liquidation values, or even cash on hand per share. Even at these extremely oversold levels rallies are viewed very skeptically by the bulk of investors, because they expect another bear-trap. However, rallies eventually begin to gain momentum, and despite the continuing disappointing business climate they climb up a wall of worry and establish the beginnings of the next bull market. Since the markets generally begin advancing three to six months before business news begins to turn positive, even these rallies are frequently viewed with caution. Eventually the market is up 10 to 20 percent above its bottom, and business news begins to turn positive This generally creates an enthusiastic wave of buying just as the market begins to drop back to consolidate its previous advance, shaking investors' fragile confidence once more.

Bear Market Risk Management Strategies

Many investors find that the hair on the back of their necks stands up and a shiver runs down their back when they first hear the dreaded "B" word, bear market, after a string of successful bull market years. The term conjures up all kinds of unpleasant images of being mauled, market panics, and the weeping, wailing, and gnashing of teeth. It's a word that carries a lot of fear, negative mental images, anxiety, and feelings of gloom and doom that can interfere with and cloud the opportunities presented by every bear market. Since bear markets occur on average about every four years and have been a regular part of the investment cycle for at least 400 years, why do we fear them so much and let them intimidate us. We don't like to talk about or even think about them. It's as if we wished they never even existed, and this is a big problem on several levels. Let me explain why.

First, if you had the supernatural power to design the perfect stock market, what would a graph of it look like over time? Most people say they'd love it to look like the chart in Figure 14.3. Take a quick look and see if that's what you'd like your ideal market to look like.

Although initially this chart looks extremely attractive and almost too good to be true, it's really only the best market for one single type of investor.

FIGURE 14.3 Best Type of Market?

Figure 14.3 is the best kind of market only for investors who have a big basket of money and invest it all at once and never make additional investments
ever again. Any investor who invests in this kind of market, over a long
period of time, accumulating and building investments over the years, pays
more and more for their investments every time they put money to work. For
these accumulators, this market is one of the worst types of markets imag-
inable. If in fact that is the case, what would an investment accumulators'
ideal market look like? To see, take a quick look at Figure 14.4.

This type of market is accumulator investors' dream come true because
they can keep investing and accumulating over a long period of time at the
same low price. Then, just as they complete their accumulation phase and
before they start their withdrawal phase, the market explodes to the upside
providing them with a 15 or 20 times or more increase in the value of their
investments. Wow. That's even better than the first ideal market isn't it?

Unfortunately, there's some bad news, in that we really don't have
supernatural powers and we can't design our own perfect investment.

We are going to have to live with the kind of market we've got, which
is illustrated in Figure 14.5.

However, when you take a close look at the market we've actually got,
and compare it to our two previous hypothetical ideal markets, it becomes
very clear that the market we actually have is the best of both of our ideal
markets. First, we have a market that has a strong uptrend bias, increasing
our wealth very nicely over time, and we also have a market that periodically
goes on sale. It very conveniently gives us the opportunity to occasionally
make new investments at discounted prices, before it goes up again. Therefore our real-world market offers us the best of both worlds because it
works very well both for one-time-only investors and also for long-term
accumulators. Why would we ever want anything different?

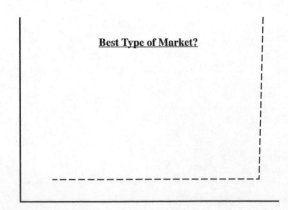

FIGURE 14.4 Best Type of Market?

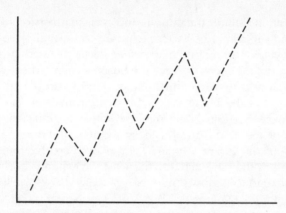

FIGURE 14.5 Best Type of Market?

During bear markets it is also of paramount importance to remember and apply the lessons we learned about risk perception/risk reality "gaps" back in Chapter 7. In order to better visualize the point, let's take another look at a diagram we referred to in that chapter, which we'll repeat as Figure 14.6.

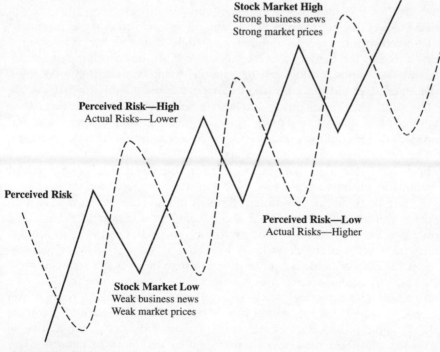

FIGURE 14.6 The Relationship of Stock Market Price Levels and Perceived Risk

This diagram illustrates the curious and cyclical inversion of our perception of risk and the actual risk we're exposed to through several complete stock market cycles. During bull markets the better the markets perform, the higher it goes, and the more positive the business news, the lower investors perceive the real risks they're taking. In fact, the risks are actually the highest when the market is the highest, yet that's when investors see the risks as the least. Conversely during bear markets when the indexes are down 20 to 30 percent or more, and the business and investment news is bad, and pessimism about the future is intense, investors perceive their risks to be the greatest when they are actually the least. So when perceived risks are high, real risks tend to be low, and when perceived risks are low, real risks tend to be higher.

These examples reinforce why market pullbacks or bear markets are usually the worst time to sell investments and actually wonderful opportunities to accumulate more investment assets at bargain basement prices. That's exactly why most experienced, long-term investors take bear markets in stride and view them as a normal part of the market cycle or as attractive opportunities to add to their favorite long-term holdings at discounted prices.

Knowledge of this very common phenomenon can be used in two ways. One method is as a self-checking or self-monitoring device. So any time you begin to feel that an investment is a sure thing, and you don't see any risks associated with it, the risks are likely very high. The other way is to observe investors and the media's attitudes, because if all they're talking about are the weak business conditions, treacherous markets, and high risks, then perceived risks are high, but the true risks are quite likely low. If, on the other hand, they're optimistic and see no risk at all, their perceived risk is low and the actual risks are quite high. The great financier, businessman, and investor Bernard Baruch may have said it best with his famous statement, "When good news about the market hits the front page of the *New York Times*, sell." Although that was well before our current bombardment of worldwide, instantaneous news, 24/7. I'm sure you get the point.

Since there are many different types of investors, some view bear markets as trading opportunities for short selling or buying and then selling on the short-term rallies. For other well-diversified investors who are just uncomfortable with the downward fluctuation of their portfolio values during periodic bear markets, the best option may be to begin reducing their exposure to equities. Some investors begin this process three to four years into a bull market, so they have less equity exposure when a bear market hits. Alternatively, as the market moves higher they may want to gradually shift holdings to higher quality investment alternatives that generate income so that any market weakness is cushioned by dividends or interest. They may also want to consider investing more heavily in high quality bonds or established recession resistant companies that pay attractive dividends. Balanced mutual funds that own a mix of stock and bonds, plus pay income distributions will usually have lower price volatility, too.

Another risk mitigation option is to consider diversifying a portion of your assets into conservative investments with return characteristics that are not correlated to stock or bond market movements. Taking that thought one step further is considering the option of implementing hedging strategies using inverse index mutual funds or inverse exchange-traded funds. Because these funds move directly the opposite their underlying index on a daily basis, if their underlying stock index goes down, they will go up an equal amount, or with leverage, more than an equal amount. However, if the market index they are based on goes up, these funds will go down and offset gains in the rest of your portfolio. Although these inverse funds have attractive hedging potential, they are sophisticated instruments that require a very good feel for market direction and frequent rebalancing in order to maintain the proper hedging ratio. It's also very important that the inverse fund you may use for hedging this way be based on an index that matches the types of stock you have in the portfolio you're hedging. For instance, if your portfolio is composed of large capitalization stocks you should only use an inverse fund to hedge that portfolio that is based on a large cap index like the S&P 500. To do otherwise will create discrepancies in your hedge that will make your necessary, regular hedge rebalancing much more complicated than necessary. So if you consider using these tools, be sure you know what you are doing or are working with an advisor who's familiar with their various applications and common pitfalls.

Finally, it may be tempting to try and time the market by selling investments in anticipation of a bear market and then buying them back at 60 or 70 cents on the dollar when the bear market bottoms. As attractive as that sounds, just keep in mind that the application of that strategy has been attempted by hundreds of thousand of investors over many decades and that successfully executing it is much easier said than done, and even if done successfully can generate serious tax consequences and extra costs.

Turn Lemons into Lemonade

Whenever a crisis event, recession, or bear market occurs, the vast majority of the public and investor reactions are to hold their hands to their heads or mouths in shock, disbelief, and horror. They say, "Ohhhh nooo," and wring their hands in anguish, fear, and sometimes panic. These reactions of shock and fear can become even more extreme if these crisis events have one or more of the factors that increase perceived risk such as sudden occurrence, broad potential impact, beyond our control, new or unfamiliar. Why does this happen again and again and again? Do most people not recognize the fact that crisis events and negative surprises happen all the time and are a normal part of reality? Do they not understand that instability, rapid change, and surprise negative events are the norm rather than the exception?

What would it be like if instead of reacting to news of a major recession, business slowdown, or crisis event in surprise, anguish, or fear they reacted by rubbing their hands together in satisfaction and said, "I've been waiting for something like this to happen for a long time, and I'm ready and prepared to take advantage of it." These people recognize that reality has both positive and negative aspects and to only live and plan for the positives in life is delusional, because they're denying 50 percent of reality. Why not look at the world as it really is, rather than pretend it's only the way you'd like it to be? Why give up control when with some extra effort, study and preparation, and flexibility you can turn the inevitable lemons into lemonade, and crisis events into opportunities. Isn't it a fuller, more confident, and enjoyable life when we have realistic expectations of what we are likely to face and understand and are fully prepared for both the positive and negative surprises life can throw at us. Remember what Sir Arthur Conan Doyle's Sherlock Holmes said in the 1902 book *The Hound of the Baskervilles* is just as true today: "that which is clearly known hath less terror than that which is hinted at and only guessed."

That quote highlights the core essence of "Risk-Wise" Investing. So don't be afraid or intimidated by crisis events, bear markets, and business slow-downs. Instead embrace them, study them, get to know them, understand and become familiar with them, and learn how to turn their power to your advantage. Their power comes from the fact that bear markets typically offer unusually attractive buying opportunities for the very reasons that the negative economic news and investment environment scare away most investors. Even though no one can pick a market bottom, crisis events are wonderful examples of periods of high perceived risk levels with low actual risk levels because prices are so depressed. In fact, one way to identify that you've actually become a savvy, true "Risk-Wise" investor is when you begin to find yourself skeptical of the conventional wisdom, wanting to invest in the opposite direction of the crowd and buying when everyone else is fearful.

Summary and Afterthoughts

Nothing in life is to be feared. It is only to be understood

Marie Curie

Fully embracing the fact that with rare exception what we know, understand, and are prepared for cannot harm us, we've surveyed a range of information directly related to investment risk and risk management. Our primary objective has been to provide practical information about risk and a user-friendly, nontechnical, easy-to-implement, risk management process. The method we've used has been to help you gain additional insights, knowledge, and understanding of this crucial subject, plus provide you with tools you can use in becoming a more knowledgeable, well prepared, and effective "Risk-Wise" Investor.

The "Risk-Wise" Process

In further support of that goal, let's review some of the highlights of our risk management studies. Let's start with the model for the "Risk-Wise" Investor risk management process, and of course that is our innate, *everyday "life-risk" management process*. Its six steps are:

1. Identify risks
2. Understand risks
3. Review risk reduction and management strategies
4. Evaluate the risk/reward tradeoffs
5. Decide to act or not act
6. Learn: continuously learn from your actual experience, how to make better and better risk/reward decisions in the future

With that process serving as our foundation and model, let's review the steps of the "Risk-Wise" Investor Risk Management Process.

1. Personal Risk Assessment
   - *Define risk* (your definition of risk is the foundation of the entire process).
   - *Identify risks* (you can't manage a risk you haven't identified as a risk).
   - *Understand risks* (their likelihood and potential personal impact).
   - *Determine which risks to avoid, accept, and/or manage.*
2. *Review risk reduction/management strategies available* (their strengths and weaknesses).
3. *Evaluate your risk/reward trade-offs* (while avoiding common evaluation pitfalls).
4. *Make your decision to act or not act—then implement* (while avoiding the common decision-making traps of many investors).
5. Effect *ongoing risk monitoring and decision making* (continuously being "on guard" for the emergence of new risks/threats and evolving nature of known risks).

Lessons from History

Following our review of the ancient past, through the Middle Ages, the Renaissance, and post-Renaissance periods, right up to our present day, a few historical lessons really stand out. *First*, instability, not stability is the norm throughout history, and creative destruction and instability are simply the by-products of growth. *Second*, surprises and rare occurrences (both negative and positive) happen all the time, and should be expected. *Third*, crisis events, bubbles, busts, panics, and crashes, wars, natural and man-made disasters are normal, happen regularly throughout history and should be planned for. *Fourth*, where risks are identified, directly faced, studied, and understood, risk management knowledge improves, which leads to more effective and reliable risk management. *Fifth*, our increasingly complex, faster-paced, and interconnected world, with more challenges, more opportunities, and more risks coming at us faster and faster means that effective, proactive risk management has never been more important.

What Is Risk?

The key to the amazing progress of science, particularly in the last 100 years, has been our deeper and deeper understanding of how our physical world actually works. That same focus on understanding all we can about the nature of risk will help us enjoy a similar level of success in the effectiveness of our risk management efforts. To that end, it is critical to first have a strong and empowering definition of risk that encompasses risks in many forms. A solid definition is so important because without one, how can you possibly know when you've found a risk, if you don't know exactly what you're looking for? Next in importance is to define risk management. Then, at the most fundamental level, it is critical to understand the true nature of risk itself, with all its different and varied characteristics.

Risk Defined

Although even many experienced investors struggle to adequately define risk, the best all-around definition of risk does not even come from the investment world, but rather from the executive suite of one of the world's most admired companies, Apple. Apple's current chief financial officer, Peter Oppenheimer defines risk as *"the degree to which an outcome varies from expectations."* The real power of that definition and why it's being used as the "Risk-Wise" Investor risk definition of choice is its inclusive nature, and the way it empowers every investor by relating risk directly to each investor's own expectations. We may not be able to totally control risk, but we have total control over our expectations, and that control gives us much greater control over risk. So the more realistic our expectations for the range of both negative and positive possibilities we face, the fewer surprises we'll experience, and the less risk we'll face.

Risk Management Defined

With risk defined, it's then necessary to define risk management. Although numerous approaches have been used over the years, the definition of risk management most appropriate to our needs is: *the culture, processes and structures that are directed toward realizing potential opportunities while managing adverse effects.* This definition is particularly effective because it focuses on the future, emphasizes a culture where risk is always kept in mind, a process focus that builds more consistent and effective results. In addition, it recognizes the balance between rewards and risk as well as the importance of advance preparation for both adverse effects and potential opportunities.

The True Nature of Risk

Now we can focus on gaining a better understanding of the true nature of risk and uncertainty. Although we have a tendency to generally think of risk as a singular phenomenon, professor Benoit Mandelbrot, in his 2004 book, *The (Mis)Behavior of Markets*, published by Basic Books, points out that uncertainty is actually more complex than that. After many decades studying uncertainty in the markets, he observed that uncertainty (risk) comes in more than one form. He came to the conclusion that it actually has three forms or states. Now initially that statement, and the concept it represents, may be a little hard to grasp. However, it may be easier to understand by comparing it to something we are all very familiar with, water. Water also has three distinct states, ice (solid), water (liquid), steam (gas). Each state of water exhibits very different physical properties and behavioral characteristics form one another, yet they are all still just on substance, water. The three states of risk identified by Dr. Mandelbrot are *mild*, *slow*, and *wild* uncertainty, and each behaves differently.

He characterizes *mild uncertainty* as being like the risk in calling a series of coin tosses. This form of risk/uncertainty adheres to the normal bell distribution. It has well defined parameters, low variability, no big surprises, and is predictable. Dr. Mandelbrot says that it "is like the solid state of matter because it has low energy and stays where you put it." It is the kind of risk, price variability and volatility periodically found during normal, random walk stock market periods. This type of risk is routine, predictable, and obvious, with no real surprises.

Wild uncertainty is the exact opposite of the mild form. It is unpredictable, irregular, outside what is normally expected, high energy, not structured, and has fast, seemingly limitless and frightening, fluctuations from one value to the next. In his book, Professor Mandelbrot states that "it's like the gaseous phase of matter, no structure, no volume, no telling what it will do." This form of risk is typical of extreme, highly unstable, hypervolatile stock markets like the one in the fall of 2008. Damage caused by earthquakes, deaths in war, death in terrorist incidents, financial markets, commodity markets, and inflation rates are typical of this type of risk. Wild uncertainty is subject to the accidental, the unseen, the unpredicted, surprises, and the extreme.

Slow Uncertainty is the form of risk between mild and wild. Professor Mandelbrot describes it as like the liquid state of matter.

Looking at risk and uncertainty in this multistate way, with each state of risk having different behavioral characteristics can be an enormous advantage in helping us understand not just the way risk works, but also the world we live in. It also helps explain the wide variances we can experience, and the range of market behaviors we can expect over time. In addition, it can greatly help us in determining and implementing effective risk management methodologies.

The Schools of Risk Management

Over time, two very different approaches, philosophies or schools of risk management have developed. One has developed and been used over the last thousand years, the other has gained prominence, popularity, and widespread use in just the last half century. Proponents of each of these two different risk management approaches tend to be dedicated believers in their particular method. They are strong proponents of what they perceive to be their chosen philosophy's numerous advantages and superiority over what they see as the inferior qualities of the other. We, however, will explore and get to know both of them for the purpose of understanding which school may better serve our needs.

Trust the Numbers

The quantitative approach to risk management initially evolved out of efforts in the late Renaissance to gain an advantage in gambling by better understanding the internal workings of games of chance. Over the centuries, once it finally evolved its comprehensive set of theories and mathematical elegance, the quantitative approach was embraced by the academic community and then by the investment management world.

Its approach to constructing, monitoring, and adjusting investment portfolios based on mathematical formulae, numerical technical measures such as alpha, beta, Sharpe Ratios, and correlation coefficients made investment management and risk management seem much more like science them art.

The quantitative approach has also become the *default* risk management approach of the majority of the global investment community. This quantification seems so logical, neat, tight, tidy, and well ... appealing. It's so gratifying and reassuring to see the highly complex, ever-changing, and complex, multidisciplinary subjects of risk and uncertainty reduced to rock-solid numbers and mathematical equations that allow us to manage risk more effectively than ever.

There is, however, one important question we have to ask. Has what works in theory and elegant equations actually worked in the real world? Fortunately, we now have over three decades of real-world experience to show us how well it works. Unfortunately, the real-world experience in using the quantitative risk management method has been mixed. Quite simply, what works beautifully in theory, in reality works sometimes and sometimes doesn't work well at all. In fact, the quantitative method works well in routine and reasonably stable markets (periods of mild uncertainty). When this approach tends not to work well or becomes less effective is when markets begin behaving badly, volatility increases, previously established relationships begin rapidly changing, and instability raises its ugly head (periods of wild risk). Of course, that is exactly when investors need effective risk management the most.

Trust Your Gut

The subjective or qualitative approach to risk management is a very natural and intuitive method of risk management. It's not a numbers-based method. In fact, it has a great deal in common with the way we adult humans manage our everyday life risks. The qualitative school is based on the belief that since the world is always changing and every situation is different, it is more effective to base risk/reward decisions on subjective degrees of belief about a subjective future rather than on the past. Although the past can be helpful in making decisions about the future, that knowledge and experience when combined with a forward-looking view and sound judgment will improve the quality of our risk/reward decision making and overall risk management success.

The heart of the subjective method is probably best described by combining the essence of the observation referenced in the introduction of this book: With rare exception, *What we know, understand, and are prepared for cannot harm us* and utilizing the full potential of the definition of risk by Peter Oppenheimer we discussed earlier, *"where risk is the degree to which and outcome differs from (your) expectation."* In combining and implementing these two profound observations we become focused on building our knowledge and understanding of risk, developing more realistic expectations, and better preparing for the risks we expect and even the ones we don't. This improvement in knowledge, understanding, and preparation, provides us more comfort, control, and flexibility in dealing the risks we are likely to face.

The qualitative approach incorporates the frequently misunderstood characteristic that the risk/reward tradeoff can often be very different from one person to the next. The level of risk can vary dramatically based on an individual's own knowledge, skill, experience, and exposure in dealing with a risk. The actual risk each individual takes, even when facing an identical threat, can range widely from little to enormous risk. The subjective risk/reward analysis can also be influenced by the relative value of what one can potentially lose versus what one might gain in taking a given risk. The qualitative method also benefits from both an individual's logical and intuitive decision-making processes. Often, with enough information knowledge, and experience, and after weighing all the factors, trusting your gut can be a very effective risk management decision-making strategy.

It is important to keep in mind that the subjective risk management method should not be confused with the practice of guessing. It's not guessing, when you're using familiarity, knowledge, and/or personal experience as the basis for your risk management decision-making process or when using the advice of an expert who's knowledgeable in the discipline appropriate to the decision. Of course, it is definitely guessing, and should always be avoided, when you're tempted to make a risk management decision with little knowledge, practical experience, or expert advice on a matter. In cases where you are making a risk management decision and lack the appropriate knowledge or have insufficient information, the decision should either be deferred until your knowledge/information gap is rectified or a knowledgeable subject matter expert can be consulted.

Which School Is Best?

Given that each of these approaches to risk management has both advantages and disadvantages, which school of risk management is best? Like so many other things in life, that it depends on you. Remember what I mentioned earlier about how critical it is for the success of any risk management method that each one of us know, thoroughly understand (both its strengths and weaknesses,) are comfortable with, and have confidence in the method we use?

The very best way to proceed may be using both methods at the same time because they complement one another so well. The quantitative method is helpful in portfolio construction and works well in mild risk environments, whereas the qualitative method is more intuitive and more effective during the inevitable periods of wild risk. Plus the subjective approach gives one more control in terms of what risks are expected (even in planning for rare or unexpected risk) and how to specifically avoid, manage, or accept those risks. Another way to benefit from both schools of risk management is to use quantitative techniques for periodic portfolio rebalancing, while using the qualitative approach to manage big picture risks and for making the occasional tactical decisions to defensively raise cash, hedge, or become more aggressive when appropriate. Just as diversification is a proven risk reduction technique in portfolio construction, and one can reduce overall portfolio risk further by owning stocks-bonds-cash, value and growth, large capitalization stocks and small caps, domestic and international, it makes the same sense to diversify your risk management methods as well.

Both Human and Beast

Our bodies have developed enormously sophisticated hard-wired automatic reflex systems to control our blood sugar and oxygen levels. Those systems also regulate heart rate, hormone levels, and thousands of other substances in order to give us the maximum opportunity to survive, reproduce, and prosper in the natural world. These natural, built-in capabilities have given us an incredible advantage in dealing with the challenges of the world our species has faced as humans navigated through their daily lives throughout history. As wonderful, amazing, and powerful as these automatic systems and built-in hard-wiring are, it is very, very important to understand how they can easily cause us to act against our best interests in the non-natural world of investments. Those same very strong, automatic systems that developed to help us survive and prosper in the natural world can often work against us because our biology has been left in the dust by the enormous advances we've made in the development of our modern lives in just the last few hundred years. Our bodies have been preprogrammed for a hunter-gatherer lifestyle and the risks and threats of the natural world that our distant ancestors faced and dealt with for more than 50,000 years. Now, however, we live in an incredibly different, extremely fast-paced world with a completely new array of challenges and issues, where our Model T biology is working overtime to help us survive and prosper in our super mobile, multitasking Internet/high-tech/space age. That divergence creates a number of challenges and potential problems that are critical to be aware of and understand if we want to manage those internally generated risks.

The investment world in particular offers special challenges and common pitfalls directly resulting from the gap between our hard-wired biology and the realities of the modern investment world, which "Risk-Wise" Investors need to address. These include pitfalls that are directly related to the automatic reflexes built into the internal hard-wiring of our brain and our body/brain interface.

The Non-Natural World of Investing

It is critical to emphasize the importance of taking into full account and understanding the basic fact that human beings have been hard-wired by evolution over tens of thousands of years to deal with the risks, rewards, and realities of life in the harsh natural world humans have lived in for over 98 percent of human existence. Our innate physiology and behavior was formed in the unforgiving natural world where the focus of life was on surviving on a day-to-day basis, and on only the here and the now. It was an environment full of countless challenges and dangers, including bloodthirsty beasts that viewed human beings more as prey than predators. It demanded focusing on the present, because the past and the future had absolutely no relevance. It was typically a life of feast or famine with relatively calm periods periodically peppered with short, surprising, highly stressful, life-threatening situations that ingrained the instinctive freeze, flight or fight responses will still posses today. The only priority was to focus on the daily struggle to pull through and live for one more day. Early humans' bodies and brains evolved to survive in that demanding, now-focused, survival-of-the-fittest kind of world. Even though our world has improved dramatically in the last few hundred years, that ancient hard-wiring still serves us reasonably well in dealing with the challenges we face in our day-to-day, natural existence.

Investing does not operate in a natural world. Instead, investing exists in a non-natural world, and the big difference is related to time. Unlike the real, natural world where we spend a lot of time and effort to hold onto and preserve the past, while living and taking action in the present, the investment world it is not at all about the past or even the present. Investing is all about, and only about, the future. Investing is not about what happened yesterday or even what is happening now. The non-natural investment world is all about the future and what is likely to happen in that future. The past and even the present may offer a convenient reference on the future, but the future will always be different from that past. To successful investors, spending too much effort on the past and even the present is pure folly, an enormous distraction, and an extremely seductive trap. Most investors, analysts, and the press spend way too much time energy and effort focusing on and analyzing the past and the present and not nearly enough time on the future and what is most realistically likely to happen over most investors' longer-term investment timeframes. When it comes right down to it, true investors are not investing today for today or even today for tomorrow. (Traders and speculators may take very short-term positions with the intention of benefiting from a few percentage points' move, but that's not investing. Those short-term speculators and trader are pure and simple, just gambling. You'll also find that their ultimate long-term success is also about the same, and about as disappointing, as any gambler's.) When you are truly investing today, you are investing in anticipation of a world 3, 4, 5, 10, 15, or 20-plus years from today. In that future world, today's news, market fluctuations, movers and shakers, and screaming headlines will be totally forgotten, and have become inconsequential and unimportant random historic noise.

Because our brain is preprogrammed for risk management in the right-now natural world and because successful investing requiring a modified future-forward approach to risk management, that mismatch can adversely impact our investment success. As a result, our ancient and trusted, internal, natural-world, hard-wired risk management circuits and automatic responses run into real difficulty in the non-natural world of investing." I use the term non-natural because the investment world is very different from the natural world in a number of important ways. As such, it requires a different set of success skills from the natural world where we spend the majority of our time. It is a critically important point to understand because our natural world hard-wiring just can't be as effective operating in a non-natural world that's so different from the one it was originally developed to address. That mismatch between the ingrained methods we use so successfully in the natural world, that work against our best interests in the investment world, is the primary reason so many investors can become frustrated, confused, and disillusioned with investing. Unless we become familiar with, and learn how to control our ingrained natural responses, and substitute them with the right non-natural approaches, we'll have problems. If we use methods appropriate for success in a natural world, it's only natural to expect that we'd be incredibly frustrated, disillusioned, and unsuccessful in the non-natural investment world.

How Your Brain Manages Risk

Of course, risk management is a very broad and very common issue in the natural world. That world strongly favors those species that can manage the risks they face successfully, because those species that are less successful risk managers just don't survive. Therefore the brain is preprogrammed to respond to dangers that can routinely occur in the life of a species, and fear/anxiety is the natural involuntary reaction to those real or potential dangers. Some of the potential threats that can activate our instinctive threat responses are falling; spiders; snakes; surprising loud noises; and facing people, places or things we've never seen before. In additions, our brains are so flexible, that we can even learn to fear potential threats like poisons, high-voltage power lines, terrorists, and other potential hazards that are not part of our instinctive hard-wiring. Our brains are so programmed to help us prepare for risks, that after exposure to a danger our brains can also learn to fear elements of the environment (the context) in which the danger occurred. This phenomenon is called *fear conditioning,* and it is so powerful that once an animal is conditioned, the context itself can generate the same kind of fear reactions as the actual danger.

Over many decades of study, behavioral science has identified many other species that share very similar risk/threat management reactions with humans. These animals include fruit flies, marine snails, lizards, pigeons, rats, cats, dogs, monkeys, and baboons. All these creatures share the same high-level, risk/threat response behaviors.

The Brain's Risk Center

The key to understanding what is happening inside the brain when the threat/risk response is activated is to understand the workings of one of the oldest parts of our brain, the limbic system. It is such an ancient part of the brain that it is sometimes referred to as the "reptile brain." The limbic system structures are located in the center of the brain and are responsible for our body's emotion and threat response systems. The seven principal parts of the limbic system are:

1. Amygdala
2. Cingulate gyrus
3. Fornix
4. Hippocampus
5. Sensory cortex
6. Mamillary bodies
7. Thalamus

The amygdala controls our emotions including love, affection, friendship, the expression of mood (mainly fear, rage, and aggression). Each amygdala contains over 20 functional areas and is also linked to brain parts that govern senses, muscles, and hormone secretion. We know the amygdalae have a controlling role and a great deal of influence on other brain structures because there are many more neurons running *to* those other structures from the amygdala then those same structures have running to the amygdala. The hippocampus is directly involved with memory and specifically with the formation of long-term memory. Scientific studies have demonstrated that the hippocampus allows animals to compare the conditions of a present potential threat with similar past experiences. This context memory enables an animal to benefit from its previous similar experience(s) and choose the best option to maximize its survival in a similar future situation.

We are fortunate to live in an age when our knowledge of the brain is increasing enormously thanks to the technological advances in brain imaging technology and the hard work of dedicated scientists. As a result, we understand more than ever before about brain function as well as how and where risk management takes place in the brain. In addition to its many other benefits, that knowledge will help you better understand and manage the risks you'll face when investing.

As a result of their continuing studies, brain and behavioral scientists have now learned that information from external stimuli travel to the amygdala along two different pathways inside the brain, not just one. The short pathway is a very fast, and nonspecific connection directly from the sensory thalamus to the amygdala. The long pathway runs from the sensory thalamus to the sensory cortex, looping in the hippocampus, before finally reaching the amygdala. Although this longer route is significantly slower, it is also more precise. In essence the shorter, more direct route provides an almost instantaneous response to a possible threat, allowing us to start preparing for it even before we know what it is. If, when the slower more detailed signal arrives at the amygdala with the sensory cortex's analysis and the hippocampus's context, and it confirms a danger, a significant time advantage has been gained. However, should the rich, slower, more information-filled signal arrive at the amygdala later and identify the perceived threat as a false alarm, that's even better. Particularly in high risk or life and death situations, that speedier reaction time of the short route, even with the risk of reacting to a false alarm, is a big advantage over taking more time and being more certain before reacting to a potential threat.

Get to Know Your Second Brain

Have you ever experienced a tense, upset, cramping stomach, stomach butterflies, a tight throat, or a strong intestinal urge before or during a stressful situation like an important job interview, presentation, a speech to a large group, an important test, or when investment prices move the wrong way? If so you're certainly not alone. In fact, all those experiences and more are very common results of the extremely long and close relationship between our body's two essential brains. Those uncomfortable feelings are the result of your normally quiet and remarkably efficient second brain letting your know it's there. Of course, you are no doubt very familiar with the brain in your head. However, you may not be as familiar with your other brain, the very important but hidden brain in your gut, known as the enteric nervous system or ENS.

Now you may be asking yourself, what does this second brain in my belly have to do with investing and risk management? The principal reason we're reviewing it is the same reason why we've already discussed the human risk management process, the history of risk management, the two basic schools of risk management, and how our first brain deals with risk and threats. Quite simply, the more we know and understand about risk, our reactions to risks/threats, risk management, and the better prepared we are, the better risk managers and the more successful investors we'll become. Since the enteric nervous system can also generate physical manifestations in our bodies when we're facing threats, risk, or stressful situations, it is imperative that we also understand as much as we can about it.

Managing Your Ingrained Risk Management Systems

All these findings about our natural and ingrained threat response systems help to explain the uncomfortable physical phenomenon many investors experience during major market drops. When humans' internal risk management systems sense a threat or danger a full complement of emotional reactions (including fear, dread, and anxiety) and physical reactions (increased acuity of the senses, laser focus on the threat, increased heart and breathing rate, elevated blood pressure, sleeplessness, queasy stomach, tense muscles, tension headaches, distrust, isolation, and threat hormone release) are rapidly generated to deal with the threat. As a result, these strong, automatic reflexive risk responses can activate investors' "freeze, flight, and fight response" and easily override or hijack their logical thinking.

Of course, two, three, or more these conditions occurring simultaneously can be very unsettling, because all your body's highly developed survival instincts are kicking in and fully energizing you to freeze, flee, or fight a possible natural world threat. You feel compelled to act, to comply with what you body is telling you to do, because not only does it feel like the right thing to do, but also taking action is the only thing you can do to neutralize the risk management urgings generated by your body.

This happens in all potential threat situations because our brain isn't hardwired to discriminate between a real-world natural risk and a non-natural world risk. It reacts the same to both. That's why it's so important to get to know, understand, and be able to identify our body's ingrained and natural risk management responses when they occur and then to use that knowledge in letting those natural responses run their course in dangerous natural world situations, while controlling them by putting them in context when the occasional non-natural risk (like a big, and always temporary, market drop) occurs.

In a potentially threatening investment situation, if you don't understand that what is happening to you is a normal and natural reaction to a potential natural world threat or if you don't know the importance of discriminating between a natural threat and a non-natural threat, then you can easily fall victim to the very common and costly investment pitfall of your animal brain overcoming your logical brain. A natural risk like a fire in your house, and a non-natural threat, like a stock market drop when you are in your forties are very different risks, requiring very different responses.

Once you gain knowledge, comfort, experience, and then confidence in your practical application of this knowledge, you can even use those tangible threat response manifestations to your advantage as confirmation of very attractive non-natural investment world opportunities.

Our Risk Perception/Reality Gap

Another of our challenges is that we humans share a common and curious tendency to perceive risks very differently from reality, because our emotions and relative experiences can impact the process so heavily. There are certainly risks that we perceive accurately. However, there are many risks that we perceive to be greater than they actually are (sometimes much greater), as well as an abundance of risks we perceive to be less than they actually are (sometimes much less). Quite simply, not understanding this very common risk/reality gap and not compensating for it can create problems in effectively managing risk. The more accurate your understanding of the true nature and characteristics of a risk and the smaller your risk perception/reality gaps, the better decisions you'll make in managing risk. The corollary is also true, in that the wider the gap between your perceived assessment of a risk and the true nature of that risk, the greater potential damage you're likely to suffer should that risk occur. That's why it's so extremely important to understand this common risk perception danger, so that you can minimize your perception/reality gaps when it comes to risk management.

Common, Widespread Risk Misperceptions about People in General

- They are more afraid of new risks than risks they have lived with for a while.
- They are less afraid of natural risks than those that are human made.
- They are less afraid of risk they choose to take than those that are imposed on them.
- They are less afraid of risks that also confer some benefits they want.
- People are more afraid of risks that can kill them in particularly awful ways.
- People are less afraid of risks they feel they have some control over.
- They are less afraid of risk that comes from sources they trust.
- They are more afraid of risks they are aware of.
- People are much more afraid of risks when uncertainty is high.
- People are less afraid when they know more.
- Parents are more afraid of risks to their children than to themselves.
- People are less afraid of risks in investments and markets that have been rising in price.
- They are more afraid of risks in investments and markets that have been falling in price.

Of course there are exceptions to these very common risk perception generalizations. These exceptions occur because we all have different experiences, upbringing, personalities, and confidence levels in the different threat situations we face. Our individual differences can either reduce or increase our particular fear level given the circumstances. These variations in individual fear levels are neither a negative nor a positive, they are just simply differences in our individual perspectives and feelings. The real problems come from the fact that we rely very heavily on our feelings in our daily decision making, leading us to sometimes trust those feelings too much when evaluating threats and risk.

Upside-Down Perceptions

Normally, our natural, innate life-risk management skills can be relied upon across a range of potential threatening real-life, natural world risk management situations. However, for reasons not yet fully understood, investing and investment markets are a different situation and a special case where the natural world rules appear to be turned upside-down. In the world of investments our tried and true, natural life-risk management skills, methods, and perceptions can actually work against us, particularly in the extreme and emotional situations markets can generate.

There are a number of theories, and although no one knows for sure, the best explanation so far is that our emotions get caught up in the negative or positive news of the day and they and our innate fear circuitry create an internal feedback loop that reinforces itself and then finally overwhelms and overrides our logic and common sense. After all, in Chapter 6 on the physiology of risk we learned that our bodies have been hard-wired since ancient times to fear first and ask questions later. Our strong and ancient survival instincts would rather we avoid potential hazards, risk missing some opportunities, and live to fight another day than expose us to something potentially harmful to us.

Doing the Opposite of Common Perceptions

What's fascinating is that there are some very successful investors who have been able to overcome their own innate hard-wiring by using their knowledge and experience to effectively rewire their mental circuits so that their logic can override their natural fear mechanisms. Warren Buffett was widely criticized during the heyday of the Internet bubble for being too behind the times (and maybe too old) for not investing in the Internet frenzy. He was also publicly criticized in October 2008 for investing heavily in some large financial services firms in the middle of the market collapse when no one knows for sure what will eventually happen. However, Mr. Buffett cannot be criticized for not following his own advice, since he has been quoted many times as saying "We simply attempt to be fearful when others are greedy and to be greedy only when others are fearful." What's fascinating is that the legendary investor and philanthropist Sir John Templeton said and did things very similar to Mr. Buffett. In commenting on his own investment beliefs Sir John said, "The time of maximum pessimism is the time to buy. The time of maximum optimism is the time to sell." Clearly an investment approach based on doing the opposite of common perceptions, shared over multiple generations by world-class investment legends which has both its proven its success and longevity, deserves to be considered even when it flies in the face of common perceptions.

Being aware of the existence of gaps between our individual perceptions of risk and reality, as well as understanding how and why they exist are very significant first steps in our efforts to make better, knowledge-based decisions about risk. Now it's up to us to apply this knowledge to our own risk reward decision making.

Decision Making Patterns and Biases

As a result of its high importance, behavioral scientists and researchers have spent increasing time and effort over the last 40 plus years, working hard to better understand how our decision-making processes work in both stable and uncertain conditions. In studying how to improve decision making in general, those scientists have discovered a number of unexpected findings and common decision-making pitfalls. They have also learned that even if you do nothing else, avoiding those common decision-making pitfalls alone could have a very positive impact on your investment success. So, in the spirit of the "Risk-Wise" Investors credo: *What we know, understand and are prepared for cannot hurt us* we'll now embark on getting to know some of those decision-making risks better. In the process we'll better understand and become better prepared for the most common of those decision-making pitfalls and be better able to avoid their negative impact on our ultimate investment success.

The foundations of these decision-making traps are found in the hard-wired circuitry of our brains. They occur at the neurological level where our neurons interconnect with each other to form interlocking systems, which then develop and grow into various thought pattern pathways. Each of our brains literally wires its own thought pathways based on the patterns of our individual thoughts, feelings, experiences, and actions. In the interest of time, and so we don't have to think too much, our brain is always learning and working to make things as easy and simple as possible for us. The brain, via learning, even goes to the point of having prewired, ready-made response patterns all set up and standing at the ready for the situations and decisions we regularly encounter. These interlocking patterns of neural circuitry become the frame of reference we use to deal with the world. They become our gut feelings. Generally these neural systems work very well. However, where they can cause us some real difficulties is when our brain spontaneously gives us an answer to a decision or problem that is close to, but still different from, the true problem we're facing.

Cognitive Reflection

We humans have a propensity to either accept our own very fast, first, and instinctive answer in making decisions or to reflect on the validity of those initial thoughts before reaching a decision. Reflecting or double-checking the answer to a question is what researchers term *cognitive reflection* or *cognitive self-monitoring*. It's a built-in process that only some people instinctively use to double-check their initial decisions in both everyday life situations as well as investing. Tests have been conducted that demonstrate and validate that over 70 percent of people tested do not naturally use cognitive reflection. These results verify the importance of developing the habit of double-checking your decisions (including investment decisions), even if those decisions feel intuitively right. These tests demonstrate that without cognitive self-monitoring the first answer that comes to mind or the easy answer can frequently be wrong. This pitfall also reinforces one of the most important reasons "Risk-Wise" Investors should work with a trusted financial advisor. Your personal advisor not only can serve as a sounding board, information resource, and provider of investment knowledge and wisdom, but can also help you double-check your investment decision making. That advice alone can prove extremely valuable in protecting against falling into our own cognitive reflection traps.

Pattern Finding in Randomness

We humans share the very common trait of not just noticing patterns but seeking out patterns in randomness and many times imagining patterns or connections when none exists. Just as movement will instinctively draw the attention of predatory animals, mankind has a very strong, hard-wired instinct that draws us to see patterns in our environments. We are continuously and subconsciously searching for patterns and meaning in all manner of random occurrences. We're so attracted to patterns in events and even natural phenomena, that we will apply meaning to them, even when there is none. It's quite common for us to see things like canals on the planet Mars, men in the moon, figures in clouds, faces on rock outcroppings, patterns in star clusters. There's disagreement among experts in human psychology as to when and where this phenomenon originated, although there is general agreement that the survival of early humans must have benefited from it. Being able to see short-, medium-, and long-term patterns in weather, seasons, river and ocean waters, the stars, and the behavior of wild animals all likely provided an edge in the battle for survival. Of course, if a survival advantage in finding patterns in randomness existed, the people who possessed it would naturally begin to outnumber the people who lacked that advantage. So, the thinking goes, it would become self-perpetuating.

We can frequently see any number of what appear to be patterns, and assume that they provide real information that we can then turn into a profit. In fact what we interpret as a pattern is simply randomness successfully fooling us into thinking we are seeing something that isn't there.

Luck, Smarts, or Both

A very common way randomness can trick us is through the methods many investors use and misuse in relying on investment track record information in selecting money managers. Long and excellent investment track records have traditionally been viewed as one of the best ways to evaluate and select investment managers. In fact, the longer and the better the track record the more appealing a manger can become to people in search of a money manager. There are however potential flaws in that assumption. That is why prospectuses and performance information always carry the admonition, required by securities regulators, that past performance is no indication of future results. Those potential flaws include whether a manager, his team, and his methods have been consistent over the time period being referenced, and whether the managers in question have been smart, lucky, or both. If both, it is even more important to determine to what degree skill or luck contributed to the manager's superior returns. As nice as it is to have money with an investment manager who has luck on his side, luck is not something an investor should count on or use in selecting a manager.

There are certainly a number of qualitative and quantitative tools investment for analysts to use to sort through these many factors in making their determinations, but the very nature of those methods relies on backward-looking, historic data, which can prove to a fragile foundation on which to build one's future. Even the well-known mutual fund rating firm Morningstar, in explaining how to use their famous star ranking system (which is based on risk adjusted, historic returns), says their star ratings are a good starting point in your fund selection process, not a summary recommendation.

Just remember and refer to these key points when you find yourself being attracted by patterns or making decisions based on patterns that appear to jump out at you, because those situations may be setting you up to fall into a classic decision-making trap:

- Randomness is much more prevalent than we realize.
- We consistently underestimate the level of randomness in everything.
- Our brains are hardwired, pattern-seeking mechanisms.
- We look for patterns instinctively, to help simplify our decision making.
- Most patterns we see just don't hold up to statistical analysis.
- What any prospectus says about past performance is true: Past performance is no indication of future returns.

Following the Herd

We humans share many biological functions, characteristics, and reactions with other animals. We have many common, deeply ingrained, hard-wired behaviors. Although we don't consider ourselves to be herd animals, we certainly have a lot in common with them. One of the most basic of those behaviors is the fact that we humans are very social animals. Although we tend to focus on ourselves and our individual needs a great deal, social interaction, being accepted by and belonging to both small and large groups, is a key motivator and driver of human behavior. None of us likes to feel like an outsider. We all want to be insiders, and we find attractive advantages to being on the inside of groups. For some animal species, the norm is to live individual, solitary lives. They are almost totally solitary except for very temporary periods of interaction when they mate or rear their offspring; then, when they are finished, they are off once again to their solitary existences. We humans are the exact opposite. We are not at all inclined to live solitary lives. In fact, people who choose to live alone or avoid social interaction are considered to have something wrong with them. They are viewed as being different, weird, or antisocial, and are often characterized by the negative term "loner." We call people who don't socialize, antisocial, and that term carries a clearly negative connotation. In fact, socializing is so normal for us that some antisocial behavior is considered a mental illness. Based on a number of studies of the life expectancies of single people, married couples, and extended families living together, living alone also has a negative impact on our very life expectancy. Taken to its most extreme, the form of punishment considered even more grievous than death is solitary confinement. People in solitary conditions long enough can even go crazy, and literally lose their minds because of lack of interaction with others.

Humans like and need to belong. We gain comfort and validation in conforming to the group. When we are uncertain as to what to do in almost any situation, we look around and do what everyone else is doing, even when it may not make sense to us. We would rather fit in with the crowd and be wrong, than be different and right.

This instinctual behavior is particularly visible in fashion, apparel, and fads of all sorts. It manifests itself in almost everything we do, including investments. In most of those situations fad and trend following is fun and works in our favor because it helps us fit in, become part of the group, and stay current with the times. The only risk is that when a new trend or fad emerges we have to shelve our old out-of-date items and stock up on the new fad product or opt out entirely from participating in fads.

In the investment world, a totally different affect occurs. If everyone else has already invested in a company, industry, investment theme, or market, the price has already been driven up by increased demand. As a result, the investment has an attractive and very compelling track record of success. Everyone likes it, is enthusiastic about it, and is making money on their investment. People start talking about it as a money-making machine and expect that it will never go down in price, even though the risks in these types of situations are extreme, most investors perceive them as low to nonexistent.

The Greater Fool

To make matters even worse, some investors because of the buying frenzy even begin using borrowed money, or leverage, to buy more. As it nears its inevitable price peak, investors begin operating on the Greater Fool Theory. They say to themselves that even though they know they're being foolish investing in this highly appreciated asset, they're counting on an even greater fool to buy it from them at an even higher price. Inevitably, the number of new buyers slows because there are just fewer and fewer people who haven't already bought. Soon the supply of all those owners who want to sell, and lock in their profits, overwhelms the demand of a diminishing number of new buyers, and prices begin to drop, and many times plunge precipitously. Then, the whole buying frenzy on the way up turns very quickly into a panic to get out on the way down, before prices go even lower and the entire situation gets ugly, which it does.

This phenomenon has occurred throughout human history so many times that it's almost hard to believe. These herd instinct–driven panics and crashes have involved assets as diverse as tulip bulbs, agricultural and indus-trial commodities, railroad and canal shares, raw land, single-family homes, golf courses, commercial office buildings, the Japanese stock market, and Sunbelt condominiums. They have also included high tech Internet com-panies, emerging markets, our own stock markets, and most recently U.S. single-family homes.

When investing, it's not just your own assessment of the future that matters, but also the combined sentiment and assessment of every other market participant as well. An accurate reading of overall market sentiment can also provide important insights into your investment decision making and cues as to the best action for you individually to take.

Common Hidden Traps

Behavioral scientists have discovered a number of other common decision making traps. Here is a list of some of them:

- *The anchoring trap* is giving extra significance to the information you receive first.
- *The status quo trap* occurs when we are attached to continuing to do what we've been doing, instead of objectively comparing it to potentially better alternatives.
- *The sunk cost trap* often happens when we resist doing something because it will verify that we made an incorrect decision in the first place.

- *The confirming evidence trap* is one of the most difficult to control because of our strong natural tendency to want to be right and not be wrong.
- *The estimating and forecasting trap* occurs when intense or recent experiences or impressions can prejudice your forecasts and estimates positively or negatively.

This last trap appears quite regularly near the extremes of the investment markets cycles. During particularly deep or extended bear markets when investor nerves are on edge, they're emotionally drained, generally depressed, and fearful that their forecasts and estimates for the future are abnormally low because of their recent unpleasant experiences. Not only are their forecasts low, they are low and wrong by a wide margin, since over the last hundred years periods of outsized positive returns regularly follow periods of negative returns. The opposite occurs after extended market advances. In these cheerful times, investors' experiences have been very encouraging, and their attitudes are positive and optimistic. Since they've enjoyed consistent, positive returns, and it's been years since a serious market decline raised its ugly head, their forecasts for the future are for more of the same, generally proving to be high and wrong. Avoiding this trap can be accomplished by becoming more familiar with and knowledgeable about investment history, the psychology of investors during the various stages of the typical market cycle, and the reality of regression to the mean.

Avoiding Common Pitfalls

How can investors avoid these common and potentially devastating investment pitfalls? First, recognize that they happen all the time and can be very challenging to resist. Second, avoid trend following and performance chasing. If anything, look in the opposite direction of the trend or conventional wisdom. Third, stick to the investment wisdom of someone like Sir John Templeton who said, "The time of maximum pessimism is the time to buy. The time of maximum optimism is the time to sell." Fourth, should you ever consider the risky strategy of borrowing money to buy investments at all (which is not recommended), only use it to buy assets that are underpriced, and be certain you can comfortably bear the debt servicing costs for at least twice as long as you think you may hold the asset. Also, never use borrowed money to buy assets that have already appreciated dramatically in price.

In the process of becoming "Risk-Wise" Investors, it's not so critical to remember the details of every single decision-making pitfall as it is to understand that risks don't just exist in the world around us; they exist inside each of us as well. In guarding against those internal risks, we can apply the same process that has proven effective in guarding against external risks. Ultimately, the fundamental principle of successful risk management is accepting and applying the power of one simple adage: What is predictable can be avoided, prevented or managed.

The Advantages of Managing Risk Categories

With our attention as investors being pulled moment by moment, from event to event by our worldwide, 24/7 news services, there are some real benefits to stepping back and taking a big picture view of the risks we face. With many types of investment-related risks that have a number of physical, financial, and behavioral characteristics in common, managing those risks within general risk categories can simplify the many complexities of managing them individually. Grouping these risks with common characteristics and managing them with common risk mitigation strategies can leverage our time, our risk management resources, and help us become more effective risk managers in the process. It doesn't mean that we should ever relax or let our guard down when it comes to the ever-evolving nature of old and new risks. It does offer a way to organize our thinking about risk and help make the job of managing risks a little easier.

Here are a few examples of risk categories that can each contain risks with common characteristics and the same basic risk management methods.

Common Risk Management Categories

- Ingrained decision making risk
  - The herd instinct
  - Decision-making biases and patterns
  - Perception vs. reality misperceptions
  - Pattern-finding biases
- Inevitable crisis events
  - Natural disasters
  - Floods/tsunamis
  - Earthquakes
  - Storms
  - Fires
  - Epidemics
- Manmade/Human Error Disasters
  - War
  - Explosions/fires
  - Nuclear
  - Terrorism

- Government or business collapses
- Assassinations/political/coup d'états
- Financial Crises
  - Recessions/business slowdowns
  - Liquidity/confidence/currency
  - Inflation/hyperinflation
  - Sudden market collapses
  - Defaults/credit crises
  - Banking crises
- Inevitable insidious risks
  - Periods of underperformance and overperformance
  - Chasing returns and outperforming asset classes
  - Opportunities that are too good to be true
  - Losing long-term focus
  - Overmanaging investments
  - Confusing investing and trading/timing

Understanding and Prioritizing Risks

The big question and even bigger potential is still how you go about effectively prioritizing risks. Many investors give their highest risk management priority to the highest-likelihood risks. Their logic is that since these risks are showing up and attacking us so frequently, it only makes sense to deal with them first and neutralize them. Even though that logic sounds reasonable, and it's gratifying to swat down some of those nuisance risks that can drive us crazy, it's actually a trap. Dealing with frequent and irritating, lower-impact risks can consume valuable risk management time and resources, leaving us even more vulnerable to the less frequent, and more harmful, higher-impact risks. Although, in the heat of the investment marketplace it can seem counterintuitive to disregard those more frequent, smaller-impact risks, it can pay off when the infrequent, high-impact, heavyweight risks arrive.

So the most effective method to use in prioritizing risks is to *prioritize risks by their impact first*, not their likelihood. In doing so, we can focus our risk management attention on the all-important, high-impact risks rather than be distracted by the frequent, low-impact risks, which we may even decide to just accept or ignore altogether. In addition, this method also exemplifies, and makes actionable, one of the basic principles of "Risk-Wise" Investing, which is to honestly recognize risks and then directly face them. As uncomfortable as that initial showdown may feel, it's the only way to gain real power over risks, as opposed to the unacceptable alternative of allowing them to have power over us. Finally, this impact-based priority ranking adheres to the venerable adage of traditional wisdom, which asserts to always hope for the best, but plan for the worst.

The example below illustrates this impact and probability risk priority ranking system, with the highest priority risk being ranked first, then the other categories ranked in descending order to the lowest-priority risks.

Risk Management Priority Ranking (Highest Impact to Lowest)

9. High impact/high probability
8. High impact/moderate probability
7. High impact/low probability
6. Moderate impact/high probability
5. Moderate impact/moderate probability
4. Moderate impact/low probability
3. Low impact/high probability
2. Low impact/moderate probability
1. Low impact/low probability

How we each choose to allocate our risk management attention and resources is ultimately our own responsibility and as individual as we are. Taking a risk management priority ranking off the shelf and implementing it without first adjusting it to your own unique situation, personal preferences, and priorities can be a big mistake The more time you spend studying and understanding the risks you face and determining which risks to avoid entirely, which to accept and manage, and which to accept outright, the more successful risk manager you'll become.

Model of Outstanding Risk Management

In reviewing the risk management approaches that have been developed and successfully implemented by the U.S. commercial airline industry and U.S. government, the armed services, and fire and law enforcement services, we found they share eight common success traits that can benefit our investment risk management efforts.

Common Lessons Learned from Outstanding Risk Management

1. Expect and plan for negative surprises
2. Face risks directly
3. Acknowledge and identify risks

4. Study and understand the nature and behavior of risks as thoroughly as you can
5. Prioritize risks in advance
6. Develop, implement, and practice risk management initiatives
7. Prepare for risks in advance (it is much more efficient than recovering after them)
8. Use checklists to avoid missing something important

Professional Financial Advice

The single most important thought to keep in mind when considering financial advice is that as valuable as good advice can be, each one of us alone has full personal responsibility for our long-term investment success, not anyone else. We have full control and full responsibility for every decision we make, every success, and every disappointment. The purpose of advice is to provide us with better-quality information in making our decisions. We can then accept the advice or discard it, but it is always our decision. As tempting as it may be to allow advisors to make decisions for us, advisors cannot and should not make our decisions. To do otherwise is to abdicate our decision-making power. We are the ones who will live with the results of our decisions, both positive and negative, and we are the only ones who should be making them. Over many decades in the investment business, I've come to learn that one of the best tests of the rightness or wrongness of any decision, after analyzing the viable options, the rewards, and the risks, and after factoring in advice from knowledgeable and trusted advisors, is the touchstone of our own personal comfort level with the decision. If you are comfortable with a particular decision, then proceed. If uncomfortable, defer your decision and work at determining what aspects of the potential action are making you uncomfortable, while you also gather additional information or advice on those discomforting aspects. Once you have enough time and information to comfortably make your decision, you are set to proceed. My observation is that life is just too short and precious to do things we are not comfortable doing.

Faux Advice

What masquerades as financial advice is just about everywhere today. From people we interact with on a regular basis, such as personal friends and business associates to barbers, hairdressers, and neighbors, casual conversations often evolve into discussions about the economy, markets, investments, and peoples' favorite investment picks. The media is now packed with pundits, soothsayers, economic forecasters, and the like who pound the table and our ears with their fearless forecasts of what to buy, own, or sell today. The fact that they are frequently wrong and many times promote the exact opposite of what they were saying a day or two before never seems to diminish their enthusiasm. They aren't talking about investing; they're talking about trading and gambling, which have very similar and unpleasant outcomes. Please do not view their comments as advice or pay any attention at all to them, except for the potential entertainment value they offer. They are not real financial advisors, and their opinions are not advice. They are entertainers trying to get and keep your attention so that their ratings stay high enough that they get to keep their entertainment jobs. True financial advice is very different. It has a several characteristics that set it dramatically apart from opinions shared with a general audience.

True Financial Advice

True financial advice can only be offered by people who meet the three following criteria. First, they are knowledgeable about and experienced in the subject for which you are seeking their advice. Second, they are thoroughly familiar with your particular personal financial situation. Third, their advice is specifically directed to you and your situation alone, and not to anyone else. As a general rule and corollary to the criteria mentioned above, any recommendations you hear that are made to a broad audience or recommendations by someone who doesn't know you and the details of your situation extremely well, even if they come from an expert source, should be immediately dismissed. Working with a financial advisor should be a real partnering, collaborative relationship. You bring unparalleled knowledge of yourself, your financial goals and needs, likes, dislikes, and tolerance for risk taking. Your financial advisor brings extensive knowledge of the investment markets and expertise in helping investors plan for and achieve their financial goals. Advisors normally have access to a wide range of investment alternatives to choose from in helping you create the right mix of investments for your particular situation.

For your joint relationship to work its best, honest and open communications between the two of you are the key. The more your advisor knows about where you are financially and where you want to go, the better they'll be in helping you reach your objective. So be as open honest and direct as possible. On the flip side of the coin, your advisors have an obligation to respect your desires and priorities, and to be as open, transparent, and direct as they can be in making you aware of the rewards, risks, uncertainties, and the fees or charges involved the investments they recommend and in you compensating them for their services.

Navigating Crisis Events and Bear Markets

Crisis events are a regular part of human existence and have been for tens of thousands of years. While some are manmade and others occur naturally, because of their unexpected and sudden occurrence, large-scale consequences, inability to control, and newness or lack of familiarity with them, they share a common ability to generate extreme emotional responses in us. These extreme emotional responses frequently generate activation of our innate, freeze/flight/fight response, and increased heart and respiration rates, elevated blood pressure, digestion shutdown, increased perspiration, heightened sensitivity to sound, sight and smell, as well as high fear and anxiety levels. When these responses occur as the result of real physical threats, they can be of enormous help in our survival because responding to physical threats is exactly what our ingrained natural responses have evolved to do. When these physical fear responses occur because of a financial crisis (or other nonphysical threat) those hard-wired instincts can actually work against our own best financial interests. Those physical world threat responses often create a negative financial effect because your body's instincts don't discriminate between a physical treat and a financial one. Our human body senses any threat, whether physical, financial, or even make believe (as in horror or action movies), as physical and directs us to initiate a physical response. While physical responses work extremely well at readying us for action in dealing with physical risks, action has been frequently been proven to be the wrong thing to do when dealing with generally short-lived financial threats. About the only way for us to comply with our body's strong instinct to flee, and get away from a perceived financial threat is to sell and get out of the market. Unfortunately that's what many investors do when a sudden crisis strikes and emotions are running. Generally speaking, that action has been a mistake in the past and one of the worst reasons and worst times to sell.

History shows us that even surprise crisis events that generate strong emotional reactions generally result in short-lived and sometimes sharp market corrections that reverse themselves within a few weeks or months. These crisis events have historically demonstrated that they are more of a buying opportunity than a reason to sell out of the market.

Crisis Summary

The best way to deal with crisis events is to expect them and prepare a plan of action for how you will deal with them, well in advance. Commercial aviation, the military, fire fighters, and other, use that technique very effectively, and you can, too. Natural crisis events, like earthquakes, hurricanes, and floods, which can impact us personally and physically must be taken very seriously and fully prepared for. From an investment perspective, their primarily local and regional impact combined with a low potential impact on the markets mean they are risks we can generally afford to accept (unless an investor has special circumstances) with no need for any extraordinary risk management initiatives.

The Relationship of Stock Market Price Levels and Perceived Risk

During bull markets, the better the markets perform, the higher it goes, and the more positive the business news, the lower investors perceive the real risks they're taking. In fact, the risks are actually the highest when the market is the highest, yet that's when investors see the risks as the least. Conversely, during bear markets when the indexes are down 20 or 30 percent or more and the business and investment news is bad, and pessimism about the future in intense, investors perceive their risks to be the greatest when they are actually the least. So when perceived risks are high, real risks are low, and when perceived risks are low, real risks are high.

These examples reinforce why market pullbacks or bear markets are the worst time sell investments and actually wonderful opportunities to accumulate more investment assets at bargain basement prices. That's exactly why most experienced, long-term investors take bear markets in stride and view them as a normal part of the market cycle or as attractive opportunities to add to their favorite long-term holdings at discounted prices.

Knowledge of this very common phenomenon can be used in two ways. One way is as a self-checking or self-monitoring device. So any time you begin to feel that an investment is a sure thing, and you don't see any risks associated with it, the risks are likely very high. The other way is to observe investors and the media's attitudes, because if all they're talking about are the weak business conditions, treacherous markets, and high risks, their perceived risks are high, but the true risks are actually low. If, by contrast, they're positive and optimistic, and see no risk at all, their perceived risk is low and the actual risks are quite high. The great financier Bernard Baruch may have said it best with his famous statement, "When good news about the market hits the front page of the *New York Times*, sell." Of course that was well before the 24/7, multi-media news avalanche we experience today. However the point is the same.

Turn Lemons into Lemonade

Whenever a crisis event, recession or bear market occurs the vast majority of the public and investor reactions are to hold their hands to their heads or mouths in shock, disbelief and horror. They say, "Oh no," and wring their hands in anguish, fear, and sometimes panic. These reactions of shock and fear can become even more extreme if these crisis events possess one or more of the factors that increase perceived risk such sudden occurrence, broad potential impact, beyond our control, new or unfamiliar. Why does this happen again and again and again? Do most people not recognize the fact that crisis events and negative surprises happen all the time and are a normal part of reality? Do they not understand that instability, rapid change, and surprise negative events are the norm rather than the exception?

What would it be like if instead of reacting to news of a major recession, business slowdown, or crisis event in surprise, anguish, or fear, they reacted by rubbing their hands together in satisfaction and said, "I've been waiting for something like this to happen for a long time and I'm ready and prepared to take advantage of it." These people recognize that reality has both positive and negative aspects and to live and plan only for the positives in life is delusional, because they're denying 50 percent of reality. Why not look at the world as it really is, rather than pretend it's only the way you'd like it to be. Why give up control, when with some extra effort, study and preparation, and flexibility you can turn the inevitable lemons into lemonade, and crisis events into opportunities? Isn't it a fuller, more confident, and enjoyable life when we have realistic expectations of what we are likely to face and understand, and are fully prepared for both the positive and negative surprises life can throw at us.

Remember what Sir Arthur Conan Doyle's Sherlock Holmes said in the 1902 book, *The Hound of the Baskervilles*, is just as true today: "That which is clearly known hath less terror than that which is hinted at and only guessed." That's the true essence of "Risk-Wise" Investing. So don't be afraid or intimidated by crisis events, bear markets, and business slowdowns. Instead embrace them, study them, get to know them, understand and become familiar with them, and learn how to turn their power to your own personal advantage.

Afterthoughts

Knowledge, understanding, and preparation give you tremendous power to effectively manage the risks you face. Remember, your outstanding life-risk management skills are highly transferable to the investment world. Continue to develop your knowledge, and keep in mind the following risk wisdom.

- Instability is the norm, and the by-product of progress in a capitalistic economy. It should be expected, and planned for.
- Expect both positive and negative surprises.
- Spend at least as much time evaluating the risks as you do the potential rewards.

- Use an empowering definition of risk.
- Expect both mild and wild uncertainty.
- Knowledge, understanding, and preparation can turn risks into inconveniences, and even opportunities.
- Work for the best, but be prepared for the worst.
- Always double-check your first answer, and the easy or obvious answer—it can frequently be wrong.
- As an individual, enjoy being part of the crowd. As an investor avoid doing what everyone else is thinking and/or doing.
- Become a student of risk and risk management.
- Both negative and positive extremes never last, since there are many forces working to revert them to the mean.
- Life and investments are cyclical by nature. Good times always follow bad times, and bad times follow good times.
- Avoid mistaking luck for skill.
- In the upside-down world of the markets, when the risks appear the greatest—remember they are generally the least, and when the risks appear the least—they are generally the greatest.
- Each of us is a gifted manager of life-risks; use those same skills and that same process in becoming "Risk-Wise" Investors.

Imagine a future where you really understand investment risk. What would it be like? You would be a more knowledgeable investor, would have more realistic expectations, and have a higher level of satisfaction. You would make fewer investment errors, and the mistakes you did make would be less severe. You would be less emotional in your investment decision making, and more likely to reach your investment goals. Overall, you would be a more realistic, successful, and happier investor. With others like you the economic future of our families, cities, states, countries, and our world would brighten as well. Isn't that a future worth spending time, energy, and effort to bring to reality? We can do it, and we now know how to do it. So let's make it happen.

Wishing you the very best, and a lifetime of successful, "Risk-Wise" Investing.

Notes

Chapter 1: The Increasing Importance of Risk-Wise Investing

1. Charles D. Ellis, *Winning the Loser's Game* (New York: McGraw-Hill, 2002).

Chapter 2: Introduction to the "Risk-Wise" Risk Management Process

1. Benoit Mandelbrot, *The (Mis)Behavior of Markets"* (New York: Basic Books, 2004).

Chapter 3: The Evolving History of Risk and Risk Management

1. The historical timeline presented in Parts 1, 2, and 3 of this chapter includes information from the following sources: Leigh Buchanan and Andrew O'Connell, "A Brief History of Decision Making," *Harvard Business Review* (January 2006); Peter L. Bernstein, *Against the Gods: The Remarkable Story of Risk* (New York: John Wiley & Sons, Inc., 1998); Peter L. Bernstein, "The New Religion of Risk Management," Harvard Business Review, March-April, 1996; Felix Kloman, "A Brief History of Risk Management" (April 2008); South Seas Bubble Collection, Baker Library Harvard Business School; Jim McWhinney, "A Brief History of the Mutual Fund," Investopedia.com/articles/ mutualfund/05/MFhistory.asp; Charles P. Kindleberger, *Manias, Panics, and Crashes: A History of Financial Crisis*, (New York: John Wiley & Sons, Inc., 1996); Mark D. Abkowitz, *Operational Risk Management: A Case Study Approach to Effective Planning & Response* (Hoboken, NJ: John Wiley & Sons, Inc., 2008); Michael Lewis, *Panic: The Story of Modern Financial Insanity* (New York: W.W. Norton & Company, 2009); Mark Gongloff, CNN/Money, "Greenspan's Changing Tune," September 18, 2002, http://money.cnn. com/ 2002 / 09 /18/news/economy/ greenspan_story/index.htm; "Setting the Record Straight of the Dow Drop," *New York Times*, October 26, 1987; Nassim Taleb, *The Black Swan* (New York, NY, Random House, 2007);"Exorcising the Ghosts of Octobers Past," *Wall Street Journal*, October 15, 2007; Thayer Watkins,

"Long Term Capital Management, Summary of the Nature of LTCM," Department of Economics, San Jose State University, www.sjsu.edu/faculty/watkins/ltcm.htm; Tyler Cowen, "Bailout of Long-Term Capital: A Bad Precedent," *New York Times*, December 26, 2008; Kevin Poulsen, "Software Bug Contributed to Blackout," *SecurityFocus*, February 11, 2004; "Interim Report on the August 14, 2003, Blackout," *New York Independent System Operator*, August 1, 2004; Andy Pasztor and Susan Carey, "Back-up System Helped Pilot Control Jet," *Wall Street Journal*, January, 29, 2009.

Chapter 4: "Risk"— What Is It, and How Does It Work?

1. David Ropeik and George Gray, *Risk* (Boston: Houghton Miflin, 2002), p. 4.
2. Mark D. Abkowitz, *Operational Risk Management* (Hoboken, NJ: John Wiley & Sons, 2008).

Chapter 12: Models Of Outstanding Risk Management

1. *A Brief History of Passenger Airlines*, Duke University Library—Digital Collection.
2. National Transportation Safety Board, "History & Mission," www.ntsb.gov/Abt_NTSB/history.htm
3. Federal Aviation Administration, "Statistics," www.FAA.gov./about/history/50th/.
4. Boeing Company, "Commercial Airline Safety," www.Boeing.com./commercial/safety/airline_role.html#aircraftMaintentance.
5. Air Traffic Organization, "2007 Annual Performance Report," www.faa.gov/search/?q=2007+annual+performance+report&x=26&y=19.
6. Gary Ballard, "Serious Business," 2002 (www.gballard.net/short.html?http%3A//www.gballard.net/port/shortbook/fire.html).

Bibliography

A Brief History of Passenger Airlines, Duke University Library-Digital Collection.

Abkowitz, Mark D. *Operational Risk Management: A Case Study Approach to Effective Planning & Response*. Hoboken, NJ: John Wiley & Sons, 2008.

About.com. "Finding a Financial Advisor." http://financialplan.about.com/od/personalfinance/a/choosingaplan.htm.

Air Traffic Organization, 2007 Annual Performance Report. www.faa.gov/airports_airtraffic.

Ballard, Gary. *Serious Business, U.S. Navy firefighter feature story*. 2002. www.gballard.net/short.html?http%3A//www.gballard.net/port/short book/fire.html.

Bernstein, Peter L. *Against The Gods: The Remarkable Story of Risk*. New York: John Wiley & Sons, 1998.

Bernstein, Peter, "The New Religion of Risk Management." *Harvard Business Review* March-April 1996.

Buchanan, Leigh, and Andrew O'Connell. "A Brief History of Decision Making." *Harvard Business Review* (January 2006).

Boeing Company. "Commercial Airline Safety." www.Boeing.com. www.boeing.com/commercial/safety/airline_role.html#aircraft Operations.

Ellis, Charles D. *Winning the Loser's Game: Timeless Strategies for Successful Investing*. New York: McGraw-Hill, 2004.

————, with Charles R. Vertin. *The Investor's Anthology: Original Ideas from the Industry's Greatest Minds*. New York: John Wiley & Sons, 1997.

Emerson, Ralph Waldo. "Essay on Courage." Complete Works of Ralph Waldo Emerson. Centenary Edition, Vol. 7.

Federal Aviation Administration. "Statistics." www.faa.gov/safety/data_statistics/.

Financial Planning Association. "Find a Planner" www.fpaforfinancialplanning.org/FindaPlanner/ChoosingaPlanner/.

"Finding a Financial Advisor." Senior Magazine Online.com.

Frederick, Shane, "Cognitive Reflection & Decision Making." *Journal of Economic Perspective* (Fall 2005). Vol. 19, No. 4, 25–42.

Freedman, Joshua. "Hijacking of the Amygdala." *EQ Today*. www .inspirations-unlimited.net/images/Hijack.pdf

Gershon, Michael D. *The Second Brain: Your Gut Has a Mind of Its Own*. New York: HarperCollins, 1998.

Gongloff, Mark. "Greenspan's Changing Tune," CNN/Money, September 18, 2002, http://money.cnn.com/2002/09/18/news/economy/greenspan_ story/index.htm.

Investment Management Consultants Association. www.IMCA.org (for CIMA designation).

Kindleberger, Charles P. *Manias, Panics, and Crashes: A History of Financial Crises*. New York: John Wiley & Sons, 1996.

Kloman, H. Felix. "A Brief History of Risk Management" April 2008. Whitepaper.

————. *The Fantods of Risk: Essays on Risk Management*. Lyme, CT: Seawrack Press, Inc., 2008.

————. *Mumpsimus Revisited: Essays on Risk Management*. Lyme, CT: Seawrack Press, Inc., 2005.

LeDoux, Joseph. *The Emotional Brain: The Mysterious Underpinnings of Emotional Life*. New York: Simon & Schuster Paperbacks, 1996.

LeDoux, Joseph. *Synaptic Self: How Our Brains Become Who We Are*. New York: Penguin Group, 2002.

Lewis, Michael. *Panic: The Story of Modern Financial Insanity*. New York: W. W. Norton & Company, 2009.

Mandelbrot, Benoit, and Richard L. Hudson, *The (Mis)Behavior of Markets: A Fractal View of Risk, Ruin, and Reward*. New York: Basic Books, 2004.

McCarthy, Mary Pat and Timothy Flynn. *Risk from the CEO and Board Perspective*. New York: McGraw Hill, 2004.

McWhinney, James. "A Brief History of the Mutual Fund." Investopedia.com.

Minsky, Hyman P. *Can "It" Happen Again: Essays on Instability and Finance*. Armonk, NY: M.E. Sharpc, Inc., 1982.

————. *John Maynard Keynes: Hyman P. Minsky's Influential Re-Interpretation of the Keynesian Revolution*. New York: McGraw-Hill, 2008.

Murphy, James D. *Flawless Execution: Use the Techniques and Systems of America's Fighter Pilots to Perform at Your Peak and Win the Battles of the Business World*. New York, NY: Harper Collins, 2005.

National Transportation Safety Board. *History & Mission*. www.ntsb.gov./Abt _NTSB/history.htm.

Pasztor, Andy, and Susan Carey. "Back-up System Helped Pilot Control Jet." *Wall Street Journal*, January 20, 2009.

Risk Management Reports, December 1999, Volume 26, No. 12.

Ropeik, David, and George Gray. *Risk: A Practical Guide for Deciding What's Really Safe and What's Really Dangerous in the World Around You*. New York: Houghton Mifflin, 2002.

Slovic, Paul, and Elke U. Webber. "Perception of Risk Posed by Extreme Events." Conference on Risk Management Strategies in an Uncertain World, Palisades, New York, April 12–13, 2002.

South Seas Bubble Collection. Baker Library Harvard Business School.

Taleb, Nassim Nicholas. *The Black Swan: The Impact of the Highly Improbable*. New York: Random House, 2007.

———. *Fooled by Randomness: The Hidden Role of Chance in Life and in the Markets*. New York: Random House, 2004.

Watkins, Thayer. "Long Term Capital Management, Summary of the Nature of LTCM," Department of Economics, San Jose State University, www.sjsu .edu/faculty/watkins/ltcm.htm.

Additional Information for Readers

P lease visit www.riskwiseinvestor.com to continue improving your understanding and management of investment risk, and to access additional information, resources, and updates for "Risk-Wise" investors, including:

- Additional Educational Resources on Risk Management
- Links to Web based Investor Resources
- Whitepapers and Special Reports on Risk and Risk Management
- "Risk-Wise" Risk Management Planning Tools & Checklists
- Alerts on "Risk-Wise" Investor Tele-seminars
- Conferences & Events
- Contact information for Speeches, Presentations, Workshops, Events, Interviews, and Consulting Services.

Note: The information in this book is general in nature and is intended for a broad audience. You should always use your own judgment and consult with your own legal, tax, and investment advisors before implementing any strategies reviewed in this book.

About the Author

With over 35 years of investment industry experience Mike Carpenter is an investment veteran. Since entering the business as a financial advisor with PaineWebber prior to the OPEC Oil Embargo of 1973, he has personally advised investors, financial professionals, and investment firms facing turbulent investment environments, ranging from raging inflation, stagflation, and stratospheric interest rates to deflation, recessions, panics, crashes, booms, and busts. His investment experience ranges from stocks, bonds, options, mutual funds, annuities, insurance, and managed money, to alternative investments, retirement plans, direct investments, private placements, ETFs, and hedging.

Over the course of his career working at the local, regional, and national levels with premier investment managers, Mike has consistently helped his firms, teams, financial advisors, and their investors meet the challenges, and capitalize on the opportunities, presented by the ever-changing investment landscape. He has conducted hundreds of investment workshops and seminars around the country for investors and financial advisors alike. He has been a guest lecturer at The Securities Industry Institute at the Wharton School of the University of Pennsylvania, and hosted investment industry programs on the campuses of Harvard and Columbia Universities. His writings have also been featured in national investment industry publications.

Mike Carpenter is known industry-wide as a creative problem solver, innovator, and outside-the-box thinker. He's a recognized professional resource to investment management firms, broker/dealers, boards, senior executives, marketers, regional and branch managers, financial advisors, and investors in helping them achieve their goals and objectives.

For over 15 years Mike has been extremely interested in the subjects of risk and risk management, and in identifying new, user-friendly, non-technical ways to help investors better understand and manage risk. With the accelerating pace of worldwide change and increasing uncertainty, he believes it is more important now than ever for investors to enhance their knowledge and understanding of risk and risk management.

Since starting his own investment industry consulting firm in 2003, Mike has also dedicated himself to identifying ways to help individual investors become as comfortable and adept at managing investment risks as they are managing their everyday life risks. This book is the result of those efforts.

Mike and his wife, who was his high school sweetheart, live near Boston. They have three children and one grandchild.

Index